THE
GREAT
BATTLES

THE
GREAT
BATTLES

GILES MacDONOGH

Quercus

CONTENTS

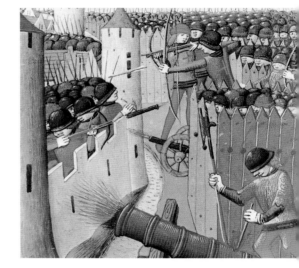

The siege of Orléans.

Previous page: D-Day landings.

Statue of Leonidas at the site of the Battle of Thermopylae.

ANZAC troops at Anzac Cove, Gallipoli

American troops on Leyte Island,
the Philippines.

INTRODUCTION

Battles are the punctuation marks in the history of the world. The first recorded battle – Megiddo – was fought three and a half millennia ago, but that should not fool us into believing that there had not been myriad military engagements before the pharaoh Thutmose faced his enemy in the field.

The battles described in this book not only detail the changes in strategic and tactical thinking that occurred through the ages, but also reveal the development of military hardware. Starting with sticks and stones, weaponry initially progressed to swords, shields and spears. Cavalry appeared with the chariot and the horse. A great leap forward was then made with the introduction of the crossbow and the longbow, and those, in turn, were superseded by the first cannon. The pike was phased out by the bayonet, just as advances in artillery sounded the death knell to old-style infantry tactics, forcing soldiers to dig trenches. In the past 100 years, air support and tanks have changed the battlefield beyond recognition. The practice of warfare has always been in a state of permanent flux, not least because only through novelty and innovation does a military commander manage take his adversary by surprise.

In the following pages, we shall look at battles as they used to be fought. They came in all shapes and sizes. Some were political battles, which had important repercussions for a nation or region. In the cases of Plassey, for example, or Calatafimi, they were little more than skirmishes – Plassey in particular had something of the comic opera about it. Yet Plassey started the process of subjecting the Mughal empire that ruled the Indian subcontinent to the British, and Calatafimi was the beginning of the end for the Kingdom of the Two Sicilies.

The Battle of Hastings completely transformed the language and culture of England. The Fall of Constantinople shut down the Byzantine empire and brought Islam within reach of Central Europe. Waterloo toppled Napoleon and redrew the map of Europe, establishing a political system that survived until the end of the First World War.

On the other hand, some great battles failed to make important changes. The Battle of Cannae, beloved of military planners and instructors, had no greater significance because Hannibal felt he lacked the men to advance on Rome. Thermopylae might have delayed the Persian army for three days, but the deciding action in the war occurred at Plataea in 479 BC. The gory engagements of the Thirty Years' War eradicated Germany politically and culturally for more than a century, but the Treaty of Westphalia of 1648 failed to satisfy the territorial lusts of any of the major powers involved.

Much as we would all like to see war wither away, the end is by no means nigh. The Middle East continues to be a hotspot: Israel has fought several wars since its creation in 1947 and there is no sign yet of it coming to terms with its neighbours, who don't always see eye-to-eye either. Lebanon was racked by civil war for decades. There was a major conflict between Iran and Iraq in the 1980s and there have been two American-led wars against Iraq since 1991. Today, peace in Iraq is ensured only by a massive foreign military presence. No bookmaker in sound mind would give you decent odds on a long period of peace in the Middle East.

As I write, there are wars smouldering further east in Afghanistan and Pakistan. India and Pakistan have been on a war footing since Pakistan was created after the Second World War and there has been a full-scale conflict between India and China too.

There have been changes; in many instances, now, soldiers are confusingly referred to in doublespeak as 'peacekeepers' and their missions called 'peacekeeping'. They act in concert with soldiers from other nations in order to prevent conflict. It can be a thankless task. They risk life and limb yet woe betide should they unleash the full force of their firepower – they will come under instant attack from those who would rather they fought with kid gloves or not at all.

Apart from its involvement in the Iraq Wars, the United States has moved on from fighting communism to fighting advocates of terrorism and radical Islam. After the Korean War, it was involved in a long-drawn-out conflict in Vietnam which ended in its defeat in the 1960s. Britain fought its last real war in the Falkland Islands in 1982. Since then, the British army has confined its activities to policing roles, as often as not in a junior partnership with the United States.

Nearer to home, it now would appear inconceivable that war should break out between the countries that constitute the European Union, but since the Cold War ended in 1989, we have experienced a bloody civil war in the former Yugoslavia. In the former Soviet Union, war has flared up in Chechnya (part of the Russian-dominated Russian Federation) and against Georgia (which is independent). These latter-day wars have something in common in that they are often short on battles and big on guerrilla tactics – pinpricks that draw blood from the Colossus that is the modern superpower.

On a positive note, nuclear deterrents may have succeeded in preventing the outbreak of major conflagrations, such as those that all but destroyed Europe in the 20th century, and shifted the balance of power to the United States and the Soviet Union.

War may prosper, but great battles seem to have had their day. Most modern warfare is conducted against irregulars who try to avoid facing the enemy. Even regular troops fight shy of engaging. The United States in particular has evolved a hands-off style, which aims to protect its soldiers from the negative PR of corpses or 'body-bags' – all hell is let loose when the 'boys' come home dead and it is even worse when there are 'girls' too. Superior technology is brought to bear to avoid a problem that might topple a government and if possible soldiers are kept out of range of enemy fire. We have reached an age when computers can control the battlefield. It may be the ultimate technological advance, but as long as man is man, warfare soldiers on.

Giles MacDonogh
2010

MEGIDDO

Pharaoh Thutmose III *v.* Durusha of Kadesh
1456 BC

MEN HAVE ALWAYS FOUGHT over a woman or a hunk of meat. Bigger issues such as the control of a cave or valley brought larger bands of warriors into the field. From the outset, to try and gain an advantage over the enemy weapons were fashioned, even from such basic materials as stones and sticks. Once these fights began to be formally planned and organized they became battles; battle-plans developed by a cunning member of the tribe became 'strategy' and the smaller ways in which the battle was fought were named 'tactics'.

Unrecorded battles and skirmishes were doubtless fought since time immemorial, but Megiddo (the fortress town is called 'Armageddon' in Hebrew) is the first recorded conflict about which historians can write with a degree of confidence. For the first time, there is documentary evidence of the classic tactics of 'shock and fire'.

BRONZE, CHARIOTS AND ARCHERS

New, more sophisticated weaponry was a prerequisite for pitched battles like Megiddo. Around 2000 BC, stone axes and clubs began to be phased out and were supplanted by bronze weapons. Warriors continued to wield axes, but the sword, introduced from the Far East, was also becoming widespread. In Egypt, it replaced the mace as the symbol of the pharoah's power. Infantrymen used spears as well and the Egyptians adopted the socket-type with a leaf-shaped head, which was already in use in Mesopotamia. Spears were used for defending ramparts, but not for throwing from chariots, which was the standard Asian practice.

Iron made its appearance later, from around 1200 BC onwards. Something akin to a regimental structure evolved too, with massed infantry units divided into smaller bodies or phalanxes composed of spear, sword and axe detachments. These were the ancestors of modern companies and platoons. Bodies of spearmen, archers and slingers required discipline to render them effective on the battlefield.

As we know from reading Homer's *Iliad*, chariots were used in the Trojan Wars, while battles in Ancient Greece were fought by a combination of infantry and charioteers. War chariots were a familiar sight in the Middle East long before 1700 BC. Yet there was an essential difference between Asian and Egyptian tactics: Asian chariots carried a charioteer and two spearmen and were used as light, manoeuvrable vehicles to harry the enemy. By contrast, Egyptian charioteers drove heavy chariots with six-spoked wheels and advanced *en masse*, sweeping the enemy before them in the manner of later cavalry charges. Egyptian chariots carried archers that were equipped with composite bows (pharaohs are often depicted in the role of charioteer bowmen), and were organized into units of 50, each under the command of an officer.

The bow was the key weapon. Because the Egyptians had craftsmen who could

turn out good bows, this gave them an advantage over the smaller kingdoms to the east. Both the chariot units and the infantry used bows. Their shafts were fashioned from reeds, while the heads were made from bronze and could pierce any contemporary armour. The quiver contained around 30 arrows.

Pharaohs of the New Kingdom period (1567–1085 BC) perfected fighting forces composed of heavy spearmen and archers. Armour was light: charioteers and bowmen alike wore coats of mail and helmets and carried either a small shield or none at all. As armour was expensive, spearmen and swordsmen wore little in the way of protection, but carried large shields.

DEFENDING EGYPT'S NEW EMPIRE

Thutmose III (r.1479–1425 BC) was the sixth ruler of the 18th Dynasty. Until the age of 21, he was co-regent with his aunt

Queen Hatshepsut. After ascending the throne as sole ruler, he remained in power for over 53 years and is regarded as Ancient Egypt's greatest warrior king.

During the 18th Dynasty, Egypt had spread its sphere of influence as far as Palestine and Syria. But Hatshepsut's death triggered uprisings in these far northeastern provinces. The chief trouble-makers were the Mitanni, with their allies, the city-states of Kadesh and Tunip. Kadesh was near Lake Homs in modern Syria, and commanded the upper valley of the River Orontes. Its king, Durusha, was rumoured to be preparing for war with Egypt. Since Kadesh controlled key overland routes to the River Euphrates and Assyria, such a conflict would seriously disrupt Egyptian trade with Asia. Durusha had the support of 330 Mitanni princes, who were with him at Megiddo.

In the first year following the death of his aunt, Thutmose led around 10,000

Ancient Egyptian relief, showing a pharaoh in the familiar guise of a chariot-mounted archer. The chariot quickly found its way into New Kingdom royal regalia, becoming a powerful symbol of military domination.

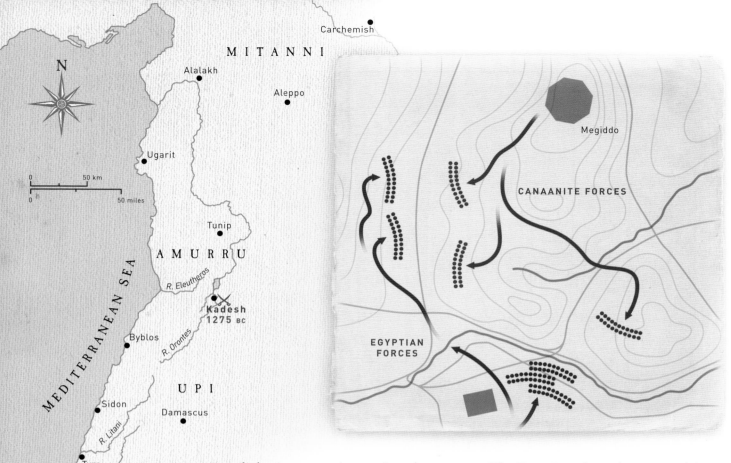

The eastern Mediterranean during the Egyptian 18th and 19th Dynasties. The Battle of Kadesh, the largest chariot battle in history, was fought between Rameses II and the Hittite empire in 1275. Inset: Deployment of forces at Megiddo.

men in a lightning campaign against the rebel chiefs. Leaving the Nile Delta on 19 April 1458 BC, the pharaoh crossed the Sinai Desert and advanced first to loyal Gaza before taking Yehem. He then passed the Carmel Range while his deputy Djehuty besieged and took Joppa (Jaffa), smuggling his troops into the city in large baskets. After a rapid march covering 16 miles (26 km) a day, Thutmose reached the southern slopes of Mount Carmel on 10 May. He then laid siege to other cities in northern Palestine (Canaan), taking them one by one.

PREPARING FOR ARMAGEDDON

A coalition of Canaanite forces under Durusha's command was encamped at the fortified city of Megiddo on the northern slope of Mt Carmel. This key site commanded the trade route to Anatolia, Syria and the Euphrates. As the British Second World War commander Field-Marshal Lord Montgomery put it: 'the battlefield was well chosen, for this ridge is the first real natural barrier to confront an army marching north out of Egypt'.

The Egyptian pharaoh's successful campaign is illustrated in the reliefs carved on the pylons at the Temple of the Imperial God Amun at Karnak, as well as on his stelae in the Cairo Museum. These 'annals' document the conquest of Megiddo. At Karnak, Thutmose is depicted as carrying out the wishes of Amun by smiting his enemies.

The Egyptians took the rebels by surprise by advancing down a narrow pass in single file on a three-day-long march rather than taking the easier, more obvious routes. Durusha was caught with his army outside the city walls, and was forced to join battle on the Plain of Megiddo. The pharaoh's army advanced in a concave, enveloping formation: the southern wing wound round the rebels at the hill of Kina while the northern one cut them off from the town of Megiddo. The pharaoh's army used shock tactics in the form of a massive chariot corps and a corps of archers. They cut communications and surrounded the enemy.

At a crucial moment, however, Thutmose lost control of his men, who

> *'... the battlefield was well chosen, for this ridge is the first real natural barrier to confront an army marching north out of Egypt.'*

FIELD-MARSHAL LORD MONTGOMERY ON THE STRATEGIC POSITION OF MEGIDDO

were so intent on plunder that they failed to prevent Durusha and his army from taking refuge in Megiddo and slamming shut the gates. Although the city's main well lay outside the town, provision had been made to ensure the garrison always had ample water. A 18-metre (60-ft) vertical shaft had been sunk from the citadel, which then accessed the water supply via a horizontal tunnel to the well. Even so, after a seven-month siege Thutmose finally managed to starve Megiddo into submission.

RELENTLESS PURSUIT

Thutmose is said to have seized impressive quantities of booty, including over 2,000 horses, chariots, armour and weaponry. Durusha escaped, but the fall of Megiddo enabled Thutmose to impose his authority as far as the River Euphrates.

Thutmose continued to pursue the rebel king of Kadesh, and six years later attacked his capital. Kadesh was the most impregnable fortress in Syria. Its formidable riverine defence network comprised the Orontes, a tributary and a canal cut between the town and the two waterways.

After an arduous siege, Thutmose captured Kadesh, thereby freeing Egypt of the immediate threat of invasion. Finally, in the 33rd year of his reign, Thutmose reconquered the land won by the Mitanni and received tributes from many cities in the region. The Mitanni were pursued beyond the Euphrates. Even so, they continued to be a thorn in the side of Egypt. When Thutmose died in 1425, the Egyptian empire was at its apogee.

LAND OF CONFLICT

A second Battle of Megiddo took place in September 1918, when the British general Sir Edmund Allenby captured the city from the Turks. The land that stretches from the Mediterranean to the Red Sea, the Dead Sea and the Sea of Galilee has seen more than its fair share of armed conflict, from Megiddo to Suez in 1956 and the Six-Day War of 1967, plus more recent battles between Israel and her Arab neighbours.

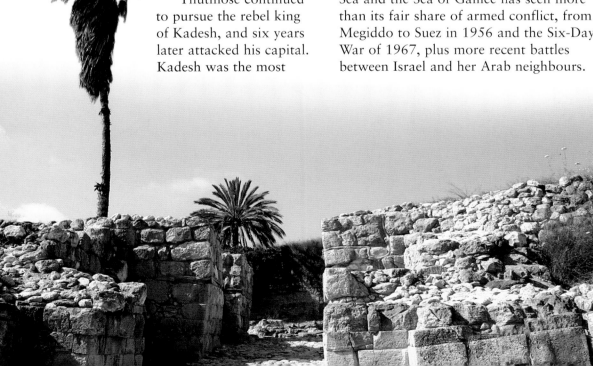

Ruins of the city gate at Megiddo (now Tel Megiddo in northern Israel). This important ancient city was made a UNESCO World Heritage Site in 2005.

THERMOPYLAE

Leonidas of Sparta *v.* Xerxes, king of Persia 480 BC

THE BATTLE OF THERMOPYLAE, fought between King Leonidas of Sparta and the Persian king Xerxes, was little more than a holding action to delay the invasion and subjugation of Greece. It tested the mettle of the Spartans, the great warrior caste of Ancient Greece, a breed comparable to the Prussians of early modern history. Indeed, the epithet 'Spartan' has flattered military leaders for more than two millennia and the martial virtues of the ancient Greek kingdom were particularly appealing to Adolf Hitler.

The selfless dedication and sacrifice that was exemplified by Leonidas of Sparta at Thermopylae appealed strongly to the Romantic sensibilities of the early 19th century. This painting by the Italian Massimo Taparelli d'Azeglio was completed in 1823, during Greece's war of independence from the Ottoman Turks, when Byron and others flocked to fight for the cause of Greek nationalism.

For Xerxes, the invasion of Greece was unfinished business. His father Darius had attempted the same, but had come unstuck at the Battle of Marathon in 490 BC. A body of Greeks – actually a tiny minority of the city-states – had agreed to bury their differences at Sparta in 481 and at Corinth in the spring of 480. This show of unity was very remarkable in itself, as the Peloponnesian Wars were to prove later. The rest of Greece had either gone over to Persia or hoped to weather the storm.

Sparta had been assigned the leadership of both land and naval forces, but in terms of numbers, the Greeks could only muster a small army to fight the Persians. Sparta had about 40,000 heavily-armed hoplites sheathed in armour and more lightly-armed troops. The name 'hoplite' derived from the characteristic round shield or *hoplon*, which was carried over the left arm, while in his right hand the warrior carried a 2.5-metre- (8-ft-) long spear.

TAKING A STAND

Aware of the overwhelming numerical superiority of the invader, the Greeks looked for a place to hold him off. The first choice was the Gorge of Tempe in Thessaly, but the Thessalians were deemed untrustworthy. The Greeks therefore decided on a tactical withdrawal, retiring to the south and leaving the Persians to invade northern Greece unopposed.

After some hesitation, the Spartans chose to face the Persians at the narrow coastal pass of Thermopylae on the southern side of the Malian Gulf, an inlet of the Aegean west of Euboea, between Thessaly and Locris. While most of the land around the bay is flat, there is one point where it is hemmed in by the Callidromus Mountains, also known as the Cliffs of Trachis.

Thermopylae lay just south of the River Asopus. The name, a compound of the words *thermo-* and *pylai* (literally 'warm gates'), alludes to the hot sulphur springs that bubble up in the mountainside there, and to three pinch points on the defile between the cliff and the sea. At those points – the East, Middle and West Gates – the track was so narrow that only a single cart could pass.

The second-century AD traveller and writer Pausanius estimates the total Greek forces at the outset of the battle as 11,200. Around 1,000 of these were Phocians guarding a path through the mountains. It is more likely, however, that the Greek army numbered a mere 5,000 men. The ancient

The pass at Thermopylae seen from the foot of mountains that in 480 BC (see map right) rose steeply along the coastline of the Malian Gulf. The road that today crosses the plain gives an indication of the ancient shoreline.

MALIAN GULF

West Gate

Thermopylae

PERSIAN FORCES

Phocian Wall **LEONIDAS** East Gate

Middle Gate

The Mound Alpeni

+
Springs

R. Asopus

Anopaea path

PERSIAN FORCES

0   2 km

0   2 miles

Mt. Callidromus

Greek historian Herodotus, who was born four years before the battle, claimed that the Persians deployed 5 million men, but this is now dismissed as a wild exaggeration. Most estimates today give Xerxes nearer 200,000, accompanied by an armada of around 1,000 ships. A request for reinforcements by the Greeks had been stymied by the Olympic festival, which had to run its course before men could be released to fight. In the end, most of the army was sent southwards to safety after Leonidas learned that the Persians had been told of a mountain path that would circumvent the Greek force. The chiefly Athenian navy, which was on hand to give the soldiers support, was helped considerably by a storm that wrecked a large proportion of the Persian fleet. Herodotus saw 'God' as having had a hand in this.

PREPARING FOR BATTLE

Leonidas, who had just succeeded to the Spartan throne after the suicide of his brother Cleomenes, was left with 300 hand-picked men (in Herodotus's words 'all fathers of living sons') and a force of 700 Thespians, together with some 400 Thebans who were unconvinced of the need to protect Greece from Persia and were brought along more as hostages than as a fighting force. The Spartan king made use of a dilapidated wall at the 'Middle Gate' as a barricade behind which he could conceal the body of his men. Before the Persians took up their positions, he had his men rebuild it.

As soon as Xerxes arrived at the pass, he sent a Persian rider to reconnoitre who was able to see some of the Spartans in front of the wall that ran from the cliff to the sea. Others were concealed behind it. 'Some of them were stripped for exercise, while others were combing their hair.' They apparently paid scant attention to him while he did his best to assess their strength.

Xerxes was baffled by his scout's report. He sent for Damaratus, a deposed Spartan king who had been granted asylum by Xerxes's father Darius. Even so, Damaratus may have retained a soft spot for his former realm, as he tipped the Spartans off about the Persian invasion by sending them a secret message hidden under a coating of wax.

A modern monument on the site of the battle at Thermopylae comprises a bronze statue of Leonidas on a plinth inscribed with the Greek words *molōn labé*. This phrase, which Leonidas is supposed to have uttered in response to the Persians' demand for his troops to lay down their weapons, means: 'Come and get them!'

'Some of them were stripped for exercise, while others were combing their hair.'

XERXES OBSERVING THE SPARTANS' PREPARATIONS FOR BATTLE

Damaratus warned Xerxes that the Spartans would be tough nuts to crack, and explained that it was the Spartan custom to groom their hair before battle, particularly if they thought they would not survive.

BRUTE FORCE VERSUS TACTICS

Herodotus tells us that Xerxes expected the Spartans to flee when they realized how hopeless their position was and how greatly outnumbered they were. When they failed to do so, he waited four or five days before losing patience and sending in the first wave of troops. These Medes and Cissians had instructions to capture the Spartans and bring them before him. The Medes were badly bloodied and were soon withdrawn and replaced with the 'Immortals', the élite Persian force commanded by Hydarnes.

In the confined space, however, Persian numerical superiority brought them no advantage, and the Greeks were able to wreak havoc with their longer spears. Moreover, the Persians could not profit from their famous cavalry or bowmen, as neither could be brought to bear against the Spartans in this narrow strip. The Spartans also employed the tactic of running away from the enemy to give them the impression they were retreating in confusion, then suddenly wheeling round to face them in good order and inflicting innumerable casualties. The dead soon began to fester in the summer sun, further sapping Persian morale. The Persians retreated to find another way of dealing with the Spartans.

A detachment of 1,000 or so Phocians had been detailed to watch the mountain pass lest the Persians discover a means of coming around the back of the Spartans at the wall. Meanwhile, a Malian by the name of Ephialtes came to the Persian camp to inform Xerxes of just such a path in the hope of gaining a rich reward.

The track began at the Asopus and ran along the Anopaea ridge before descending behind Black-Buttocks' Stone to Alpeni, close to the East Gate at the rear of the Spartan warriors. The Persian Immortals marched by night, the Oeta Mountains on their right and the Cliffs of Trachis on their left. By dawn they sighted the Phocian force stationed at the top of the pass. Taken by surprise, the Phocians were unable to organize their defences before coming under fire from the Persian archers, and withdrew in disarray further up the mountain.

GLORIOUS DEFEAT

The Spartans defending Thermopylae had their first inkling of their coming defeat when a seer named Megistias read the sacrificial entrails (augury was common practice in ancient times). Messengers arriving during the night confirmed his prophecies. With the exception of the Spartans, the Thespians and the captive Thebans, who elected to fight on, the other Greeks withdrew to defend the Isthmus at Corinth. Leonidas may have deliberately decided to sacrifice himself and his men since he had been told by the Delphic Oracle that a Spartan king would first have to fall if Sparta herself was to be spared destruction.

Knowing their fate, the Spartans and the Thespians fought to the last. They went out into the plain in front of the wall to face Xerxes's army. Herodotus tells us that: 'Many of the barbarians fell; behind them

'Go tell the Spartans, passer-by,
That here, obedient to her laws we lie.'

SIMONIDES – EPITAPH FOR THE SPARTANS WHO FELL AT THERMOPYLAE

the enemy commanders plied their whips indiscriminately, driving the men on. Many fell into the sea and were drowned, and still more were trampled to death by one another. No one could count the number of the dead. The Greeks, who knew that the enemy were on their way round by the mountain track and that death was inevitable, exerted all their strength and fought with fury and desperation. By this time most of their spears were broken, and they were killing Persians with their swords.'

King Leonidas fell in the battle together with several members of the Persian royal house. The Greeks fought to protect the king's body and four times they drove the Persians off. It was only when the Persian forces arrived from behind that they had to fall back on the wall in a single compact group and fight with their hands and teeth when they could no longer wield their swords. The Persians won the day with a hail of missiles from their archers. The Spartan Dienekes deserves special mention for his cool response on being told that the impending torrent of Persian arrows would blot out the sun: 'If the Persians hide the sun we will fight in the shade.'

After the battle Xerxes ordered his men to find Leonidas's body, sever his head and fix it on a stake. Only one Spartan survived according to Herodotus's account, and that was because he was recovering from an eye infection during the battle. Nor did the Thebans manage to convince the Persians immediately that they were mere hostages, and many were killed.

Thermopylae was a defeat with no major military significance: it held up the Persian advance for just three days, barely enough to create a new defensive line. It is also doubtful that the Greeks killed 20,000 Persians – the tally attributed by Herodotus. If the battle has a significance, it is that it taught the Greeks and subsequent generations of the dignity of personal sacrifice and the need to take a stand against tyranny.

Stone relief carving of Xerxes (I) the Great (r.485–465 BC) on the wall of his palace at Persepolis, capital of the Achaemenid (Persian) empire.

SALAMIS

SOME POSITIVE FACTORS EMERGED FROM THE DEFEAT at Thermopylae: the Athenian fleet had passed muster and, man for man, the hoplites had proved more than a match for Persian infantrymen. Even so, the Persians had only been delayed, not beaten: the real battle was still to be fought. In the face of the Persian advance, the Greeks withdrew from their first line of defence, abandoning Attica. Their plan was to fall back on the Isthmus of Corinth and to defend the Peloponnese.

The population fled too, seeking refuge behind the Greek lines. The Persians raped and pillaged those who remained behind, and were only prevented from violating the holy places at Delphi by the supposed divine intervention of Zeus, who sent two huge rocks crashing down on the invaders approaching the shrine. The survivors fled in disarray. The Delphic Oracle had been sending out contradictory messages, urging the Greeks to flee, while advising the Athenians to put their faith in a 'wall of wood'. Some interpreted this as a call to strengthen the city's defences with a wooden palisade, while others saw it as a reference to the navy.

The Greeks fell back in waves. First Boeotia was abandoned to its fate. Then the Athenians quit their city at the Persian approach. A small number of poor, old or infirm Athenians remained on the Acropolis, but that yielded to Persian besiegers, who sacked and burned the Holy of Holies and murdered those who had sought asylum under its aegis.

It now fell to the brilliant – but allegedly venal – Athenian commander Themistocles to rally the Greeks. Themistocles had risen through the ranks by virtue of his martial prowess, but he was not a member of the old Athenian élite, and may have been seen as untrustworthy as a result. His later fate – ostracism and exile – seemed to bear this out.

A SEABORNE TRADING EMPIRE

The Graeco-Roman historian Plutarch calls Themistocles the 'Father of the Athenian Navy'. Prior to the Persian invasion, he had persuaded his people to use the money from a newly discovered silver mine to build a fleet of 100 triremes, to supplement those they already possessed. As these vessels were expensive to run, it was ordained that the wealthiest Athenians should pay for the upkeep of one ship each – a sort of supertax aimed at the rich. Athens, argued Themistocles, could never hope to win on land, but with a powerful navy they could both 'keep the Persians at bay and make themselves masters of Greece'.

Where the Spartans were the greatest warriors among the Greeks, Athens was a state that had grown rich on trade, much like the later British empire, which could only be sustained by a huge navy. Athenian commercial interests throughout the Mediterranean dictated the necessity of a good fleet. Sparta had the largest army, but Athens was the most powerful city-state on the water. At Salamis, more than half the fleet of 370 or so ships belonged to Athens.

RALLYING SUPPORT

Themistocles must have been aware that he had only had a small minority of Greeks on his side: most had gone over to the enemy. Only a fifth of the city-states had chosen to fight the Persians, the others had pledged support to the enemy in order to save their land and people. He also needed to be cunning to counteract the Persians' overwhelming numerical superiority: first he had to cajole the other generals into accepting his plan and then mislead the Persians by feeding them disinformation. He began by trying to lure away from the Persian camp Greeks from Asia Minor like the Ionians and Carians.

Themistocles could count on the Persians dancing to his tune: all but one of Xerxes's commanders were in favour of fighting at sea. The only dissenter was Queen Artemisia of Halicarnassus, who pointed out that the Greeks were more experienced in this form of warfare, and by taking Athens the Persians had already fulfilled their war aims. Xerxes, though, heeded the majority of his commanders – there was to be a naval battle.

Artemisia's later apparent bravery in the battle (in fact, according to Herodotus, her ship rammed and sank a Greek trireme by accident, while fleeing from another) prompted a baffled Xerxes to exclaim: 'My men have turned into women, my women into men.'

Meanwhile, the Greeks continued to bicker. Resistance to the idea of an Athenian commanding the fleet had led to the appointment of the Spartan Eurybiades as admiral. Themistocles was for fighting at Salamis, not least because many Athenians had taken refuge on the island opposite Athens and were still extremely vulnerable to the Persians across the bay.

The naval clash at Salamis, as seen by a 19th-century illustrator. The Athenian triremes that took part in the engagement were manned by crews of 170 oarsmen together with 18-man-strong detachments of marines, made up of four archers and 14 hoplites. Salamis was essentially a land battle fought at sea.

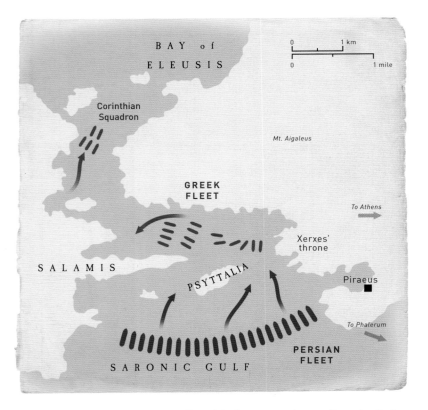

BAY of ELEUSIS

0   1 km
0   1 mile

Corinthian Squadron

Mt. Aigaleus

GREEK FLEET

To Athens

Xerxes' throne

SALAMIS

PSYTTALIA

Piraeus

To Phalerum

SARONIC GULF

PERSIAN FLEET

Run-up to the Battle of Salamis. As the Persian fleet closed in on Psyttalia, the Greek force under Themistocles feigned disarray, with some ships – the Corinthian squadron – even breaking off north as if to head for the bay of Eleusis.

Eurybiades wanted to sail to the Isthmus and reinforce the Greek line of defence there. He proved pusillanimous when it came to the crunch. Not so Themistocles. 'Themistocles,' chided Eurybiades, 'at the games they whip those who are too quick off the mark.' The Athenian replied: 'Yes, but they award no prizes to those who get left behind.'

The Persians arrived at dusk and took up position opposite the Greek fleet. Their army was on the march towards the Peloponnese. At this point, Themistocles employed a daring subterfuge. He sent Sicinnus, his children's tutor and a former Persian slave, over to the Persian fleet, telling him to inform them that his master was actually on their side. Sicinnus claimed that the Greeks were fearful and disunited and that most would either slip away or join forces with the Persians. Herodotus reports that the Persians were taken in, and blocked the Greeks' escape route so that they were forced to stand and fight.

The action took place between modern Ambelákia on Salamis and Pérama in Attica. According to the Greek playwright Aeschylus, the Persians faced the Greeks

with 1,207 ships, but only around 700 were moored at Phalerum ready to fight. Some 200 Egyptian vessels were sent to seal off the western approaches to the bay, while 400 troops were landed on the island of Psyttalia, where they were massacred the day after the battle.

TIME, TIDE AND TACTICS

Bad weather had done much to whittle down the Persian expeditionary force: many of its ships were sunk off Euboea. In an indecisive skirmish at Artemisium, Themistocles's choice of a tight position had thwarted the numerically superior Persian flotilla. The Greek force then fell back on Salamis.

He knew the Athenians had to fight by sea, and chose the place with care: once again, the strait between Salamis and the mainland was too narrow for the Persians to bring their superiority to bear – they outnumbered the Greeks three to one.

Themistocles delivered a stirring oration to the mariners before they boarded their ships. According to Plutarch, it was not just the position of Themistocles's fleet, but his tactics that won the day. The Greeks lay in wait behind Psyttalia, while the Persians came in from the open sea. Xerxes watched the entire drama play out seated on a golden stool on Mount Aigaleus.

The Athenian commander made it appear to the Persians that his fleet was in disarray. He only deployed his ships at the time of day when the wind blew up. This had no effect on the Greek vessels, as they were light and sat low in the water, but the wind slewed round the higher, heavier Persian ships and made them turn their flanks towards the enemy.

Some say that Pallas Athena, patron goddess of the city, appeared in person to egg the Athenians on. Others claim it was Dionysus. At first the Greek fleet backed off, almost running aground in the process, then Ameinias of Pallene and Socles of

Piraeus, commanding an Athenian vessel, moved forward to ram the Persian flagship captained by Xerxes's brother Ariamenes. According to Plutarch: 'the ships collided, prow to prow and their bronze beaks became firmly entangled together, but Ameinias and Socles made a stand against him and hit him so hard with their spears that he fell into the sea.'

Other ships came forward to assist Ameinias. Time and again, the Greeks rammed into the Persians' exposed sides, breaking their oars and leaving the vessels stranded. The Persians sent in squadron after squadron, but the ships got in each other's way, causing utter chaos. The Greek victory was total. The enemy was destroyed. Xerxes's fleet was broken, along with his nerve, and the Persians turned sail and fled.

PUT TO FLIGHT

The Persians lost over 200 ships, while Greek losses amounted to about 40. As they turned to flee, the Persians collided with their own ships again, causing mayhem. Those that escaped the mêlée were intercepted by the Aeginetan Squadron. Indeed, the battle honours were awarded to Aegina, rather than Athens, with Polycritus of Aegina, Eumenes of Anagyrus and Ameinias of Pallene singled out as the most valiant. Most of the Greeks survived the fight, Herodotus tells us, because they could swim over to Salamis. The Persians could not, and drowned.

Leaving Mardonius behind with a sizable army, Xerxes took Artemisia's advice and went home. Plutarch claims it was Themistocles who frightened him away by sending a eunuch to tell him that the Greeks were on their way to the Hellespont to burn the bridge of boats. His once proud army was decimated by disease and ravaged by hunger. Only a fraction made it back to the Hellespont. Mardonius's army was defeated at Plataea and the Persian menace to Greece evaporated.

Plutarch regarded Salamis as the greatest sea battle ever fought. It was the victory of Themistocles's 'sound judgement and ingenuity'.

Battle is joined at Salamis. The Persians fell for Themistocles's ruse and sailed into the narrows. Meanwhile, the Greeks had regrouped and suddenly rowed hard into the attack, ramming the Persian triremes. The Corinthian squadron changed course and sailed back to rejoin the main force.

'A king sat on the rocky brow / Which looks o'er sea-born Salamis; / And ships, by thousands, lay below, / And men in nations; all were his! / He counted them at break of day, / And when the sun set – where were they?'

LORD BYRON, 'THE ISLES OF GREECE', ON XERXES'S CRUSHING DEFEAT AT SALAMIS

PELOPONNESIAN CAMPAIGNS

Athens v. Sparta 431–404 BC

THE PELOPONNESIAN WARS ranged Athens (centring on Attica) and its allies on one side, and Sparta and its satellites (based in the Peloponnesian Peninsula) on the other in a battle for supremacy in Greece. According to historian J. E. Lendon, it was 'a war of cruel accidents and fleeting chances'. The First Peloponnesian War broke out in 460 BC and lasted until 446 BC. It was caused by the Athenians and culminated in an invasion of Attica by a Peloponnesian army. Athens concluded a peace that lasted for a generation.

The two catalysts for the Second Peloponnesian War were the battles of Corcyra in 435 and Potidaea in 432 BC when Athens clashed with Corinth. At the Battle of Potidaea, the philosopher Socrates and the future Athenian commander Alcibiades shared a tent. Potidaea paid tribute to Athens, but refused to pull down its walls at the Athenians' demand. Corinth appealed to Sparta to help the Potidaeans, and the result was a formal declaration of war.

SHIFTING FORTUNES

A short-lived peace was ruptured by a Theban attack on Plataea, which was allied to Athens, in 431 BC. A Theban force of just 300 entered the city by night thanks to the help of a traitor, and Plataea was only saved through the swift reaction of the city's inhabitants. This attack clearly violated the truce, and the war began afresh. Virtually all mainland Greece sided with the Spartans, while the islands of Greece and Asia Minor backed the Athenians.

Eighty days after the Theban attack, a Peloponnesian army overran Attica, an event that was to be repeated five times up to 425 BC. The initial response of the Athenian leader Pericles was to take refuge within the city walls. Athenian military action was confined to the odd show of bravura by their cavalry. Their navy was so powerful that they could launch their attacks on the Peloponnese by ship. After Pericles's death, Athens became more aggressive in its response to Sparta.

In 425, the Spartans and their allies invaded Attica once again and laid waste to the country. The Athenians under Demosthenes seized the headland of Pylos on the southwest of the Peloponnese and fortified it, forcing the Peloponnesians under King Agis to return home. Sixty Peloponnesian ships were sent to the spot where Demosthenes exhorted the Athenians with a rousing speech ('beat back the enemy at the water's edge') and prepared to mount a spirited defence, but it was the Athenian fleet that carried the day. After the battle, 420 Spartan hoplites were trapped on Sphacteria, an island to the south. They were eventually forced to capitulate when

Detail from an Attic amphora (fifth century BC), showing close-quarters combat between hoplites. The armed forces of the ancient Greek city-states were made up of all free men of fighting age; many poets and philosophers served their time as hoplites.

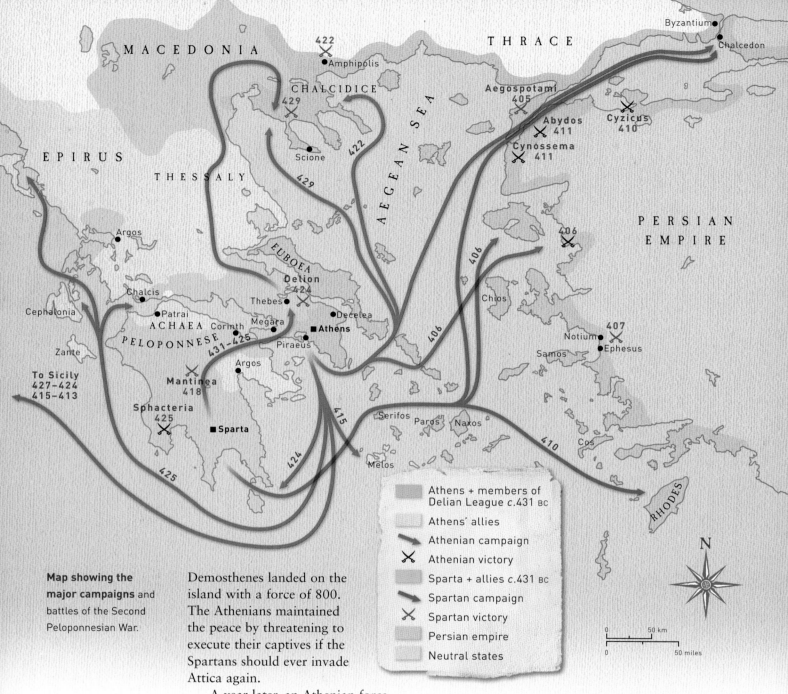

Map showing the major campaigns and battles of the Second Peloponnesian War.

Demosthenes landed on the island with a force of 800. The Athenians maintained the peace by threatening to execute their captives if the Spartans should ever invade Attica again.

A year later, an Athenian force commanded by Hippocrates suffered a major defeat at the hands of the Boeotians and Thebans under General Pagondas at Delion (modern Dhilesi). The Athenians were intent on gaining control of the city – site of an important shrine to Apollo – in order to try and provoke an uprising by democrats throughout Boeotia. The plot crumbled when the Boeotian revolt failed to take place, and some 1,000 Athenian hoplites were killed. Once again, Alcibiades and Socrates were present in subaltern roles.

The victorious enemy harassed and picked off the Athenian army as they retreated.

A brief peace was concluded in 421 after the deaths of the Spartan leader Brasidas and the Athenian Cleon, but Athens and its allies were soon whipped up again by the colourful and controversial figure of Alcibiades, a wealthy Athenian who had been adopted by the leading political force in the city, Pericles, in whose home he grew to manhood. Alcibiades might even have been named Pericles's heir had it not been for

> *'For when a king is in the field all commands proceed from him: he gives word to the Polemarchs; they to the Lochagoi; these to the Pentecotyes; these again to the Enomotarchs, and these last to the Enomoties.'*

THUCYDIDES, CHRONICLER OF THE PELOPONNESIAN WAR, ON THE SPARTAN CHAIN OF COMMAND

his irreverent and sacrilegious lifestyle. He vaingloriously styled himself a descendant of the mythical Greek hero Ajax. Nevertheless, most people had to concede that he was an outstanding commander on land and at sea.

MORALE-BOOSTING VICTORY

At Mantinea in 418 BC, the Spartans won a resounding victory over a combined force from Athens and Argos. However, this battle took place far from Athens – according to Plutarch: 'in a place where victory brought the Lacedaemonians (Spartans) no significant additional advantage, and where, had they been defeated, the position of Lacedaemon would have been precarious'. The Spartans had been taken by surprise, but succeeded in rallying and turning the tide.

The following description of the battle by the Greek writer Thucydides, author of *The History of the Peloponnesian War*, affords us an insight into the Spartan command structure: 'The Spartans … returning to their old encampment by the temple of Hercules, suddenly saw their adversaries close in front of them, all in battle order … there was scant time for preparation, and they instantly and hastily fell into their ranks, under the direction of their king, Agis, according to law. For when a king is in the field all commands proceed from him: he gives word to the Polemarchs; they to the Lochagoi; these to the Pentecotyes; these again to the Enomotarchs, and these last to the Enomoties.'

The Spartans advanced on the Argives accompanied by flute-players, who were 'meant to make them advance evenly, stepping in time, without breaking their order as large armies are apt to do in the moment of engaging'. The Spartan shields were locked together. One Spartan wing was routed, but the 300 troops of the king's bodyguard charged the Argive veterans and routed them. When a messenger brought news of the victory back to Sparta, he was rewarded with nothing more than a piece of meat. Yet joy was unconfined among the Spartan forces: 'for it is said that before this the men had felt so ashamed of the defeats they had suffered that they had not even been able to look their wives in the face' (Plutarch).

AMBITION AND TREACHERY

Alcibiades was able to win the common people of Argos over to the Athenian side when the city-state's oligarchy went over to the Spartans. Once the city was secure, he shipped stone from Athens to help them extend its defensive walls down to the sea. Peace returned to much of Greece, but the Spartans remained aloof, as they were hoping to acquire the land of Messene. Alcibiades himself was bogged down in preparations for the disastrous Sicilian campaign against Syracuse (415–413 BC), which aimed to establish an Athenian colony on the island. In Alcibiades's eyes, Sicily was only the beginning of a huge Athenian empire that would ultimately take in Carthage, Libya, Italy and the Peloponnese. Alcibiades had managed to fire up the young men of Athens with these ideas, 'the upshot [of which] was that in the wrestling-schools and alcoves people would commonly be seen sitting and mapping out the shape of Sicily and the position of Libya and Carthage' (Plutarch).

Aside from being a military fiasco, the Sicilian campaign ruined Alcibiades's reputation, when he fled to Sparta rather than face accusations of immorality at home. While there, he proposed an alliance between Sparta and Persia. He also fortified Decelea in Attica, placing a permanent garrison there to hold Athens in a state of siege. He wooed the Ionian cities away from their allegiance to Athens, tipping the scales of war in Sparta's favour. But despite performing all these services for his new masters, Alcibiades still found no friends among the Spartans. They distrusted him, suspecting he would return to his native land one day. Fearing that plans were afoot to assassinate him, Alcibiades decided to jump ship.

PLOTTING HIS RETURN

From Sparta, Alcibiades went to Persia, taking refuge with Tissaphernes, one of King Darius's prefects. From Persia, he was able to channel help towards his native city against Sparta, thereby fulfilling the Spartans' worst fears. He also negotiated with Athens in the hope that it might pardon him. To this end,

he held secret talks with Pisander, an Athenian commander on Samos, who favoured aristocrats like Alcibiades and the overthrow of democracy in Athens.

Agitiation by the oligarchs of Samos brought regime change in Athens in 411 BC, when an oligarchy known as the Four Hundred supplanted the democratic order. This development was ultimately to lead to Alcibiades's recall from exile – though ironically not by the city's new rulers. In the meantime, Alcibiades formed a triumvirate with the democratic generals Thrasybulus and Theramenes to oppose the Spartans. This alliance enjoyed great military success.

CYZICUS AND AFTER

Most importantly, at the Battle of Cyzicus in 410 BC, they destroyed the Spartan fleet that was threatening vital Athenian grain supplies from the Hellespont. The Athenian fleet numbered 86 vessels, the Spartans only six fewer.

Before the battle, the Athenians moved under cover of darkness and moored off the island of Proconnesus. Alcibiades delivered a

'Ships lost. Mindarus dead. Men starving.
No idea what to do.'

rousing speech to the Athenians, telling them they would not only have to fight at sea or on land, but even lay siege to the enemy in his fortresses; also there was no money in the treasury to pay them unless they won them all. With that he got them to board their ships. Chaereas was put in charge of the Athenian army, while Alcibiades, Theramenes and Thrasybulus took charge of the naval squadrons.

When Alcibiades sailed boldly into the western harbour of Cyzicus with his squadron of around 40 ships, the Spartan admiral Mindarus assumed this represented the entirety of the Athenian navy. He therefore set off with his full fleet in pursuit of Alcibiades as he made for the Artace Headland. At the agreed moment, Alcibiades wheeled round and Theramenes and Thrasybulus attacked Mindarus from concealed positions to his rear.

Mindarus fled to Cleri, where his Persian ally Pharnabazus had his army.

Alcibiades was able to destroy some of the Spartan vessels, but it was only when Theramenes joined up with Chaereas's forces that the Athenians were able to rescue Alcibiades and the Persian general ordered his men to retreat. Mindarus was killed not long after and the Spartans scattered. Cyzicus was abandoned to its fate, and the Athenians secured the Hellespont and swept the Spartans from the seas. A typically laconic despatch was sent back to Sparta: 'Ships lost. Mindarus dead. Men starving. No idea what to do.'

In the wake of the victory at Cyzicus, the unpopular oligarchic government in Athens was replaced by a restored democracy. In 407 BC, Alcibiades returned in triumph. But barely a year later, he was unfairly blamed for the Athenian defeat at the Battle of Notium and banished anew. Athens lost the Second Peloponnesian War in 404 BC. A few weeks after the cessation of hostilities, Alcibiades was murdered in Phrygia.

The Temple of Poseidon at Sounion on the southernmost tip of the Attic Peninsula, south of Athens. In 413 BC, the Athenians fortified this site to prevent it from falling into Spartan hands. Control of the promontory was vital for ensuring the safe passage of Athens' seaborne grain supply from Euboea.

CHAERONEA

Philip of Macedon *v.* the Hellenic League 338 BC

THE KINGDOM OF MACEDON in northern Greece rose to power under Philip II and reached its zenith under his son Alexander the Great. One of the principal innovations of this warlike state was to supplant the 'soldier-citizen' hoplites maintained by the Greek city-states with a more professional standing force. This 'new model' army was equipped with long pikes (*sarissai*) made from two lengths of tough wood, probably cherry. Under inspired leadership, the Macedonians became a power to be reckoned with.

In addition, Philip's troops were reinforced by Agrianian and Thracian javelin throwers and Cretan archers, as well as proto-regiments with titles like the 'Royal Foot Companions' and the 'Royal Shield Bearers'. The employment this army gave to the peasants made them loyal to their king rather than to the local nobles.

WARRIOR STATE

Like Prussia under Frederick William I (the 'Soldier King'), Macedon was conceived as a military state. The fact that Philip's men were banned from taking hot baths compounds this image of stern martial discipline. Slaves worked the land and mines, while native Macedonians were trained from an early age in the arts of war, especially how to use their spears.

Macedonian soldiers were more lightly armed than hoplites. They wore leg-armour and metal helmets in the form of Phrygian bonnets. Shields were small to allow them to wield their spears. Infantry units initially comprised 10 ranks of 16 men each, but evolved into 16 x 16, a total of 256 men. A phalanx was a force of 10,500, which was subdivided into seven 1,500-strong squadrons, or 'taxies', each commanded by a Macedonian noble.

Defeat of the Persian king Darius III by Alexander the Great at the Battle of Issus in 333 BC (scene from a Roman mosaic). In the background can be seen the principal fighting weapon of the Macedonian army, the long pike or *sarissa*.

The unprotected right flank was accompanied by a unit of shield bearers, who wore full armour. These were Philip's crack troops when he was forced to retreat from the plains. They were flanked by the cavalry, who were naturally also positioned on the left flank. Mounted units formed a wedge shape among the Macedonians and a diamond among their Thessalian allies. These shapes were intended to help the units turn. The cavalry wore no stirrups, but sported breastplates and leather skirts, and carried short swords called *kopis* in one hand and a 2.7-metre (9-ft) spear called a *xyston* in the other. The spear was brought to bear first, and once it had hit home was cast aside in favour of the slashing sword. Philip led the cavalry in person.

SECURING THE KINGDOM

In an effort to consolidate his kingdom, Philip of Macedon pushed north and west as far as the Danube to subdue the Thracians and Illyrians and as far as the Black Sea in the east. Philip had learned the arts of war from Epaminondas of Thebes, the greatest general of his age, who was an early advocate of cavalry and infantry formations up to 48 ranks in depth.

Emulating Epaminondas, Philip re-formed his own cavalry as a first-wave shock force, charging at the enemy and throwing them into confusion with a concerted spear attack. The infantry would then move in to finish them off. We may liken this use of cavalry to an early form of artillery barrage.

Another key weapon in Philip's armoury was the siege engine, which helped him to conquer no fewer than 32 northern Greek towns including Amphipolis, Potidaea, Pydna and Methone. He resettled these conquered lands with Macedonian farmers, who in turn bred horses and rode them in his armies. A similar idea would later resurface in Hitler's concept of *Lebensraum* ('living space').

Philip allied himself to the Thebans and Thessalians in a 'sacred war' against the Phocians and razed the city of Olynthus to the ground after it had defied him in a siege lasting a year.

Yet Philip was fully aware that he would eventually have to take on the Thebans and Athenians. Late in 339, he encamped at Chaeronea in Boeotia, on the Phocian borders some 30 miles (48 km) north of Thebes, which dominated the Cephissus Valley, an important land route though the rocky terrain south of Thermopylae. Historian Ian Worthington has succinctly summed up what was at stake here: 'The battle was to decide the fate of Greece: if the Greeks won, they calculated that they would retain their freedom and

> *'The battle was to decide the fate of Greece: if the Greeks won, they calculated that they would retain their freedom and autonomy ... If Philip won, Greece was his. It was as simple as that.'*
>
> HISTORIAN IAN WORTHINGTON

autonomy... If Philip won, Greece was his. It was as simple as that.'

ROUT AT CHAERONEA

The Hellenic League was slow to respond, so the battle did not take place until 22 August the following year, probably on a field between the River Cephissus and the Acropolis of Chaeronea. The site was narrow – about 2 miles (3 km) wide – and was bisected by a number of rivers, with hills to the north and south. To the east, there were marshes. The border of the plain was the river. It had been chosen to inhibit Philip's lethal cavalry. Should the line break, it was easy to retreat up the Cerata Pass.

Philip moved up from Elatea to Parapotamii and on to Chaeronea. His son Alexander pitched his tent under an oak that was still known as 'Alexander's Oak' in Plutarch's day. Philip is reputed to have possessed an army of 30,000 infantry and 2,000 cavalry, slightly more than his adversaries in the Greek camp. About 24,000 of these were Macedonians, while the rest were supplied by Philip's allies. The Athenians under the command of Chares, Lysicles and Stratocles held the left of the line, the Thebans under Theagenes the right. They had a slight numerical advantage over their foe: 30,000 infantry and 3,800 cavalry. Boeotia had sent 12,000 hoplites, including the Sacred Band of Thebes, an élite infantry corps of 254 men.

The units were arranged ethnically and each flank was anchored in a river. Alexander's cavalry faced the Sacred Band. It looked as if the battle would be decided by the infantry, as the front was too narrow to give advantage to the cavalry. It began shortly after dawn on 1 or 4 August 338. The Macedonians had more experience of fighting and the Athenians had never met the Macedonians in the field before. Details are uncertain, but it is believed that Philip's right wing

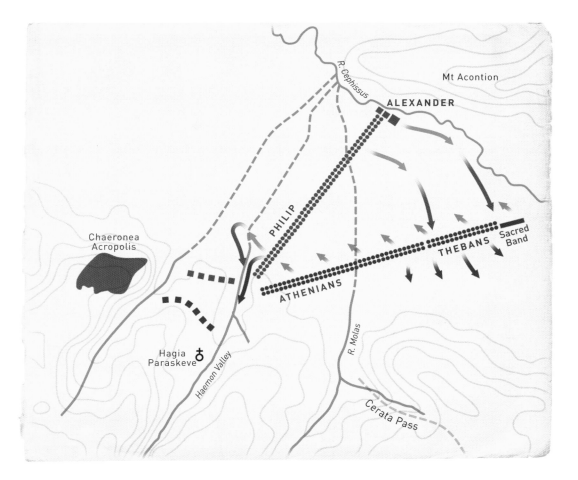

feigned a retreat, leading the Athenians on the left to break ranks and pursue them. This opened up a gap in the allied line, which had to contract in order to close it. Only the Sacred Band did not adjust its line and another gap opened. Philip retreated for 30 metres (100 ft). At that point, however, Philip launched his cavalry, commanded by his son Alexander, into the gap. He quickly surrounded and annihilated the Sacred Band, who fought to the last man. Their brave but futile resistance supposedly moved the austere Macedonian king to tears.

In the meantime, Philip's phalanx had stopped his feint and advanced again. His *sarissai* meant that the allies could get nowhere near his men. He drove the Athenians back into the river valley. Around 1,000 were killed and another 2,000 taken prisoner. The River Haemon was said to have run red with blood. Although elements of the allied forces fought with great bravery, the battle turned into a rout. Some survivors

managed to escape through the Cerata Pass. Philip reputedly commented wryly: 'The Athenians do not know how to win a victory.'

DAWN OF A NEW ORDER

The battle was nothing short of a catastrophe for Athens and Thebes. The latter had suffered even greater casualties than the Athenians. In Athens, General Lysicles was put on trial; the prosecutor referred to him as 'a living monument of our country's shame and disgrace' and he was condemned to death. The victory meant that most Greek cities now joined the League of Corinth, which accepted Macedonian leadership and subscribed to Philip's war on Persia. Chaeronea was a truly Clausewitzian victory, as it suppressed Greek liberties and kept the former city-states under the Macedonian thumb for a full century and a half.

Philip II was assassinated two years later at the Macedonian capital of Vergina and was succeeded by Alexander.

CANNAE

Hannibal *v.* the Roman Republic
2 August **216** BC

STRATEGISTS WHO TEACH AT MILITARY ACADEMIES consider the Battle of Cannae in southern Italy, at which the Carthaginian general Hannibal routed a Roman force against all odds, as the perfect battle. All subsequent battles are measured against the yardstick of this exemplary engagement.

The Punic Wars were the long-running conflict between Rome and Carthage for mastery of the Mediterranean. The first Punic War (264–241 BC) was fought when Rome was a comparatively weak fledgling state and not yet in full control of the Italian peninsula. Its catalyst was a struggle for control over the grain-rich island of Sicily and the city of Messina. It ended in Carthaginian defeat after a series of naval battles.

The Second Punic War (218–201 BC) came about through Carthage's desire for revenge. Indeed, Hannibal's father made his son swear 'never to bear goodwill to the Romans'.

A RISKY STRATEGY

Like Alexander the Great, who had inherited a magnificent army from Philip of Macedon, Hannibal had the use of a splendid fighting force put together by his father Hamilcar Barca. Like Alexander, Hannibal was essentially a cavalry leader. In 219, he began his march through Spain to engage the enemy in their homeland. His decision to take the long and perilous land route was to avoid a conflict at sea, which the Romans would inevitably win.

In 218, he crossed the Alps with his army of Libyan infantrymen, Numidian horsemen, Balearic slingers and assorted

Spaniards together – famously – with 37 elephants. (He was not the first general to use war-elephants: Alexander had used them too.) Although his arduous mountain trek had the advantage of surprise, it cost him over half his army, who 'perished by reason of the cold and lack of food; many also returned home'. So grievous were these losses that they almost scuppered his invasion plans.

Once in Italy, he harassed the Romans in their camp on the Trebbia, a tributary of the Po. The Romans gave battle, but their line was broken by Hannibal's cavalry. But it was not a total defeat, and 10,000 Romans were able to take refuge in Placentia (now Piacenza).

On the foggy morning of 21 June 217 BC, Hannibal ambushed the 25,000-strong army of Consul Flaminius between the southern Tuscan hills and Lake Trasimene and destroyed the bulk of the enemy. Only around 6,000 men escaped, and even they were rounded up later.

DATE WITH DESTINY

Despite these victories, Hannibal's army was in a parlous state. He didn't trust his men – a ragtag army whom the Roman writer Livy called 'the sweepings of every nation' – and was short of supplies. He considered retreating to Gaul, but instead

Roman calamity.
Cannae (now Canne della Battaglia in Apulia) was the most famous battle in ancient history and the worst defeat ever suffered by the Roman Republic. This painting of the clash is by the 19th-century French artist François-Nicolas Chifflart.

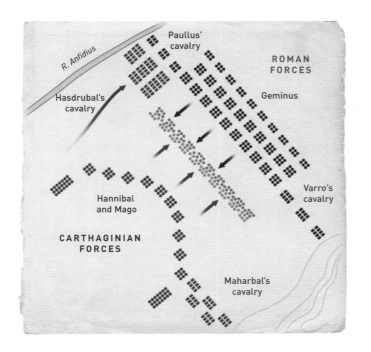

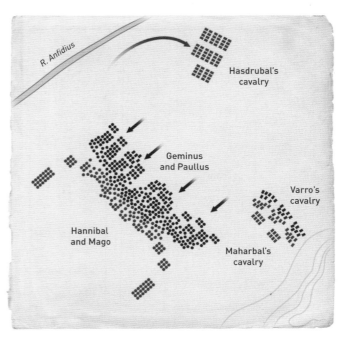

First two phases of the battle: the tactic devised by Hannibal to roll up and annihilate the Roman force facing him at Cannae came to be known as 'double envelopment'. As the infantry of Hannibal and Mago (Hannibal's brother) worked around the undefended flanks of the Roman legions, Hadrubal's cavalry fell upon their rear, completely surrounding them.

marched south to Apulia, because the harvest came earlier there. Commanding the Roman army sent to crush him once and for all were the consuls Gaius Terentius Varro and Lucius Aemilius Paullus. Posterity has judged these two men harshly, especially the impetuous Varro. The Roman army was almost twice the strength of the Carthaginian, but still, against Paullus's better judgement, let itself be drawn into fighting on Hannibal's terms. As Livy put it 'destiny itself was at its heels'.

The Carthaginian commander had around 46,000 infantry, made up of Celts, Spaniards, North Africans and Numidians, plus about 10,000 cavalry. The Roman army numbered eight whole legions – or 86,000 men.

Hannibal positioned his troops with their backs to the prevailing wind, which drove stinging dust over the plains of Cannae. The Roman historian Cassius Dio confirms how well this ploy worked during the battle, as the Romans found their vision and breathing impaired.

Raring to join battle, Hannibal tried to coax the Romans into attacking him. His plan was to send in his cavalry, the arm in which he excelled, 'to provoke the enemy by small-scale rapid charges'. Meanwhile, Paullus and Varro bickered about tactics.

SURROUND AND DESTROY

Hannibal began by feigning a retreat and then despatching his cavalry to harass the Romans at the watering-places right outside their camp gates. The cautious Paullus, whose 'turn' it was to command that day, wisely restrained his men from taking the bait. But on the following day, 2 August 216, Varro summarily gave the order to engage the enemy without even consulting his colleague. The two Roman camps joined together, with the cavalry on the right wing and the legionaries on their left. The javelins and light auxiliaries formed the centre under the command of consul Gnaeus Servillus Geminus. They adhered to their usual three-line infantry formation flanked by cavalry. Hannibal had the Gallic and Spanish horse on his left and the Numidians on his right. The infantry was in the centre: Gauls and Spaniards with African troops on each flank. The Africans were well equipped with Roman arms, the spoils of Trasimene.

After an inconclusive morning, Hannibal lured the Romans into a trap by bulging out his centre and strengthening his wings. He then sent his cavalry forward to the left to sweep the untrained Roman civilian cavalry from the confined field – they were hemmed in by the River Anfidius.

Hannibal then rode around the back of the Roman infantry to give help to the

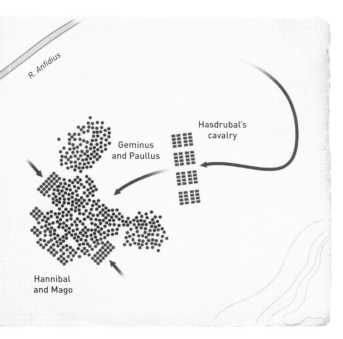

R. Anfidius

Hasdrubal's cavalry

Geminus and Paullus

Hannibal and Mago

The final phase of the battle, in which the huge Roman army was enveloped and wiped out.

Numidians on his right wing who were facing the allied cavalry. According to Livy's account, about 500 Numidians pretended to desert. They concealed their swords under their tunics and rode up to the Romans with their shields slung behind their backs. The Romans then conducted them to the rear.

Once there, however, the Numidians picked up their shields and fell upon the Roman line from behind. As the Roman infantry pushed forward in the centre of the line, the Africans in Hannibal's army were able to attack them in the flank. Spanish and Celtic horsemen under Hasdrubal then galloped around the rear of the Roman army, encircling it. Some 48,200 men were killed, including one consul, two quaestors, and 29 tribunes, as well as many ex-consuls, praetors, aediles and other high-ranking Romans. Nearly 20,000 more were taken prisoner. The devastation of the old Roman élite was graphically illustrated by the 'bushels' of finger-rings that Hannibal gathered from the dead and sent to Sicily.

Varro escaped, but Paullus fell: he was hit by a stone from a slingshot right at the beginning of the engagement, but fought on bravely until his strength gave out. The tribune Lentulus is said to have seen him sitting on a rock, bleeding profusely, and told him: 'you alone, in the sight of Heaven, are blameless for this day's disaster.' Paullus waved him off, telling him to ride to Rome and fortify the city.

WAR OF ATTRITION

Military commanders from Schlieffen to Eisenhower have described Cannae as the classic battle of annihilation. Yet Hannibal failed to bring the war to a successful conclusion after his fabulous victory when he declined to attack a defenceless Rome, claiming his army was too weak. The Romans now fell back on a strategy of attrition developed by Quintus Fabius Maximus. This general, whose cautious approach earned him the derogatory nickname of *cunctator* ('delayer'), refused to engage Hannibal in the field, opting instead to retake bases once the Carthaginian general had moved on. These 'Fabian' tactics gradually wore down an enemy racked by disease and desertion. Hannibal could find no reinforcements for his dwindling band. In 212–211 BC, the tables were turned when first Capua and then Syracuse fell to Rome.

The Second Punic War was brought to an end by the resounding victory of Publius Cornelius Scipio ('Scipio Africanus') in 202 BC at the Battle of Zama, after which Hannibal sued for peace. He was driven into exile, dying by his own hand in 183 BC.

The Third Punic War (149–146 BC) finally rid Rome of the Carthaginian menace when a Roman army took the city and razed it to the ground. Obeying the Senate's dictum that 'Carthage must be destroyed' (*Carthago delenda est*), salt was strewn in the ruins to stop anything growing and the people were sold into slavery.

Column marking the site of the Battle of Cannae. The flat plains of this region allowed Hannibal to use his cavalry to devastating effect.

PHARSALUS

Julius Caesar *v.* Pompey the Great 48 BC

THE BATTLE OF PHARSALUS – now Farsala in northern Greece – consolidated Julius Caesar's power by destroying that of his erstwhile ally and longstanding rival Pompey the Great. Now Caesar was on course to become the sole master of Rome, paving the way for the foundation of the Roman empire.

Gnaeus Pompeius Magnus was once the darling of Rome. The son of Pompeius Strabo – a leading figure in Rome's wars of domination over her Italian neighbours – Pompey was a far more adept politician than his father. He carefully groomed his image, styling himself on his hero Alexander the Great. Blessed with good looks and bravado, he followed Alexander in favouring cavalry charges and scored notable victories over Rome's enemies. Yet as Pharsalus was to prove, cavalry was still not always a match for well-trained and experienced Roman foot-soldiers.

In 81 BC, at the tender age of 25, Pompey was granted his first triumph by the dictator Sulla after waging a successful campaign against the Numidians in the Roman province of Africa. Pompey's youth and lack of status actually rendered him ineligible for such an honour, but he insisted. He planned to enter Rome on a chariot drawn by an elephant – a clear reference to his African exploits – but it would not fit through the city gate. This incident was an early sign of Pompey's overweening pride and ambition.

JOCKEYING FOR POSITION
In the first century BC, the Roman Republic was beset by an incessant round of political infighting and civil war. In 60 BC, the three most powerful figures in

Rome – Pompey, Julius Caesar and Marcus Licinius Crassus (one of Sulla's former generals) – formed the First Triumvirate. Caesar then returned to his ongoing task of subduing a revolt in the Roman province of Gaul. The triumvirate was fated to be a fragile alliance, as Pompey and Crassus were deadly rivals. Caesar had played Pompey off against Crassus for political advantage to win a consulship. Caesar's machinations also involved aligning himself with Pompey through marriage, by offering him the hand of his daughter Julia. This bond was later broken when she died in childbirth. Finally, Crassus' death on a doomed military adventure in Asia Minor in 53 BC removed the only buffer between Pompey and Caesar. From that moment on, the stage was set for bloody conflict between Rome's two titans.

Pompey had shown himself skilled at manipulating public opinion: in the mid-60s, after pirates raided the Italian coast and seized two Roman magistrates, Pompey used this minor incident to his advantage, appointing himself admiral and claiming outright victory over the corsairs within a year. But Caesar was also well-versed in playing to the mob. Plutarch called his behaviour 'cunning and underhand'. He used his victories in the Gallic Wars as a stage to win popularity.

Julius Caesar (shown here in a statue in Rome) was the outstanding military commander of his age. His exploits in fighting the Gallic Wars soon outstripped those of his older contemporary Pompey.

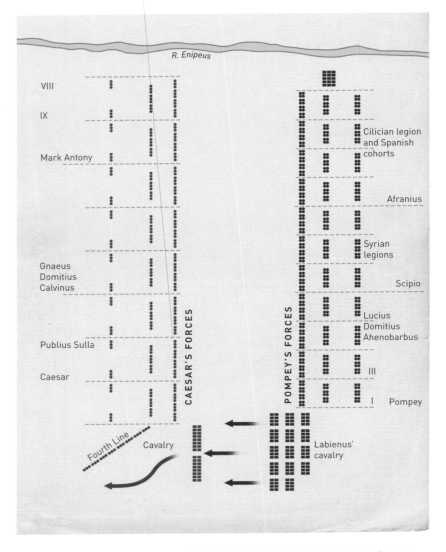

VIII			
IX			
Mark Antony			
Gnaeus Domitius Calvinus			
Publius Sulla			
Caesar			

CAESAR'S FORCES

POMPEY'S FORCES

Cilician legion and Spanish cohorts

Afranius

Syrian legions

Scipio

Lucius Domitius Ahenobarbus

III

I Pompey

Fourth Line Cavalry

Labienus' cavalry

First stage of the Battle of Pharsalus.
Pompey enjoyed overwhelming superiority in numbers, with just over twice as many troops as Caesar. However, Caesar's forces were battle-hardened from their years in Gaul.

CROSSING THE RUBICON

In 50 BC, Caesar quit Gaul in alarm at the news that Pompey and his friends were trying to prevent him from resuming public office in Rome. Roman generals were forbidden from crossing the Rubicon – the stream separating Italy from Cisalpine Gaul – at the head of an army. In January of 49 BC, Caesar famously dared to, exclaiming 'the die is cast' (*iacta alea est*). After marching on Rome and occupying the city, he defeated Pompey's armies in Spain. Back in Rome, he proceeded to woo the mob – the *populares*, while Pompey aligned himself with the old nobles, or *optimates*.

Pompey raised what forces he could and fled to Brundisium (Brindisi) before embarking for Greece. His plan was to join up with other loyal forces from Rome's eastern provinces and confront Caesar, but his authority was crumbling. Caesar criticised Pompey's tactics at Brundisium, claiming he was emulating Themistocles, who had abandoned Athens, and not Pericles, who had prepared the city for siege. Having no ships, however, Caesar returned to Rome and subdued the rest of Italy in just 60 days.

Pompey, though, defended his decision to make a stand in Greece: 'It was his opinion that the more a man cared for Rome, the further away he fought for her and the more he saw to it that she never experienced or even heard about the evils of war, but just waited patiently to see who would finally possess her.'

THE CAMPAIGN IN GREECE

Caesar had one huge advantage over his rival. His armies were war veterans, skilled in the use of the javelin (*pilum*) and in close-quarters combat with the short, stabbing sword (*gladius*). In contrast, Pompey's force had been rapidly assembled and lacked battle experience. Yet first blood went to Pompey.

Caesar crossed to Macedonia and fought several skirmishes against Pompey's forces, but presently ran short of food. An attempt to capture Pompey's supplies at Dyrrachium in present-day Albania ended in ignominious defeat, with the loss of over 1,000 men. Pompey crucially failed to exploit his victory, however, and shied away from fighting a pitched battle. His officers tried to embolden him by calling him 'Agamemnon' or 'king of kings', but it seems he had already lost his nerve. Plutarch reports how Caesar mocked his adversary's lack of resolve: 'Today the enemy would have won if they had had a winner for a commander.' But the writer goes on to reveal that Caesar's bravado hid a deep-seated anxiety at the setback, which he called 'the most harrowing night of my life'.

Caesar's fortunes were low. When the town of Gomphi refused to admit him, he showed his ruthlessness by letting his troops off the leash, who subjected the city to an orgy of rape and pillage. The other cities in the region did not need to be told twice. Pompey was still reluctant to join battle, preferring to try and wear down Caesar, whom he knew lacked vital supplies. He was also wary of Caesar's hardened veterans and was unwilling to leave his father-in-law Metellus Scipio – who had yet to join up with Pompey's main force – in the lurch. Pompey eventually gave in to the pressure from his own commanders; once Scipio had arrived, he advanced to meet Caesar in Thessaly.

SHOWDOWN AT PHARSALUS

Pompey initially camped on high ground above the Plain of Pharsalus, which was bounded to the south by the River Enipeus. Caesar was reluctant to give battle while Pompey held such a commanding position. But suddenly, and quite unexpectedly, Pompey decamped to the flat land. After seeking the advice of his lieutenants, Caesar resolved to engage the enemy the next day. To solicit the gods' help in securing victory, he spent the night performing sacrifices to Mars and Venus.

The following morning the two armies moved into battle order: opposite Mark Antony, flanking the river, Afranius had command of Pompey's right wing. Scipio faced Gnaeus Domitius Calvinus while Lucius Domitius Ahenobarbus was on Pompey's left, facing Publius Sulla. Caesar

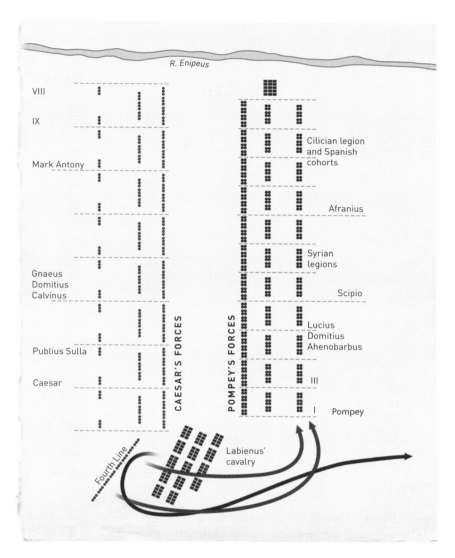

stayed close to his best troops: the 10th Legion. The Pompeian cohorts were tightly packed, inhibiting them from throwing their javelins. Pompey's left flank contained most of the cavalry – 6,400 men under Labienus – who were positioned so as to face the formidable 10th Legion. In total, Pompey had 45,000 troops ranged against Caesar's 22,000.

Battle commenced with a charge by 120 of Caesar's men led by the centurion

The turning point.
Labienus's cavalrymen charged, but their lack of discipline soon saw them wilt under pressure and beat a retreat. As they did so, Caesar's fourth line swung round against the left flank of Pompey's infantry, starting a rout.

> '*Today the enemy would have won if they had had a winner for a commander.*'

CAESAR ON POMPEY'S FAILURE TO FOLLOW THROUGH ON HIS VICTORY AT DYRRACHIUM

Gaius Crassianus. Crassianus was instantly struck down by a sword thrust that pierced his throat from front to back. Unfazed, Caesar's forces stood their ground, a mark of the extraordinary loyalty he inspired in them.

Pompey's cavalry was supposed to attack and break through to the rear of Caesar's positions, thereby rolling up Caesar's line. Caesar had surreptitiously fortified his left wing with six cohorts of reserves extracted from the *triplex acies,* or third line, and positioned at an oblique angle. Each side had a password to avoid confusion: Caesar's was 'Venus, Bringer of Victory' (he claimed divine descent from

Venus) while Pompey's was 'Hercules the Unconquered'. Caesar's positions were looser and more manoeuvrable.

At a distance of 14 metres (15 yds), Caesar's men threw their javelins. They expected the Pompeians to come forward, but Pompey had ordered his troops to stand firm. Caesar later criticized this decision, deeming it a grave error, 'to ignore the fact that blows gain in force when the first clash with the enemy occurs at full tilt, and that fighting spirit is kindled by a charge and blazes up at the point of impact'. When they realized the enemy would not advance to meet them, Caesar's legions charged, sword in hand.

THE TURNING POINT

Now was the moment for Pompey's cavalry commander Labienus to charge. His squadrons massively outnumbered Caesar's, whose horsemen withdrew, leading the enemy further towards the Caesarian line. The soldiers on Caesar's left flank had been ordered to run through the front line and jab at the riders' eyes with their javelins. Caesar was convinced that the riders – many of them raw young aristocrats – would be too vain to hold their ground if they thought their good looks would be marred. It was a shrewd calculation: the discipline of Labienus's cavalry faltered even before they ran into Caesar's reserves, and they broke ranks and fled. This left Caesar's infantry free to focus on the weakest point in Pompey's line, turning their front in the process.

When Caesar brought up fresh cohorts from the third line, Pompey's men turned and fled. Caesar kept some of his troops back to storm Pompey's camp, but urged them not to slaughter their fellow Romans if it could be avoided. Even so, between 6,000 and 15,000 soldiers from Pompey's army were killed, including the general Lucius Domitius Ahenobarbus. Caesar lost just 200 men and 30 centurions.

Seeing his armies reduced to chaos, Pompey himself quit the battle early and slunk off back to his tent. His age may have been the reason for his disappointing performance: he was 58, no longer an ideal age for front-line command. By the time Caesar's forces reached the camp, Pompey was gone. He had stripped off his general's insignia and abandoned his men in a manner unfitting of a Roman general. Caesar's troops were appalled at the opulence of Pompey's quarters.

AN INGLORIOUS DEATH

Pompey fled to the coast with a small party and made his way to Egypt. He may have thought that there was a chance of restoring his fortunes there. When his ship arrived in Alexandria, the counsellors of King Ptolemy XIII, who was still too young to rule, debated how they should receive him. An advisor named Pothinus the Eunuch, who knew that Caesar was already on his way there in pursuit, decided against offering Pompey refuge. The Roman general's fate was sealed.

Unsuspecting, Pompey boarded a small fishing boat that came to ferry him to shore. As the boat pulled away, one of the men on board, a former comrade-in-arms of Pompey named Septimius, stabbed the general to death. From the railing of their ship, Pompey's wife Cornelia watched in horror as the hero who had celebrated three triumphs and been consul three times collapsed and died. His head was cut off to present to Caesar, his naked body contemptuously tossed onto the beach. Caesar was appalled when he learned of Pompey's fate. By a ghastly irony, the statue of Pompey the Great was to look down on his own assassination in Rome four years later by the conspirators led by Brutus and Cassius.

'... *during the morning watch a great light shone out above the camp of Caesar ... and a flaming torch rose from it and darted down upon the camp of Pompey.*'

PLUTARCH, ON A FAVOURABLE OMEN FOR CAESAR BEFORE THE BATTLE OF PHARSALUS

TEUTOBURG FOREST

Arminius *v.* Quinctilius Varus AD 9

THE BATTLE OF TEUTOBURG FOREST – known in German as the *Varusschlacht* ('Varus battle') and in Latin as the *clades Variana* ('Varian disaster') – dealt a devastating blow to Roman self-esteem. Military defeat at the hands of a barbarian – the German chieftain Arminius – traumatized Rome, while victory held the German people in thrall right up to the time of the Third Reich. Arminius can be seen as the archetype of the freedom-fighter rising up against oppression; as he commented to his brother: 'the wages of slavery are low.'

Arminius slaying the Romans under Varus at the Battle of Teutoburg Forest. This highly romanticized depiction, by the artist Johann Peter Theodor Janssen, was painted shortly after the founding of the German Second empire in 1871. Arminius's great victory was eagerly adopted as a symbol of German national identity and military prowess.

Even in a Germany that has firmly renounced its militaristic past, the 53-metre- (175-ft-) tall monument to 'Hermann' (the Germanized form of Arminius) near Detmold remains a popular tourist attraction. Stripped of all nationalistic associations, the Battle of Teutoburg Forest is the story of a military juggernaut halted by a combination of tactics and courage.

The devastating defeat caused a public scandal in Rome at the time. Augustus banned the few survivors from entering the city, while the three legions (XVII, XVIII and XIX) that were lost were never replaced. Several decades later, the historian Tacitus used Varus's defeat to castigate the decadence of Rome: only Roman weakness could have allowed such a humiliation to come to pass.

FROM ALLY TO ENEMY
The catastrophe occurred when the Romans left the safe havens they had established on the Rhine and pushed further into the territory of the Germanic tribes. In AD 6, Publius Quinctilius Varus had been charged with consolidating the progress that Augustus's son-in-law, the future emperor Tiberius, had already made in pacifying this region. He was assigned five legions, plus command of some German auxiliary units, one of which was led by Arminius, a chief of the Cherusci tribe.

Arminius (also known as Armin, or even the fully Roman-sounding Gaius Julius Arminius) was the son of the chieftain Segimerus and was born in around 18 BC. The Cherusci were one of the main tribes living between the Elbe and the Weser rivers, which run roughly north–south across the north German plain. From AD 4–9, the Cherusci co-operated with the Roman occupiers. The terms of the treaty signed between Tiberius and the Cherusci stipulated that the tribe were to provide the Romans with auxiliary forces. We also know that Arminius fought with the Romans in the northern Balkans to quell the Pannonian uprisings. He commanded his own detachment, spoke Latin, was made a Roman citizen and even raised to the Equestrian Order. He therefore knew full well how the Roman army worked.

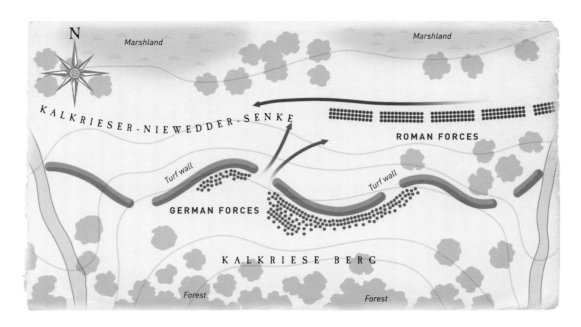

As the Roman legions marched through the narrow defile between marshland and the Kalkriese Berg, they entered a deadly ambush carefully prepared by their erstwhile ally Arminius.

Records show that his brother Flavus, who lost an eye serving under Tiberius, was still in Roman service in AD 16.

PLOTTING SEDITION

In around AD 7, Arminius returned to Germany. It is fair to assume that he had been assigned a role in the ongoing Romanization of the country being implemented by the governor, Varus. However, this programme was badly mismanaged: the Romans not only treated the Germans as menials, but also exacted money in return for bestowing on them the benefits of Roman culture.

Far from promoting the Roman cause, Arminius now began secretly to assemble a coalition of tribes opposed to the occupation: the Cherusci, Marsi, Chatii, Bructeri, Chauci and Sicambri. Yet even among the leaders of the Cherusci, there was no consensus on whether, let alone how, to stage an uprising. While his uncle Inguiomerus sat on the fence, Arminius began to take an ever harder line against Roman rule.

In AD 9, Varus was operating with three legions, six auxiliary units (including the one led by Arminius) and three cavalry battalions east of the River Weser near the modern town of Minden. The loyal Cheruscan leader Segestes had warned Varus that Arminius was not to be trusted, but Varus still refused to believe that this valued confederate would rebel.

Varus set out to return to his winter quarters with some 12,000–15,000 men, their progress impeded by a baggage train and camp-followers. In appalling weather, they marched between the Weihengebirge and the Great Moor along a path that grew ever narrower. The pouring rain soaked the bow-strings of the Roman archers, making their weapons largely useless, and the wicker shields they carried became waterlogged, heavy and unwieldy.

CAUGHT IN A TRAP

Arminius persuaded Varus to let him and his men scout ahead. He may even have suggested a detour to ensure the safety of the column. Trusting him, Varus failed to send out his own reconnaissance party. Presently Arminius and his troops melted away and the Roman force – the cavalry in particular – began to come under increasingly heavy guerrilla attack.

The two sides were roughly equal in strength. The Romans continued along a three-mile- (4.8-km-) long pass called the Kalkrieser-Niewedder-Senke, an important route between the Rhine and the Weser. This swampy corridor was just 182 metres (200 yds) wide. On the heavily wooded Kalkriese Hill overlooking it, the

'Quinctilius Varus, give me back my legions!'

AUGUSTUS

Cherusci had constructed a serpentine turf wall with sand ramparts. Once in the pass, the Romans were caught in a trap. From behind the wall the Cherusci now began to rain arrows and javelins down on the enemy, who had no room to form up into lines. A unit of Varus's men tried to storm the rampart, but were buried underneath it when it collapsed. His second-in-command, Numonius Vala, did manage to escape with the cavalry, but Arminius's riders soon caught up with them and cut them down. Eventually, when all was lost, Varus committed suicide. Extensive archaeological finds at the battle site confirm that most of the dead were Roman.

GERMANY RISES UP

Although Segestes remained loyal to Rome, his daughter Thusnelda subsequently became pregnant by Arminius (despite being betrothed to another). Segestes and Thusnelda were captured by Germanicus, the new Roman commander in Germany, and sent to Ravenna, where the rebel's son was born. This action so enraged Arminius that he took up arms once more ('my fighting …

has been against armed men, not pregnant women') and nearly succeeded in wiping out a further four legions.

The destruction of Varus's legions at the Battle of Teutoburg Forest prompted Germanic tribes to rise up and slaughter Romans wherever they could. Thus began a major rebellion that lasted for seven years. In AD 16, Arminius faced the Romans for the last time at the Battle of Idistaviso on the Weser. He used Roman tactics to good effect, squeezing his enemy's front and limiting their field of action. Even so, Arminius was ultimately defeated at this engagement, and only escaped by smearing his face with blood to disguise himself. Presently, Germanicus was recalled to Rome and the advantage was lost.

Arminius now directed his forces against Rome's Bohemian ally Maraboduus. This campaign ended in stalemate. In AD 21, aged just 37, Arminius was murdered by opponents within his own tribe.

Contemporaries and later commentators were unanimous in their condemnation of Varus. The biographer Suetonius reports that Tiberius blamed the defeat on his 'rashness and neglect of precautions against surprise'. When the ageing emperor Augustus learned of the disaster, he is said to have hit his head repeatedly against a wall, exclaiming: *'Quinctili Vare, legiones redde!'* ('Quinctilius Varus, give me back my legions!').

Even nowadays, woodland covers much of the region around Minden and Osnabrück, near the site of the famous battle, which the 19th-century German nationalist historian Theodor Mommsen called 'the turning point in Germany's national destiny'. In Roman times, the dense primeval German forest provided ideal terrain for guerrilla warfare.

SACK OF ROME

Visigoths v. Romans 24 August AD 410

IN THE FOURTH AND FIFTH CENTURIES, waves of Barbarian invasions from the East put the Western Roman empire under intolerable pressure. Unlike imperial Rome in its heyday, this moribund and weakened state now found itself unable to resist its enemies.

For the 18th-century British historian Edward Gibbon, author of *Decline and Fall of the Roman Empire*, the arrival of the Visigoths in the Holy of Holies was unquestionably the greatest of tragedies. But writing a century later, the German historical novelist Felix Dahn reached quite different conclusions. Dahn condemned the last Romans as duplicitous and decadent, while the Goths offered new virtues to the people of Italy.

The Western Roman emperor at the time – a feckless and weak man named Honorius – was not present in Rome during its sacking. He had taken refuge in the impregnable city of Ravenna, which was protected by walls and swamps, and open only to the sea.

THE BARBARIAN INVASIONS
From the late fourth century onwards Germanic tribes from Eastern Europe were driven westward after their lands were invaded by the Huns of central Asia. One of these tribal groupings, the Visigoths (made up of the Tervingi and the Greuthingi peoples), settled on the northern bank of the Danube, from where the Roman emperor Valens (364–378) was powerless to dislodge them, as he was at war with Persia. Besides, it was thought that these migrants might prove useful in the face of population decline and a lack of Roman subjects prepared to man the army.

In 378, Valens made peace with Persia. This freed his armies to deal with the Visigoths, who in the interim had turned to brigandry and threatened Roman interests. Valens attacked the Visigoths at Adrianople in Thrace, but his forces were defeated and he was killed along with two-thirds of his army. Eventually, his successor Theodosius I (the last emperor of a unified Roman empire) allowed the Goths to settle in Thrace (modern Bulgaria) as Roman 'confederates' (*foederati*).

THE RISE OF ALARIC
The Visigoth commander Alaric was a member of the Tervingi tribe, born some time between AD 360 and 370. He was not of noble lineage, but rather rose to pre-eminence through his own abilities. In 391, he almost captured Theodosius in an ambush. Shortly after, however, Alaric was persuaded to join forces with Theodosius and served under him in his war against the usurper Eugenius, who had taken control of Rome. This campaign ended with Eugenius's capture and execution at the Battle of the Frigidus in the Julian Alps. After Theodosius died in 395, the empire was divided between his two sons Arcadius, who ruled from Constantinople and Honorius, who took over in the West. As Honorius was only ten, Stilicho, a general of mixed Vandal and Roman ancestry, became regent.

Ruins of the Roman Forum. The destruction of ancient Rome took place over several centuries. When Alaric and the Visigoths invaded in August 410, they left the fabric of the city, and its inhabitants, relatively unscathed.

Alaric felt hard done by after Frigidus. The Visigoths had suffered heavy casualties and he had been sent home without being assigned a regular command. His response was to attack Constantinople. After failing to take the well-defended city, he conducted a campaign of pillage around the Aegean.

Stilicho led an army across the Alps to confront Alaric, but the Visigoth king eluded him. In 397, the eunuch Eutropius, who effectively governed the empire in the east, reached an accord with Alaric, appointing him a general and allowing him to raise taxes in Thrace and Macedonia. These concessions, however, proved unpopular in Constantinople and two years later Eutropius was overthrown and executed, and the licence made to Alaric declared null and void.

Rape and pillage. This 1890 painting of the sack of Rome by Alaric conveys the traditional view of the event as a disastrous collapse of civilization in the face of a barbarian onslaught. The truth is now known to be more complex.

Seville

ALARIC LOOKS WEST
Denied in the east, Alaric returned to harass the Western Roman empire. He crossed the Julian Alps before the snows closed the passes in November 401 and descended as far as the valley of the River Po. Driving Honorius from the imperial court at Milan, he besieged the emperor at the city of Asta. On Easter Sunday, 6 April 402, Stilicho arrived and attacked the Christian Visigoths as they attended Mass at Pollentia (modern Pollenzo in Piedmont). The Romans captured Alaric's

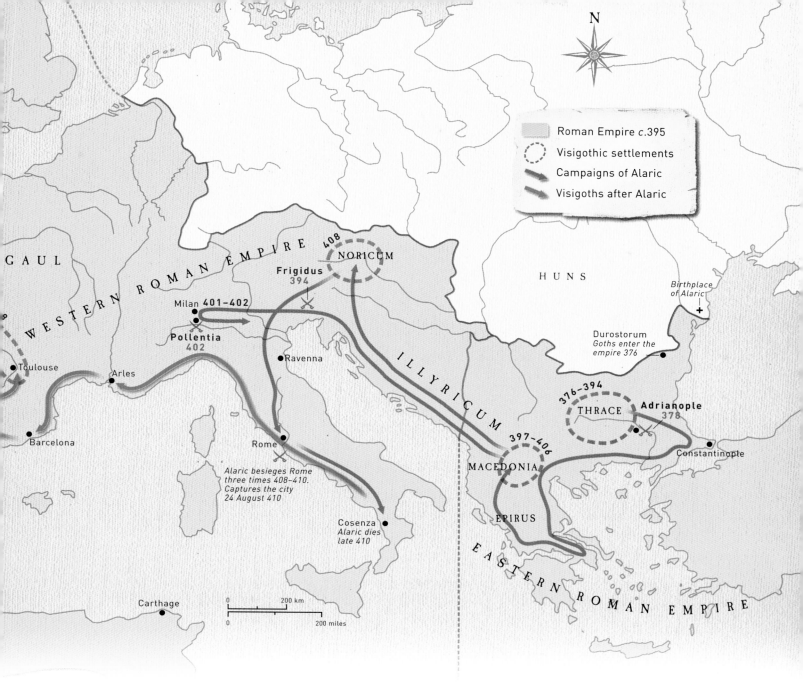

Map showing the campaigns of Alaric and the Visigoths in the late fourth and early fifth centuries AD. A Visigothic kingdom was eventually established in Spain and southern France, flourishing until the Moorish invasions in the eighth century.

baggage train containing his plunder together with his wife and children. He was bruised a second time by Stilicho at Verona before withdrawing to the Balkans. The main outcome of Alaric's invasion was that Honorius moved his capital north to Ravenna.

For four and a half years, Alaric licked his wounds, but in 406 Stilicho approached him as a potential ally in his plan to wrest Illyricum from the Eastern emperor. Stilicho calculated that control of this province would give him a useful

source of manpower for his army, which was now looking weak in the face of new threats from other central European tribes. Alaric was offered official status and the right to raise taxes once more.

But before Stilicho could unite his forces with Alaric's at Epirus, a joint army of Vandals, Suevi and Alans crossed the frozen Rhine and invaded Gaul, while the usurper Constantine crossed from Britain. Stilicho had to alter his course and once again left Alaric in the lurch. Alaric settled in Noricum in the eastern Alps and demanded tribute to keep the peace. Displeased at the way Stilicho had handled matters, and driven by a deep-seated anti-German prejudice, the Senate had him arrested and executed, while even more calamitously, Roman soldiers massacred their German comrades-in-arms and their families. The survivors fled to Alaric's camp.

Alaric now invaded Italy for a second time, plundering as he went. By November 408, his army stood before the walls of Rome, blockading the city until the youthful emperor agreed to his terms. In Gibbon's account: 'Alaric encompassed the walls, commanded the twelve principal gates, intercepted all communication with the adjacent country, and vigilantly guarded the navigation of the Tiber, from which the Romans derived the surest and most plentiful supply of provisions.' He wanted ransom, and now proceeded to starve the Romans out. Alaric's ranks had swelled with runaway slaves giving him an army of around 40,000.

When a delegation from the Senate visited him in his camp, they warned him that Rome was populous and that its men were trained in arms. Alaric is said to have replied: 'The thicker the hay, the easier it is mowed.' He then named his price – a homeland for his people in Noricum, plus large quantities of gold and grain. The senators asked: 'If such, O king are your demands, what do you intend to leave us?' 'Your lives!' was Alaric's pitiless answer.

For a year, the Romans continued to negotiate with their powerful enemy. Meanwhile Honorius, secure behind the walls of Ravenna, and now grown to manhood, was saving his troops for a confrontation with Constantine in Gaul.

PREVARICATION AND PLUNDER

In 409, seeking a pragmatic solution to the impasse, the Senate appointed their own emperor – Priscus Attalus, prefect of the port of Ostia. Yet Attalus had no real power to fulfil Alaric's demands. Losing patience, in July 410 Alaric marched to Ravenna to try and force Honorius to deal with him. But after being ambushed and losing several of his men, he returned to Rome and renewed the siege. During the night of 24 August 410, finding that a sympathizer had left open the Salarian Gate on the northeastern side of the city, the Visigoths entered Rome.

The plunder lasted for three days before Alaric withdrew. Edward Gibbon describes at length the despoiling of the Eternal City: 'The palaces of Rome were rudely stripped of their splendid and costly furniture. The sideboards of massy plate, and the variegated wardrobes of silk and purple, were irregularly piled in the wagons that always followed the march of the Gothic army.'

Yet most modern commentators agree that Alaric's army was remarkably restrained in its actions. The Visigoth

'The decline of Rome was the natural and inevitable effect of immoderate greatness … instead of inquiring why the Roman Empire was destroyed we should rather be surprised that it has subsisted for so long.'

EDWARD GIBBON ON THE UNDERLYING CAUSE OF ROME'S FALL TO ALARIC IN AD 410

soldiers were forbidden from entering churches and were ordered to concentrate only on what they could easily carry and to avoid bloodshed and destruction. The basilicas of St Peter and Paul were designated sanctuaries and some treasure, allegedly belonging to St Peter's, was even taken there by the Goths themselves. Undoubtedly a number of Roman citizens did lose their lives, most likely patricians killed by slaves keen to avenge harsh treatment by their masters. Gibbon's sources cited widespread rape as well, but in general the barbarians seem to have behaved well. There are even reports of them escorting nuns to safety.

Prisoners were taken, including the emperor's sister Galla Placidia, while others were sold into slavery. The only building to be seriously damaged was the Senate, whose members bore the brunt of

the blame for failing to stave off the disaster. Yet only one senator is said to have perished during the sack of the city.

A SYMBOLIC BLOW

The sack of Rome had no strategic importance, as the city was now only a symbol – albeit a powerful one. But it was a devastating blow to the Roman psyche: the city had been founded in 753 BC and had not been invaded since the Gauls 800 years before. Popular outrage was directed at Serena, the widow of Stilicho, the niece of Theodosius and Honorius's aunt who was strangled on orders of the Senate after a rumour blew up she was communicating with the enemy.

Still Honorius refused to give Alaric what he wanted, and the Visigoth king carried on plundering the south of Italy, where he died later that year.

The Roman emperor Honorius, feeding pigeons and guinea fowl in his palace at Ravenna. Detail from the painting *The Favourites of Honorius,* by the Victorian artist J.W. Waterhouse.

CATALAUNIAN PLAINS

Flavius Aetius *v.* Attila the Hun AD 451

IN A MASSIVE ATTACK ON THE VISIGOTHS, the Huns overran Gaul and burned over a dozen cities before laying siege to Orléans. The invaders brought their own quaint customs to the West: they 'ate drank, defecated and even gave judgement from the saddle'.

Flavius Aetius was the last of the great Roman generals. A typical product of the late Roman empire, he was from the Balkans, where his father Gaudentius, a common soldier who had served in the élite Praetorian Guard had attained high rank in the cavalry and married into a senatorial family. It was a union between old and new, vital and decadent. Aetius also served in the Praetorians. He had the ill fortune to be taken hostage by both Alaric and the Huns, but he used his time in captivity well. While he was with the Huns, he learned to ride and use a bow like them and became friendly with their king, Ruga, and his nephew Attila. He married a Visigothic princess, and one of their sons, Carpillo was also taken prisoner by Ruga and educated in the camp of Attila. Close contact with the Visigoths and Huns gave him many advantages in later life.

A contemporary Roman commander and historian, Renatus Profuturus Frigeridus, gives the following thumbnail sketch of Aetius: 'The graceful figure of Aetius was not above the middle stature; but his manly limbs were admirably formed for strength, beauty and agility; and he excelled in the martial exercises of managing a horse, drawing a bow and

darting the javelin. He could patiently endure the want of food or of sleep; and his mind and body were alike capable of the most laborious efforts. He possessed the genuine courage that can despise not only dangers, but injuries: and it was impossible either to corrupt, or deceive, or intimidate the firm integrity of his soul.'

POWER STRUGGLES

The year AD 423 saw the death of Honorius, the irresolute western Roman emperor who had allowed Alaric to sack Rome. As he had no male heir, the emperor in the East, Theodosius II, appointed Honorius's four-year-old nephew Valentinian III to that office, under the regency of his mother Galla Placidia. Her rule lasted for 25 years.

Western Roman officials rebelled against the idea of a boy-emperor and installed an official called John to rule in Valentinian's place. Theodosius provided Placidia with an army to assert his will, while John despatched his general Aetius (who had served Galla Placidia's former husband Constantius) to recruit Hunnish mercenaries. By the time Aetius returned, 'at the head of 60,000 barbarians,' John had been deposed and executed, but Placidia, no doubt swayed by this show of

Fresco of Flavius Aetius, the conqueror of Attila the Hun. Having spent much of his youth as a hostage of the Goths and Huns, Aetius had a genuine knowledge of the 'barbarians' with whom he had to deal in later life.

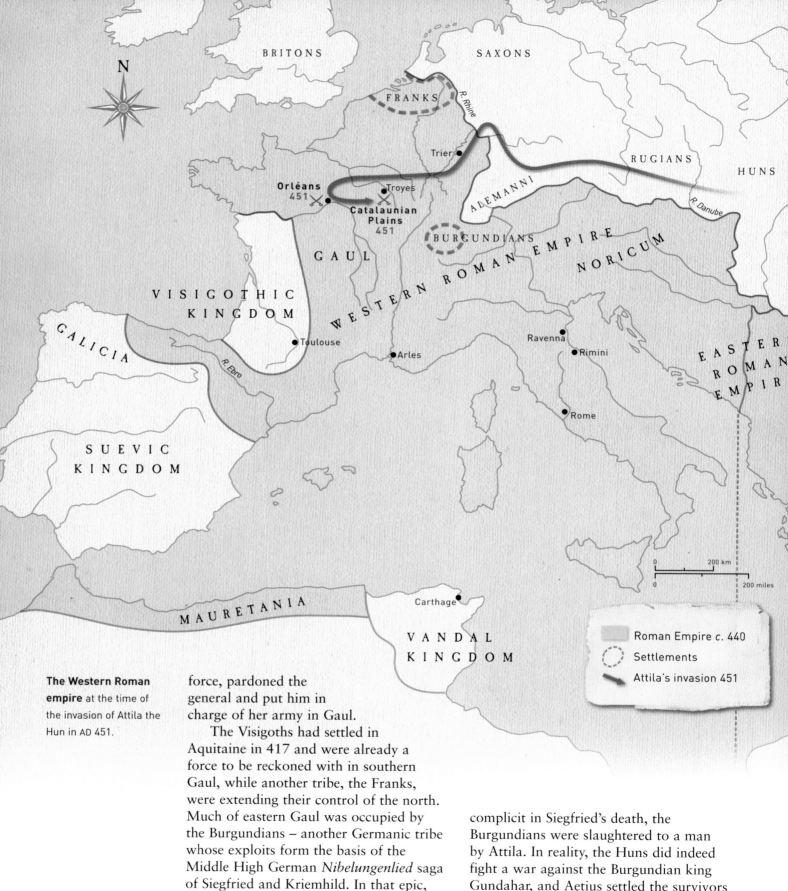

BRITONS SAXONS

FRANKS

RUGIANS

HUNS

Trier

GAUL

Orléans
451

Troyes

Catalaunian
Plains
451

ALEMANNI

BURGUNDIANS

WESTERN ROMAN EMPIRE NORICUM

R. Rhine

R. Danube

VISIGOTHIC
KINGDOM

GALICIA

Ravenna

Rimini

EASTERN
ROMAN
EMPIRE

Toulouse

Arles

R. Ebro

SUEVIC
KINGDOM

Rome

200 km

200 miles

MAURETANIA

Carthage

VANDAL
KINGDOM

Roman Empire *c.* 440

Settlements

Attila's invasion 451

**The Western Roman
empire** at the time of
the invasion of Attila the
Hun in AD 451.

force, pardoned the
general and put him in
charge of her army in Gaul.

The Visigoths had settled in
Aquitaine in 417 and were already a
force to be reckoned with in southern
Gaul, while another tribe, the Franks,
were extending their control of the north.
Much of eastern Gaul was occupied by
the Burgundians – another Germanic tribe
whose exploits form the basis of the
Middle High German *Nibelungenlied* saga
of Siegfried and Kriemhild. In that epic,
after their king, Gunther, was found to be

complicit in Siegfried's death, the
Burgundians were slaughtered to a man
by Attila. In reality, the Huns did indeed
fight a war against the Burgundian king
Gundahar, and Aetius settled the survivors
in land south of Lake Geneva.

> *'The graceful figure of Aetius was not above the middle stature; but his manly limbs were admirably formed for strength, beauty and agility; and he excelled in the martial exercises of managing a horse, drawing a bow and darting the javelin.'*

RENATUS PROFUTURUS FRIGERIDUS

PACIFYING GAUL

Aetius had only around 45,000 men supplemented by Hunnish mercenaries to police Gaul. His success was largely due to the presence of these feared fighters in his ranks. He spent a decade gaining control of the region. In 425–426, he defeated the Visigoth king Theodoric – son of Alaric – outside Arles, while the next year he stopped the Franks from advancing to the Somme.

In 430, he prevented the Alemanni from establishing a foothold across the Rhine. Other triumphs followed: the suppression of a rebellion in Noricum (modern Austria south of the Danube) plus further victories over the Visigoths and Franks. In 432, in reward for his service, Aetius was made consul in Rome.

FACING THE VANDALS AND HUNS

Yet Galla Placidia still bore Aetius a grudge and he soon found himself removed from office, replaced by the African commander, Boniface. Aetius sought aid from the Huns and defeated Boniface in battle. He was promptly reinstated and made a patrician. When Valentinian III came of age in 437, his mother was sidelined and Aetius became the effective ruler of the Western empire.

The barbarian tribes still posed a major threat. The Vandal king Genseric advanced from Spain into North Africa and conquered the whole of Mauretania by 435. Meanwhile Aetius's campaign against the Vandals and the Suevi in Spain culminated in a victory at the battle of Snake Mountain in 438. He also restored the Gallic frontier at the Rhine.

Even so, Genseric remained a thorn in his side. In 439, he seized Carthage. This city and the surrounding region was Rome's bread basket, and its fall meant the loss of huge amounts of tax revenue. Edward Gibbon was perhaps right to believe Genseric deserved equal rank with Alaric and Attila in the annals of the fall of Rome. Aetius was forced to appeal to Theodoric for help. In 440, a combined army from the Eastern and Western empire assembled in Sicily, but before they could begin the reconquest, Attila started his invasion of the Balkans and the mission had to be aborted.

The personal friendship between Aetius and Attila endured until 451, but then they fell out. In that year, Attila launched an attack on the Visigoths. With considerable diplomatic skill, Aetius managed to convince the great Visigothic king Theodoric of the common danger. Theodoric put their past enmity behind

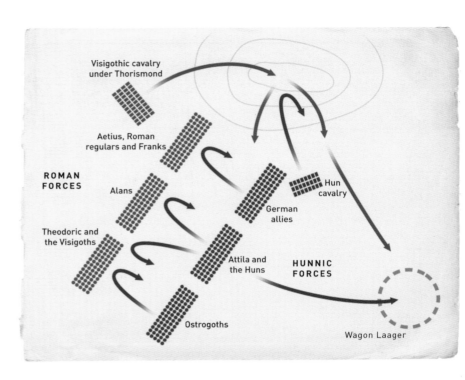

him and their joint armies proceeded to Orléans, where Attila, who had travelled all the way from modern Hungary, was laying siege. If he could take the city, he would have mastery over the whole of the Loire Valley.

Aetius was also able to prevail upon the Burgundians, Saxons and Alans for support. Faced with such a strong coalition, Attila raised the siege and retreated to the Seine while the vanguard of Aetius's and Theodoric's forces harassed his rear. He looked for a site where he could find the open plains and grasslands that suited his cavalry tactics and located it on the Catalaunian Plains near Châtres, between Châlons-sur-Marne and Troyes in the Champagne region.

It was to be Aetius's last battle. The Roman–Visigoth army greatly outnumbered the joint forces of the Huns and Ostrogoths. Attila began with a speech: 'I myself … will throw the first javelin, and the wretch who refuses to imitate the example of the sovereign is devoted to inevitable death.'

THE COURSE OF THE BATTLE

The battle began at about 3 p.m. with a struggle to gain possession of the sole piece of high ground. Aetius spotted it first and sent in the Visigoth cavalry, commanded by Theodoric's son Thorismond. He was now facing Attila's left flank. In the centre of their line, Aetius and Theodoric had placed their Alans, who were considered of doubtful loyalty, and needed to be watched over. Their king, Sangiban, had been in league with Attila, so he too was placed in the

line. They faced Attila's Huns presided over by Attila in person. Spreading out from Attila's people were his allies and subject peoples: Rugians, Heruli, Thuringians, Franks and Burgundians. His right wing was commanded by Ardaric, king of the Gepidae, while his left was controlled by the Ostrogoths who faced their Visigoth kinsmen. As Gibbon put it: 'The nations from the Volga to the Atlantic were assembled on the plain of Châlons.'

The Alans were swiftly broken by a Hunnish cavalry charge. Having scattered them, the Huns wheeled left and charged the Visigoths under Theodoric. Theodoric was hit by a javelin thrown by Angages the Ostrogoth, pitched from his horse and trampled to death by his own men; but Thorismond counter-attacked and drove Attila's Ostrogoths from the field. He almost suffered the same fate as his father, sustaining a head wound and being thrown from his mount, but he was rescued by one of his men. Aetius's soldiers withstood the onslaught of the Huns by locking their shields together in the old Roman manner, so Attila concentrated his attacks on the Germans in the Roman army. Aetius reined in his men at dusk. Attila took refuge in his wagon camp and was forced to retreat the next day, preparing to take his own life on a funeral pyre of saddles. His archers, however, kept the Romans at bay and the Huns were able to beat a retreat. Casualties had been heavy on both sides, though the traditionally quoted death toll of 165,000 is surely an exaggeration.

This was Attila's first defeat, but Aetius, possibly intentionally, did not press home his advantage. Attila was keen to marry the Emperor's sister Honoria and took off for Italy, ravaging and pillaging all the way. He died in mysterious circumstances the following year.

BLOODY DOWNFALL

The departure of the Huns spelt disaster for Aetius, for they had maintained the balance of power. He was also losing his influence at court. Valentinian was keen to reunite the two halves of the empire under his sole rule. Conversely, Aetius was determined to avert this as he knew that it would lead to civil war. The general was also trying to marry off his son Gaudentius to Valentinian's daughter Placidia. As Valentinian had no male heirs, that meant placing Aetius's progeny on the throne at some future date. Valentinian showed his distaste for the scheme by drawing his sword at a conference on taxes on 22 or 25 September 454 and murdering Aetius.

On 16 March 455, it was the emperor's turn. He was assassinated by two officers loyal to Aetius while he practised archery. The empire in the West limped on until 476, when it was finally brought to an end by the installation of Odoacer, a Germanic *foederatus* general, as king of Italy.

Aetius served as the model for the character Cethegus in German writer Felix Dahn's 1876 novel *Struggle for Rome*, while the sixth-century Byzantine historian Procopius called him 'the last of the Romans' – a title seconded by Gibbon.

Aetius lost only one battle throughout his illustrious career and was adored by his troops, but he relied too heavily on the friendship of the Huns.

Attila the Hun beating a retreat at the Battle of the Catalaunian Plains. Attila died the next year, supposedly after bursting a blood vessel at his own wedding.

HASTINGS

Harold Godwinson *v.* William of Normandy
14 October **1066**

MANY HAVE SEEN THE BATTLE OF HASTINGS as signalling a change in style of warfare. Was this the dawn of the age of the knight? Others ask whether Hastings marks the end of the 'Infantry Cycle' that characterized warfare in the Ancient World. And did the French duke William's victory introduce feudalism to the British Isles?

The truth is, as ever, highly complex. For a start, this was not the French–English conflict of popular myth. The Normans were descendants of the Vikings, while the Saxons who opposed them came from continental Europe – albeit several hundred years before. And the Saxons already had a semi-feudal system in the form of the *fyrd* (militia). Where tactics are concerned, there is evidence that the Normans mounted cavalry charges; equally, though, we also know that they often dismounted to fight.

THE NORMAN KNIGHTLY CASTE

What is beyond dispute is that the Battle of Hastings was won by William's cavalry. Their tactics were to first charge with their lances and, once the shock of this assault had been blunted, to fight with sword, axe or mace. They had adopted their fighting methods from the feudal armies of Western Europe; but the knights who crossed the Channel with William were often soldiers of fortune, hoping to gain fiefdoms for their families in return for military service. In this, they followed a pattern established by Charlemagne's knights in the 8th–9th centuries.

The changes in the nature of warfare gave rise to escalating costs: the armoured horseman was costly to maintain (hence the need to get him to pay for himself and his peasants). At Hastings he wore the long (and expensive) mail shirt or 'hauberk'. He also needed a warhorse or 'destrier' capable of carrying him and his equipment. The knight was self-financing: the award of a fiefdom meant that he paid homage and owed service, just as the peasant paid homage and owed service to his seigneur.

Post-Hastings England was remade, as it were, from the ground up, with the entire country up for grabs by those who had helped William secure his victory. By 1166, there were 5,000 knight's 'fees' (fiefdoms), but the largest number ever called out was 228 knights. By the 15th century and the Battle of Agincourt, this purely feudal system was already being replaced by one that put patriotism first.

RIVAL CLAIMANTS

The claims of Duke William of Normandy (a.k.a. William the Bastard – his father Duke Robert II of Normandy never married William's mother) to the English throne were legitimate, but he was just one of several pretenders. When William visited the heir-less Edward the Confessor in 1051, the English king gave him a clear promise that he would inherit the throne.

The Bayeux Tapestry was commissioned by Bishop Odo of Bayeux in 1086 and is thought to have been embroidered in England. This famous section shows the Saxon commander Harold Godwinson being shot through the eye with an arrow, before he was cut down by William's knights.

On the other hand, he also offered it to Svein of Denmark, plus there was always a chance that Queen Edith might still bear him a son. In the light of this, neither offer can have been meant very seriously. Should Edward die childless, a regency council would award the throne to whoever appeared to have the best claim. That was probably Edward the Exile, the son of Edward's half-brother, who had been living in Hungary, but he died in mysterious circumstances soon after returning to England in 1057. After the Exile's death the chief claimant was Edward's great nephew Edgar Aetheling.

Later, another contender emerged: Edward's brother-in-law, Harold Godwinson, earl of Essex. Harold fell into William's hands when he was shipwrecked or taken prisoner off Ponthieu in 1064 or 1065. William rescued him and he thus became the duke's vassal. According to the Bayeux Tapestry, William obliged Harold to back William's claims to the English crown. This may indeed be true.

> *'The Norman Conquest meant that England received not just a new royal family, but also a new ruling class, a new culture and a new language.'*
>
> John Gillingham, on the impact of Hastings

But it is also possible the mission had nothing to do with the succession. The main source of the story, William of Poitiers, is unreliable, as his account is essentially Norman propaganda.

Harold may also have simply been playing for time to try to extricate himself from a difficult situation. But whatever promise he made provided William with the pretext he needed to seek papal support for the invasion. On his deathbed, Edward the Confessor seems to have changed his mind and chosen Harold: invasion threatened on all sides.

A SEASONED CAMPAIGNER

William was every inch a military leader, who had been campaigning for 20 years before he faced Harold Godwinson. His greatest victory to date had been the seizure of the castle at Domfront on the borders of Maine (1055). While besieging Domfront he proceeded to Alençon, which he had heard was poorly defended. The defenders incensed him by calling his mother's honour into question. When he took the fort, he punished them by having their hands and feet amputated.

William was a great advocate of shock and fire. In the former, brutality figured large and he made great use of both in his conquest of the region of Maine, centring on Le Mans, 'sowing terror in the land by frequent and sustained invasion'.

Edward the Confessor's state was falling apart at his death as a result of the lack of a clear successor. Once he heard the news, William began preparing for invasion by building boats in unprecedented numbers, as shown in the Bayeux Tapestry. In response, Harold posted units of his army and navy along the south coast. In August, William assembled an army at Dives-sur-Mer and waited for favourable winds, or possibly just for Harold to lose patience and send his soldiers home. This Harold did on 8 September.

William put to sea three days later, but the wind was against him and after some of his ships sank he was forced to seek shelter in the mouth of the Somme. It was then that he heard the remarkable news of a Norwegian attack on the north of England. King Harald Hardrada – yet another claimant to the throne – had made a bold surprise move to seize the crown.

FIGHTING ON TWO FRONTS

To counter the Norwegian threat, Harold Godwinson marched north to Tadcaster, which he reached on 24 September. The next day he defeated Hardrada at the

Battle of Stamford Bridge near York. He also slew Tostig, who was not only his brother, but also the brother of Edward the Confessor's widow Edith. But the Saxons had little time to savour their victory. Within days, Harold learned that William had received the wind he craved and had set sail on the 28th. William disembarked his forces unopposed from 500 ships at Pevensey Bay and proceeded to strengthen the Roman fort there and build a wooden one at Hastings. He also sent out scavenging parties and scouts. The latter were William's trump card. He was a master of battlefield intelligence.

He now needed to force Harold to give fight quickly, lest he find his throne stolen from under his feet in Normandy. (Something similar did indeed occur a few years later, when Le Mans threw off his rule while he was away in England.)

After a gruelling seven-day march south from Yorkshire, Harold arrived in London on 6 October, where he joined forces with

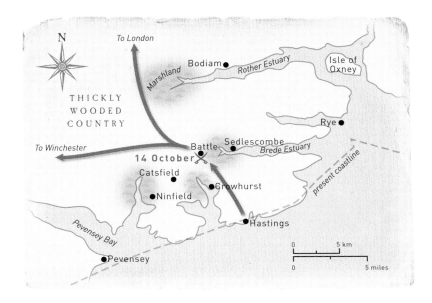

his brothers, Gyrth and Leofwin. Five days later he set off south again, to a rendezvous point at Caldbec Hill northwest of Hastings, which he reached on the 13th. William's scouts informed him of Harold's arrival and the duke, fearing a night attack, recalled his foragers. It is said he was so nervous that he put his hauberk on back to front.

Lie of the land. Above: Map showing the location of Pevensey Bay, the site of the Battle of Hastings and the direction of London and Winchester.. Below: The 13th-century Abbot's house is located on the site of the ruins of Battle Abbey on Senlac Ridge near Hastings. William ordered the abbey to be built in 1095.

AT A DISADVANTAGE

Whereas Harold had taken Hardrada by surprise, William was fully forewarned and drew up his forces by first light to face Harold in strength. The Saxon king had taken up position on Senlac (now Battle) Ridge. Harold had lost some of his best men while fighting in the north and his *fyrd* had yet to assemble in full. With his housecarls (military retainers), thegns (the minor nobles roughly equivalent of feudal seigneurs) and fyrdmen (the militia recruited among the peasantry), his forces numbered just under 10,000. It seems he was also joined by some local peasants armed with clubs, desirous of revenge for William's harrying of their land and beasts.

All the elements of Harold's army used horses, but they dismounted to fight. Also, being out of step with the latest European military technology, they were unaware of the devastating power of the longbow. William, on the other hand, 'was familiar with every device of continental warfare' (Sir Frank Stenton). He was 'a knight and leader of knights'. William commanded 2,000 cavalry, 4,000 heavy infantry and 1,500 archers. The army was made up of volunteers, chiefly landless knights, opportunists from all over Western Europe.

The archers took on the role of artillery, opening the battle by firing salvoes of arrows into the Saxon ranks. The Saxons fought a defensive battle, lacking bowmen and cavalry. Harold and his best men were grouped on a promontory situated more or less where the high altar of Battle Abbey stands today. From there the land fell away and the Normans occupied the next ridge, slightly lower than the Saxons. Badly mauled by the two-bladed axes that easily cut through shield and mail, the Normans at first turned in flight back down the hill with the Saxons in pursuit. But it was then that the cavalry was able to turn the rout to their advantage.

Rallying the troops.
Fragment of the Bayeux Tapestry showing Odo, half-brother of William and later bishop of Bayeux, astride a black 'destrier' (warhorse) urging on the Norman forces. Aside from the legend above, the ornate chain mail marks out this figure as a leading commander.

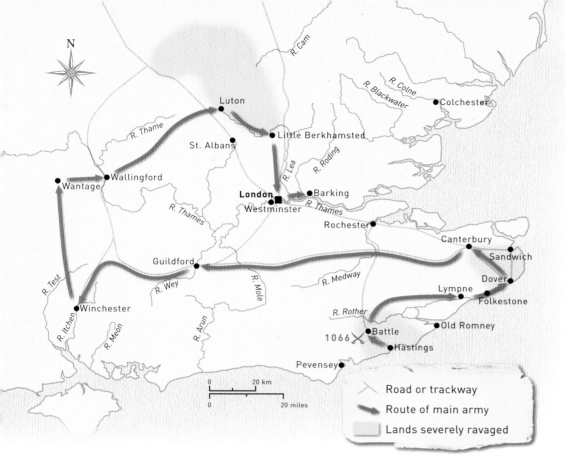

Road or trackway

Route of main army

Lands severely ravaged

TURNING THE TABLES

Once the effectivenness of the tactic became clear, the Normans used it time and again to good effect. The lie of the land gave William the advantage, and all Harold could do was compact his lines and hope that the Normans would exhaust themselves in the attack. According to William of Poitiers, these were so tightly packed that even when men were killed they remained upright.

The Norman cavalry failed to break the housecarls, who continued to wreak havoc with their axes. A rumour that William had been killed spread panic among the Bretons on the Norman left flank and William had to identify himself by raising his helmet to rally them. William of Poitiers claims the duke had three horses killed under him. William turned the tables with his feigned flights, which saw the Saxons cut down every time they pursued the enemy. Meanwhile, the Norman archers kept thinning out the English line. It was growing dark when Harold's death ended the battle: he was wounded in the eye before being cut down by William's knights. The day culminated in a massacre of the survivors, probably intended as a warning to William's new subjects that he would not tolerate any resistance.

'A strange manner of battle, where the one side works by constant motion and ceaseless charges, while the other can but endure passively as it stands fixed to the soil.'

Norman Chronicler William of Poitiers (c.1075)

ANTIOCH

Bohemond of Taranto *v.* Kerbogha 1098

THE SIEGE OF ANTIOCH took place during the First Crusade (1095–99). Liberating land that had been wrongly seized from the Church appealed to the principles of chivalry and feudalism; yet it is by no means clear to what extent the Crusaders were seeking personal gain or were motivated solely by the idea of Holy War. As Bohemond's case proves, many knights clearly saw expeditions to the Holy Land as a means of acquiring fiefdoms. These campaigns promised not just booty, but also glorious seigneuries well beyond the reach of the established princes of Europe.

In November 1095, 100,000 men took up arms and joined the First Crusade after Pope Urban II called for a military expedition against the Turks at the Synod of Clermont. Its ostensible aim was rapprochement with Byzantium. The Byzantine emperor Alexius had urgently sought Urban's help in defending his empire against the Seljuk Turks. The prize for the knights who took part would be the remission of their sins. In 1097, 60,000 Christian soldiers entered Asia Minor. Defeat of the Seljuks provided a springboard for invasion of the Holy Land. The main objective, Jerusalem, eventually fell on 15 July 1099, just two weeks before the pope's death.

In its capture of Jerusalem, which many thought had been lost forever to the Christian world, the First Crusade proved the high-water mark of these punitive campaigns, which lasted until the late 13th century. Even so, Christianity's holiest city was soon retaken by Islamic forces, never to be regained. Exalted leaders, including Philip II of France, Conrad III and Frederick Barbarossa of Germany and Richard I ('the Lionheart') of England, would try and fail to emulate the success of the First Crusade.

A GIFTED LEADER

The outstanding military commander of the first expedition to the Holy Land was Bohemond of Taranto. He was born Mark Guiscard, the eldest son of Robert, a Norman adventurer who had settled in southern Italy. Bohemond (possibly an allusion to 'Behemoth') was a nickname that poked fun at his diminutive size. He rose to become second-in-command to his father in his duchies of Apulia and Calabria.

After an audience with Urban II, Bohemond made himself a papal vassal. Heeding the pope's call, he assembled several hundred knights, including his nephew Tancred, and set sail for Constantinople. Despite having asked for help, Alexius was alarmed by the huge force of Catholic knights that converged on his capital. Moreover, Bohemond was his sworn enemy, having fought alongside his father in an attack on the Byzantine empire in 1080–85. Alexius extracted a promise from the Crusaders to return any former Byzantine lands they conquered, and made them all swear an oath of fealty. In return, they would be given food, guides and military assistance.

The Franks – a term used by both Muslims and Christians of the time to

describe the early Crusaders, deriving from the claims of many knights to having descended from Charlemagne – fought their first fierce engagement at Dorylaeum on 30 June 1097. Bohemond's column was attacked by Seljuk archers. He was relieved by the forces commanded by Raymond de Saint-Gilles and Godfrey de Bouillon. The Crusaders were also seriously hampered by their lack of horses – many had perished en route from Byzantium, particularly while crossing the arid Anatolian Plateau.

GATEWAY TO THE HOLY LAND

They reached Antioch on the River Orontes in what is now northwest Syria in the autumn of 1097. The city was the gateway to the Holy Land and had only been conquered by Islamic Turcomen a dozen years before.

Antioch was a huge place, and the Crusader force was too small to invest it properly. They were also hampered by quarrels with Byzantium, which made the overland supply route unreliable.

Laying siege. This illustration, from William of Tyre's *History of Outremer* (c.1250), depicts the Crusaders using a rock-throwing catapult to batter the walls of Antioch. In the background, the city's Muslim defenders are seen shooting and hurling missiles down from the ramparts.

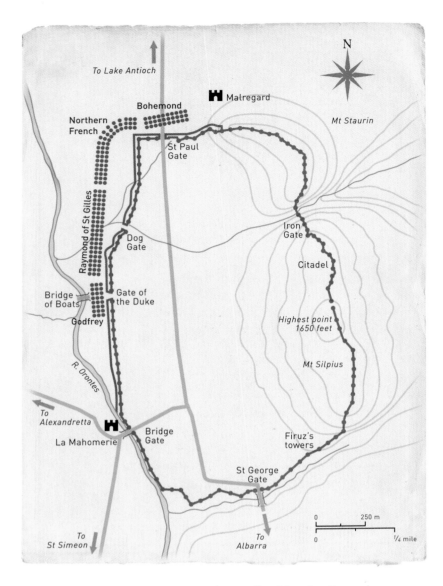

To Lake Antioch

N

Malregard

Bohemond

Mt Staurin

Northern French

St Paul Gate

Raymond of St Gilles

Dog Gate

Iron Gate

Citadel

Bridge of Boats

Gate of the Duke

Godfrey

Highest point 1650 feet

Mt Silpius

R. Orontes

To Alexandretta

La Mahomerie

Bridge Gate

Firuz's towers

St George Gate

To St Simeon

To Albarra

0   250 m

0   ¼ mile

Map of Antioch in October 1097–June 1098, showing the deployment of the besieging Frankish forces and the elevated position of the Citadel, the last part of the city to fall to the Crusaders.

On the credit side, the Crusaders were united in a strong belief in their cause. They also established key bridgeheads on the Levantine coast (notably Edessa and Tripoli) that ensured supplies by sea.

This made for a comfortable siege in the first months, with plentiful food and wine. But by the early winter supplies were dwindling and Bohemond was keen to finish the job. In December 1097, while out on a foraging expedition, he ran into a larger force of Muslims coming to relieve Antioch. He charged with his cavalry and scattered them.

Yet Bohemond's troubles were far from over. His camp was plagued by desertions and then news came of an army under Ridwan approaching from Aleppo. He rode out to confront them near Lake

Antioch. To offset the fact that he was outnumbered, he placed his men in a strong defensive position between the river and the marshes bordering the lake. Ridwan's army was still compact and had not had time to deploy, when Bohemond dispersed them with a well-timed cavalry charge.

THE BESIEGERS BESIEGED

The siege continued until early summer 1098, when Bohemond tried a ruse that had once worked for his father at the siege of Durazzo 16 years previously. Approaching Firuz, the Armenian warden of the towers above the city, he promised him a fortune in gold if he let the invaders into the city. Bohemond also reached an agreement with his allies that if he should find a way into the city then he could keep it for himself, promising that he would give it to Alexius in due course. On 3 June, Firuz let a troop of Bohemond's men pass, who promptly fought their way into the city. Once inside they went on a bloody spree of indiscriminate slaughter.

Christian joy was short-lived, however. Not only did the imposing Citadel remain in enemy hands, but almost as soon as the Franks had entered Antioch a relieving army under Kerbogha, the Turcoman ruler of Mosul, appeared outside the walls to invest the city. From besiegers, they suddenly became the besieged. Kerbogha's relief mission was personally authorized by the caliph of Baghdad, who had grown alarmed at the increasing fragmentation of the Muslim world and was determined to put a stop to Christian incursions.

Once Kerbogha invested the city, the Muslims in the Citadel also joined in the attack. Many Crusaders fled while they still could. The lucky ones among those trapped in the city were forced to eat their horses; the poor ate thistles. Alexius was already underway to relieve the city, but deserters convinced him this was pointless, and he turned back. His decision was also

SUCCESSFUL BREAKOUT

In mid-June the Crusaders found an object they identified as the 'Holy Lance' that had pierced Christ's side on the Cross. Discovery of this sacred relic gave them the same kind of morale boost as the appearance of Pallas Athena to the Athenians at Salamis. They resolved to attempt a breakout.

On 28 June, the Crusaders marched out of the city. Their cavalry numbered a paltry 200 chargers that had escaped being eaten. Bohemond divided his forces in five groups, holding his own unit at the back in reserve. The Turcomen had made the error of stretching out their men thinly around the entire perimeter of the city. They fired a volley of arrows followed by a cavalry charge. When Bohemond saw his men begin to panic he threw himself into the fight, shouting: 'Charge at speed like a brave man and fight valiantly for God and the Holy Sepulchre!' According to the *Gesta Francorum* (a Latin chronicle of the First Crusade, written in 1100) he hit the Turks 'like a lion that has been starving for three or four days, [that] comes out of its cave roaring and thirsting for the blood of the cattle and recklessly falls upon the flocks, tearing the sheep apart as they flee in all directions'.

His men regained their courage and threw the enemy back, killing and looting as they went. Despite their desperate state, they remained well disciplined. After resisting the first Muslim attacks, they charged and drove the enemy from the field. Seeing their co-religionists routed, the force in the Citadel surrendered. The Crusaders were now free to proceed to Jerusalem. Under pressure from pilgrims anxious to reach the Holy City, the force set off, without Bohemond, who was reluctant to lose control of his prize. He was already styling himself 'Prince of Antioch', and the city became an independent Christian principality. He justified his actions by pointing out that the Byzantines had failed to provide the promised assistance during the siege. Only at Christmas 1099, did he make his own pilgrimage to Jerusalem.

A PRINCE'S RANSOM

Bohemond extended his domain, but in 1100 he was ambushed and captured by the Turks. They were thrilled with their prize whom they believed the most powerful of all the Franks. He was held prisoner for three years and ransomed for 100,000 pieces of gold.

When Bohemond was released, Antioch once again found itself under threat, and so he decided to tour Italy and France to raise support. He was fêted wherever he went. Some people even took to calling him Boamundus Magnus or 'Bohemond the Great', echoing the titles bestowed on Alexander of Macedon, Pompey and Charlemagne. Men flocked to his banner and in 1107 he was ready to return to the Crusades. First, he attacked the Byzantines in Albania and besieged Durazzo. The attack ended in a failure and he was obliged to sign a treaty with Alexius in which he agreed that he held Antioch as an imperial vassal. He died in 1111 and was buried at Canosa in Puglia.

'Charge at speed like a brave man and fight valiantly for God and the Holy Sepulchre!'

BOHEMOND, AT THE LIFTING OF THE SIEGE OF ANTIOCH

POITIERS

Edward the 'Black Prince' *v.* John II of France
17 September 1356

THE HUNDRED YEARS' WAR (1337–1453) was the conflict fought between the English and the French for control of France. In its early stages, the English won the Battle of Crécy and captured the port of Calais, which remained in English hands until January 1558.

The greatest English commander of the war was Edward Prince of Wales, the eldest son of King Edward III. The epithet by which he is most often known, 'the Black Prince', dates only from the 16th century, but his cult status was firmly established even in his own lifetime, when he was known simply as 'the Prince'. As historian Jonathan Sumption has written: '...Edward was unquestionably the greatest general of his day, one of the greatest of the European middle ages...at the Battle of Poitiers he captured John II of France and won one of the most complete military victories of the Hundred Years' War.'

CHANGING TACTICS

The prince performed his military miracles in the context of evolving battlefield tactics. The heavy cavalry charge, with knights dressed in chain-mail and armour, was fast becoming obsolete. Horsemen on slow mounts were vulnerable to well-trained infantry, and particularly to archers. Archers had first shown their mettle against cavalry in July 1302 at the Battle of Courtrai, when the Flemish routed the French. (This engagement is also known as the Battle of the Golden Spurs, from the numerous trophies collected from fallen riders at the end of the battle.) It was not just bowmen who had proved their worth on the battlefield:

the Scots had also shown how effective pikemen could be at the Battle of Bannockburn against the English in 1314.

Another innovation at this time, which came from England, was the use of dismounted cavalry. Once armies arrived at the appointed field, the horses were kept back until the end and used only in the rout and to pursue the enemy. Conversely, if things went badly, they could provide a getaway. Dismounted cavalry was supported by companies of archers, mustered in ever-increasing strength.

BAPTISM OF FIRE

It was also the English who perfected the use of the longbow. These powerful weapons could fire arrows great distances and be reloaded at speed, on both counts outclassing the crossbows with which European armies were equipped. By the mid-14th century, there was no standard infantry left to speak of. Edward III triumphed using these tactics fighting the Scots at Halidon Hill in 1333 and the French at Crécy in 1346. After that the French started fighting back by adopting the tactics of their enemies.

The Black Prince learned these techniques from his father and put them into practice when he tasted blood for the first time at Crécy. Aged just 16, he was in command of one of three divisions in a 14,000-man

force. It was an arduous campaign that took the army from Normandy to the Seine and from Paris to Picardy.

Crécy was a brutal object lesson in the new arts of warfare. The French cavalry charged in chaotic disarray, while the English bowmen mowed down the Genoese crossbowmen. Ultimately, the Franco-Genoese army was overrun by a far smaller, much more disciplined force. It is thought that the prince wore black

armour on that day, giving rise to his famous soubriquet. In any event, his impressive feats of arms continued. He was present at the Siege of Calais, which fell to English arms after 11 months. He was still only 20 when he led his troops into battle outside Calais and when he engaged the French at sea off Winchelsea.

In 1355, at the age of 25, he became his father's viceroy in the province of Aquitaine, which had been English since

The rout of French forces at the Battle of Potiers, as imagined by the French Romantic painter Eugène Delacroix in 1830.

the marriage of Eleanor to Henry II in 1152. Most of the Black Prince's soldiers were Gascons, as he arrived in Bordeaux with just 800 soldiers and 1,400 mounted archers. This did not stop him from raiding Languedoc, pillaging Avignonet and Castelnaudary and sacking Carcassonne and Narbonne. The following year, he turned north and ravaged the Auvergne and the regions of the Limousin and the Berry.

The Black Prince was supposed to join forces with his father in the French campaign, which went ahead in 1356. The idea was hatched by Edward III and his cousin the duke of Lancaster. They planned to invade France with three armies. The Black Prince would advance north from Bordeaux while Lancaster pushed south from Normandy. They would then join forces with Edward's troops in Brittany and French rebels under the king of Navarre. Meanwhile, Edward III himself would cross the Channel and land at Calais with the main English army. The three armies would meet at the Loire.

The Black Prince set out in August with 6,000–7,000 men, two-thirds of them Gascon cavalry, plus about 1,000 English archers. They marched to the Loire, but the king was not at the rendezvous: he had been forced to abandon his part of the pincer movement. For his part, Lancaster had set out from Normandy as arranged, but found himself unable to cross the River Loire.

The prince now discovered he was heavily outnumbered by John II of France, who had 8,000 cavalry and 3,000 infantry. The Prince decided to fall back on Bordeaux, but John gave chase. On 16 September, he caught and outflanked Edward on the plains east of Poitiers. The Prince offered terms, but refused to surrender his person.

That evening, the French held a council of war, at which they decided to abandon their traditional tactic of the cavalry charge in favour of advancing on foot. They did this on the advice of a Scot, Sir William Douglas, who told them of the mistakes the English had made at Bannockburn.

DEFENSIVE STRONGHOLD

Dawn on the 17th revealed that the English had dug in on high ground to the south of the advancing French army. Their troops were positioned behind a hawthorn hedge, with the archers in the wings. Deep trenches on one side and marshes on the other provided further protection.

Despite this strong defensive position, the English had run out of food and were preparing to retreat when the French cavalry attacked their wings. Their aim was to scatter the English archers. With difficulty, the archers re-formed and proceeded to inflict great carnage on the attackers. The main French force saw nothing of this, as the action was concealed by the brow of the hill. Led by the *dauphin*, they continued to advance on

'...*Edward was unquestionably the greatest general of his day, one of the greatest of the European middle ages ... at the Battle of Poitiers he captured John II of France and won one of the most complete military victories of the Hundred Years' War.*'

HISTORIAN JONATHAN SUMPTION ON THE BLACK PRINCE

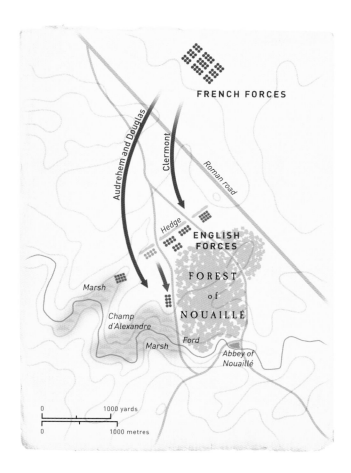

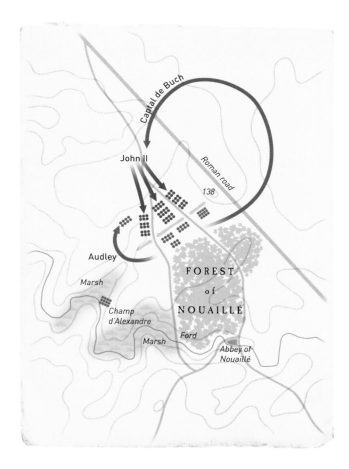

the hawthorn hedge, cramming themselves through the gaps. After two hours of close fighting, they were forced to retreat. As the *dauphin* was being led to safety, the rest of the French line took this as a signal to retreat. King John tried to save the day by leading in his reserves, but he was driven down the hill and enveloped by the English, with Gascon troops attacking the French king from the rear and English cavalry under Sir James Audley enfilading from the side. Many French were taken prisoner, including the king himself.

MILITARY PROWESS

Edward had demonstrated the pragmatism and flexibility required of a great general. By contrast, John issued commands and expected them to be carried out to the letter. There was no hope of adapting them once the battle took an unexpected turn. Yet Poitiers proved little more than a pinprick against the French elephant, as

the Prince had no way of consolidating his great victory. All he could do was take John back to Bordeaux and hold him hostage for four years in the hope of a large ransom.

In 1360, Edward III and John II signed the Treaty of Brétigny. This granted the English vast new territories in France and installed the Prince as ruler of the newly expanded territory of Aquitaine.

The Black Prince went on to perform other great feats of arms. At Nájera in Castile in 1367, he led an Anglo-Gascon army to victory against the pretender to the Castilian throne, Henry of Trastámara.

Not long thereafter, the French rallied and began to win back much of the territory lost at Brétigny. In response, the prince laid siege to Limoges in 1370, slaughtering its inhabitants when it fell. He returned to England the following year, but was plagued by illness and died in 1376, a year before his father.

Phases of the Battle of Poitiers. French forces led by King John II advanced across the Roman road from Poitiers to Bordeaux. After they had tried in vain to penetrate the English defences, cavalry detachments under the Gascon Captal de Buch and the Englishman Sir James Audley caught the French in a deadly pincer movement.

AGINCOURT

Henry V of England *v.* Charles VI of France
25th October **1415**

AGINCOURT WAS THE GREATEST ENGLISH VICTORY of all time, resulting in a 'Fall of France' every bit as humiliating as that of 1940. Like many before it, the battle was carried by the archers; but it was one of the last fights where bowmen would decide the course of history, for very soon the longbow would be superseded by artillery.

Like his great-uncle the Black Prince, King Henry V began his apprenticeship young. At the age of just 16, he played an important role at the Battle of Shrewsbury, and was badly wounded in the face by an arrow. On ascending the throne in 1413, Henry demanded the return of territory ceded by England at the Treaty of Brétigny (1360) together with the Norman and Angevin lands as a precondition for marrying Catherine of Valois. He saw his role as uniting France, which was riven by factions.

HENRY'S FRENCH CAMPAIGN

After immense preparations involving the assembly of 10,000 men and a vast armoury of longbows and arrows, ships and cannons, he sailed from Southampton on 11 August 1415. The strictest discipline was maintained: there was to be no looting, and respect paid to women and the Church. He took the port of Harfleur by the end of September and challenged the *dauphin* (the French king's eldest son) to single combat.

As winter loomed, however, Henry's army was badly depleted by dysentery and the reserves due to arrive by sea had been scattered by a storm. The campaigning season was drawing to a close, so he marched through driving rain towards Calais with some 6,000 soldiers, intent on

returning to England. He found his way blocked by two French armies, which had joined outside the town of Bapaume. After futile negotiations, Henry took up a position above the River Ternoise at Blagny, where he saw the size of the French force for the first time 'as large as a swarm of locusts'.

Aware that the armies would have to give battle, the accompanying priests were kept busy granting absolution. When a knight, Sir Walter Hungerford, remarked that he could do with another 10,000 archers, Henry replied that since God was there to protect his people they would make do with what they had. The king then released his prisoners, probably fearing they might attack him in the rear. In the ensuing battle, Henry fought an army perhaps three times the size of his own at the village of Agincourt (now Azincourt) on 25 October: the feast of St Crispin. The king himself commanded the centre, while the duke of York led the van. The king's left was under the command of Lord Camoys. It had been another wet night, which would play into Henry's hands – just as the weather helped Arminius in the Teutoburg Forest and would come to the aid of Wellington at Waterloo.

Henry drew up his archers. The French had taken up position half a mile to the right with a small valley between the two armies, wider at the French end. Henry repositioned

A 15th-century manuscript illumination shows the decisive victory of Henry V's forces (right) at Agincourt. The *fleur-de-lys* on the English battle standard symbolized England's claim to French territories.

his forces as he suspected the French would try to come round the back of the wood and surprise them. As night fell, he quartered his army in the village of Maisoncelles.

DEATH FROM THE SKIES

The pious Henry heard three Masses the next morning. He arranged his men-at-arms four deep in a single line divided into three 'battles' or battalions. Between the battalions he placed his bowmen, as well as in a forward position on the wings with room enough to withdraw at the moment of impact. The archers drove stakes into the ground chest-high to the horses.

The French rode into a bottleneck. Henry had woods to the left and the right and half the land to his rear was woodland too. Henry rode up and down the line, rallying his men. Then he dismounted and took up his position in the centre of the line.

The French advanced on foot from Tramecourt. What little mounted cavalry they had was in the third of their 'battles', although there were some mounted cavalry on the wings whose job it was to take out the English archers. The battle in the van contained the high nobles and office holders. Their crossbowmen, archers and gunners were pushed to the back. In contrast to the English army, the French was essentially leaderless, as the commanders were positioned in the van. Henry delivered a rousing address to his men: 'Nowe is gode tyme, for alle Engelond prayeth for us; therefore be of gode chere, and lette us go to our iorney… In the name of Almyghti God and Saynt George, avaunt banarer! And Saynte George, this day thyn help!' He then ordered his archers to pull up their stakes and advance, halting within bowshot of the enemy: 230–275 metres (250–300 yds). They drove in their stakes again and reformed.

At this point, the English marshal, Sir Thomas Erpingham, hurled his baton in the air and the archers fired their first volley.

Some of the French force rode into the attack, but most came on foot. The ground was soft and slippery from the rain and wrought havoc on those moving in heavy armour. The cavalry aimed to roll up the archers on the wings. But as they approached, they were halted in their tracks by the stakes and met by salvoes of arrows, which killed or wounded many. Some of the horses impaled themselves upon the stakes. Those riders who could, turned tail – and rode headlong into the dismounted troops. Chaos prevented the men from going forward or back. They hit the English line, but Henry's soldiers did not yield. The archers threw down their bows and joined in the fray with their swords and battle-hammers. Now the English moved in for the kill: the French dead were piled up in heaps while their living soldiers were increasingly squeezed between the English ranks and were unable to swing their swords. In these conditions, the numerical superiority of the French actually told against them. Those who were not cut down surrendered *en masse*.

The French were routed with great slaughter: the English army lost between 300 and 400 dead, but the French lost several thousand men, killed or taken prisoner. At one stage, rumours spread that the baggage train had been raided and that the French were about to mount a fresh attack using their third, unharmed battle. At this news, Henry is said to have ordered 200 archers to kill all the prisoners. Some

Portrait of Henry V by an unknown artist. Henry was a brilliant tactician and audacious commander. He is said to have ridden into the Battle of Agincourt wearing a basinet (a type of helmet with a pointed crown and visor) topped with an ostentatious golden crown, supposedly to draw the enemy's fire.

accounts claim up to 1,000 men were slain, all of them nobles. There is, however, no evidence to support this; the true figure is unlikely to have exceeded 100. Once Henry was confident that the French would not try to mount another attack, he seems to have called off the executions.

Some very prominent noblemen were taken prisoner. They included Charles, duke of Orléans, the duke of Bourbon, the count of Vendôme and the duke of Brittany's brother, the count of Richemont. The battle was over by 2 p.m. Henry had lost important men too, including the duke of York and the earl of Suffolk.

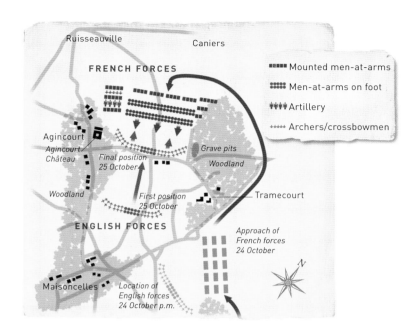

Map of the Battle of Agincourt, showing the deployment of the opposing armies.

CONQUERING HERO

Henry was a ruthless general. His most famous utterance – 'war without fire is like sausage without mustard' – says it all. Like the great victory of the Black Prince at Poitiers 70 years before, Agincourt was a testimony to skilled leadership and showed what a small, well-disciplined army could do against a poorly led one, albeit of superior strength. Henry was never rash, but planned everything in minute detail. Having secured victory at Agincourt, he marched to Calais and sailed back to England.

Yet Henry was far from finished with France. In 1416, he returned to Normandy and captured Caen, leading the assault in person after despatching his lieutenants to take Cherbourg, Coutances, Avranches and Evreux. He then laid siege to Rouen, which finally fell in 1419. At this time, he shrewdly forged an alliance with the dukes of Burgundy.

At the Treaty of Troyes of 1420, Henry was declared heir to Charles VI of France and married Catherine while the *dauphin* (later Charles VII) was disinherited. Henry directed the siege of Melun and after defeating its governor, the sire de Barbazan, in single combat entered Paris in triumph in December 1420.

Henry continued to enjoy great military success: in 1421, he relieved Chartres, drove the *dauphin* back across the Loire and took Meaux. But the following year, while on his way to help the Burgundians, he fell victim to dysentery at the Château de Vincennes, just outside Paris. Aged not quite 35, he was even younger than the Black Prince. More tragically, by dying six weeks and a day before his rival Charles VI, he failed to inherit the throne of France.

'Nowe is gode tyme, for alle Engelond prayeth for us; therefore be of gode chere, and lette us go to our iorney ... In the name of Almyghti God and Saynt George, avaunt banarer! And Saynte George, this day thyn help!'

HENRY V – ADDRESS TO HIS TROOPS BEFORE AGINCOURT

THE SIEGE OF ORLÉANS

Joan of Arc *v.* the English April–May **1429**

AFTER THE DEATH OF HENRY V IN 1422, English fortunes in the Hundred Years' War began to wane, though not immediately. Competent generals prosecuted the war on behalf of the infant heir to the thrones of England and France, Henry VI, winning notable victories at Cravant (1423) and Verneuil (1424). By 1428, the English had extended the borders of their French provinces to the Loire and began to lay siege to the city of Orléans. Then came the first major setback, when one of their most talented commanders, Thomas, earl of Salisbury, was killed.

France then witnessed an extraordinary national revival, which was largely the result of the inspirational leadership of Joan of Arc or *la Pucelle* ('the Virgin'), as she is sometimes known. In May 1429, she pulled off a remarkable feat in raising the siege of Orléans.

DIVINE GUIDANCE

Joan, a simple peasant girl from Lorraine, had long been subject to visions, in which she claimed that various saints including St Michael and St Catherine appeared to her, imploring her to save France. When the local *seigneur*, Robert de Baudricourt, heard the story, he sent her packing. Soon afterwards the Burgundians – allies of the English – arrived in her home village and she was forced to take refuge in the local town of Neufchâteau.

The voices in her head now grew more urgent, telling her to relieve Orléans. Under her incessant petitioning, de Baudricourt began to listen. He furnished her with a horse and sword and sent her

to see the *dauphin* at Chinon on the River Vienne, a few miles south of the Loire. She arrived there on 4 March 1429.

The English siege became bogged down after Salisbury's death. Even so, supplies were assured after the victory of Sir John Fastolf – one of the models for the character of Falstaff in Shakespeare's *Henry V* – at the so-called 'Battle of the Herrings' at Rouvray in February 1429. The *dauphin* now tried to drive a wedge between the English and their Burgundian allies. This strategy was successful to the extent that the Burgundians withdrew their troops from Orléans, giving the French a glimmer of hope that they might be able to raise the siege.

Joan was granted her first audience with the *dauphin* on 6 March. He was naturally superstitious and open to suggestion, but demanded proof of her virginity before he provided her with soldiers. His mother-in-law examined her and she was deemed fit 'to show a sign of divine approval before Orléans'.

Aside from trusting in divine intervention, Joan also took her military preparations very seriously. She learned to ride a horse and wield a lance. The king gave her specially designed armour and a sword, together with a standard bearing the image of 'our Saviour sitting in judgement on the clouds of heaven … an angel holding in his hands a *fleur de lys* which the image of Christ was blessing'.

This standard proved to be her trump card, acting as a rallying point for the hesitant French. Her aim was to rid France of the English, as she made clear in a letter dictated on 22 March. The army left for Orléans with a posse of priests walking ahead of the van chanting '*veni creator spiritus*'.

Joan arrived at Orléans in April. By this time, the English siege was faltering.

English cannon and bowmen in siege towers batter the walls of the French city of Orléans in 1429. Scene from a contemporary manuscript illumination.

The city was too large to invest completely, and now they had lost their Burgundian auxiliaries. They had erected a series of temporary fortresses, but they were few and far between on the city's eastern side.

Joan and the relieving forces crossed the Loire by boat. At her second trial, the success of this endeavour was hailed as a miracle, but the safe landing probably had more to do with the fact that the defenders had distracted the English by a sortie against their position at Saint Loup. The relief forces entered the city on the 29th.

RAISING THE SIEGE

Joan wanted to engage the English straight away, but the city's commandant Dunois was against it. For the time being, Joan contented herself with haranguing the English with religious invective. She targeted William Glasdale and his men in particular, who were defending Les Tourelles at the end of the bridge crossing the Loire to the south.

While continuing to raise morale within the city, she probed the English defences. Successful sorties captured two outlying English positions: Saint Loup, and two days later Les Augustins. On 8 May, she directed the French to attack Les Tourelles, the bridgehead on the southern bank of the

Loire. In this action, she was wounded in the neck by an arrow. The fighting was so fierce that Dunois advised retreat, but Joan stood her ground and asked him to defer until she had spoken to God. She came back and rallied the French forces around her standard.

As fear spread among the English, French courage grew. It was Joan who placed the first ladder against the wall. A pitched battle ended in English defeat. Shortly afterwards, the siege was raised and Orléans was saved. The departure of the English army was the cue for two days of thanksgiving and cheering for *la Pucelle* and her troops.

Now that Orléans was secure, Joan set about clearing the Loire Valley of the English and pushing them back to Normandy. She literally struck the fear of God into the enemy, who recoiled before this unusual vision on the battlefield. Rumours began to spread among the English that God had deserted their cause. In rapid succession, the garrisons at Jargeau, Beaugency and Meung-sur-Loire fell to the French. Whether these actions were divinely ordained or not, a more prosaic reason lay behind the French victory at the Battle at Patay on 18 June: the use of artillery. Since Crécy and Agincourt, English longbowman had dictated terms on the battlefield. But they were now superseded by a deadly new weapon that would change the face of war.

Modern view of Orléans seen from the far side of the River Loire. Joan of Arc's relief force crossed this obstacle without difficulty after a diversionary action by the city's defenders.

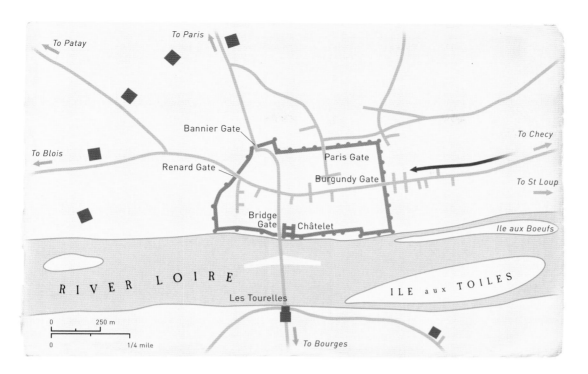

Map showing the walls of Orléans and the temporary fortresses constructed around the city by the besiegers. A shortage of English troops left the city's eastern side poorly defended, so allowing the relief force relatively free passage into Orléans in April 1429.

THE TIDE TURNS

After Orléans, the tide turned, as the French recorded a series of important victories against the English. Patay was crucial, since it liberated the territory east of Paris. French morale and military strength increased, culminating in the Battle of Castillon in 1453, when the armies commanded by John Talbot, earl of Shrewsbury were overwhelmed north of Bordeaux. This defeat ended three centuries of English rule in Aquitaine and brought the Hundred Years' War to a close.

A FALLING STAR

On 17 July 1429, Charles VII was crowned in Reims. Joan stood by the king's side at the anointing with her banner in her hand. Her divine mission had been fulfilled, but more important even than her military victories had been the sense of national unity they had instilled.

However, Charles's main concern was now to bring the Burgundians over to his side, a task that Joan's strident militancy might only hinder. Moreover, the myth of her invulnerability in battle was exploded. As she led an army against Paris, she was wounded in the leg by a crossbow bolt at the Port St Honoré. Soon afterwards, the king ordered her to withdraw.

In April 1430, Joan moved north to Compiègne, which was being threatened by the Burgundians. She was captured during a skirmish on 23 May. Religious scholars at the University of Paris advised that she should be submitted to the inquisition, but instead in November she was sold to the English and taken to Rouen just before Christmas. Charles VII failed to come up with any offer of a ransom to free her.

In January 1431, Joan was put on trial in Rouen for heresy. The proceedings were a foregone conclusion, and she was found guilty and burned at the stake on 30 May. At a second trial in 1456, after the French had swept the English enemy from their lands, she was posthumously rehabilitated. The Roman Catholic Church canonized her in 1920.

Charles VII belatedly acknowledged the enormous debt he owed Joan of Arc. Her brothers were raised to the nobility and her home village of Domrémy was exempted from paying taxes right up to the French Revolution.

The 'Maid of Orléans' had inspired the military and political revival of an entire nation. Tellingly, though, she insisted at her trial that she had not commanded the troops for the king, but for God.

THE FALL OF CONSTANTINOPLE

Sultan Mehmet II *v.* Emperor Constantine XI
29 May **1453**

THE CITY OF CONSTANTINOPLE WAS FOUNDED IN AD 324 by the emperor Constantine on the site of the ancient city of Byzantium. His 'new Rome' (*Nova Roma*) was designed as a bulwark against the barbarians threatening the empire. Its position at the end of a triangular peninsula and surrounded by water on three sides made it virtually impregnable. Strengthened by Theodosius II in the early fifth century, its formidable landward and seaward defences ran for 14 miles (22.5 km), comprising double walls and 192 towers.

For centuries, the Byzantine empire (heir to the eastern Roman empire) had found itself under threat from its Muslim neighbours the Seljuk Turks and their successors, the Ottomans. The final push to take Constantinople occurred after the 18-year-old Mehmet II ascended the Ottoman throne in 1451. Prior to this, Constantinople had been sacked only once before – by Venetian troops on the Fourth Crusade in 1204.

RISING TENSION

The immediate catalyst for the attack was the Byzantine emperor Constantine XI Palaeologus's demand for an increase in the annual stipend paid for safe passage through the Bosphorus (the narrow sea lane, guarded by the city, between the Black Sea and the Dardanelles Straits). Yet since childhood, Mehmet had dreamed of conquering Constantinople, thereby achieving total Ottoman hegemony over Asia Minor and the Balkans. In 1451–52, he ordered a sea blockade and began building a castle at

Asomaton (Rumeli Hisar), 5 miles (8 km) outside the city on the European shore of the Bosphorus. This was to be the base for his operations against Constantinople. The emperor protested in vain that the fort lay within Byzantine territory; the last envoys he sent to Mehmet were beheaded.

Some 5,000 labourers were engaged in building the castle. It was finished in four and a half months and named *Boghaz Kesen* 'the cutter of the throat'. Mehmet manned it with 500 troops, and having ostentatiously inspected the walls of Constantinople, rode back to his capital at Adrianople (Edirne). Henceforth any boat travelling through the straits had to drop anchor and pay a tax to the sultan, on pain of being blown apart by a fearsome arsenal of cannon that Mehmet built up and stationed at *Boghaz Kesen* and 13 other batteries along the shore.

ORBAN'S METAL MONSTERS

Mehmet's cannon were the work of a Hungarian or German (Gibbon suggests he might have been a Dane) gun founder

Mehmet II's entry into Constantinople, in an 1876 painting by the French artist Benjamin Constant.

called Orban (or Urban), who had initially offered his services to the emperor. As Constantine could not afford his fees, he approached the sultan, who had both the funds and the desire for new weapons.

Orban promised him a gun that could breach the walls of Constantinople, and in three months produced a bronze behemoth 8 metres (27 ft) long with a bore of 76 cm (2.5 ft), dubbed the 'Basilica Gun'. At its first trial it fired a cannonball weighing 360 kg (800 lbs) over a mile. On impact, the projectile buried itself in the earth to a depth of 1.8 metres (6 ft).

The Basilica was cast at the sultan's foundry in Edirne, and was dragged by 60 oxen 140 miles (225 km) to be installed opposite Constantinople in the spring of 1453. In all, Orban and his foundrymen turned out 70 guns for Mehmet. This was the first time the east had seen artillery on such a scale. (In the west, field guns had been known for a century or more and had made old-style castles obsolete.)

As well as his guns, Mehmet assembled siege engines and mines for his assault on Constantinople. His army numbered 100,000 men drawn from throughout his empire, including 12,000 Janissaries (an élite unit of soldiers conscripted as boys from Christian lands under Ottoman control). This force was twice as large as the entire population of Constantinople, which had an army of just 7,000, just under a third of whom were Venetians and Genoese. These troops were spread thinly around the city walls.

That winter Mehmet was like a cat on a hot tin roof, waiting for the ideal moment to seize the city. For his part, the emperor engaged Giovanni Giustiniani, a Genoese engineer, to strengthen the city's defences with a force of 700 men. He had been promised the island of Lemnos as a reward.

Mehmet knew that to gain his prize he had to attack the city from both land and sea. He set about assembling a naval force of some 125 vessels under the command of Bulgarian admiral Baltha Ogli. It outnumbered the emperor's fleet five to one.

THE ASSAULT BEGINS

With the onset of spring, Mehmet marched his army to the Bosphorus, arriving on Easter Monday, 2 April 1453. He established his position at the centre of the land walls with his Janissaries and three huge cannon, including Orban's monster. Asian troops formed the right of the line, Europeans the left. A smaller army invested Galata with its population of Genoese. The emperor was opposite at the Gate of St Romanus with the Genoese troops commanded by Giustiniani. The Greeks had some cannon of their own, but they were frightened to discharge them lest they weaken the ancient walls.

Despite his pleas, no one came to the emperor's aid – Western Christendom was seemingly indifferent to Constantinople's fate – and 700 Venetians quietly sailed away. The emperor did not despair, 'but if his courage were equal to the peril, his

> '*A circumstance that distinguishes the siege of Constantinople is the reunion of the ancient and modern artillery. The cannon were intermingled with the mechanical engines for casting stones and darts; the bullet and the battering ram were directed against the same walls; nor had the discovery of gunpowder superseded the use of liquid and unextinguishable fire.*'

EDWARD GIBBON ON MILITARY TECHNOLOGY AT THE SIEGE OF CONSTANTINOPLE

strength was inadequate to the contest' (Gibbon). Constantine shut the gates and withdrew the bridges over the moat. The remaining population prayed for deliverance. After a week the sultan, in accordance with Muslim law, sent messengers offering a truce. He would grant the population their lives under Ottoman protection. The offer was refused and the bombardment began on 6 April. It would continue relentlessly for six weeks.

The old walls proved remarkably resilient to the sultan's cannon, mortars and catapults and Giustiniani and his men were quick to conduct running repairs to any breaches. The sultan's navy also failed to force the chain boom that the Genoese had built across the Golden Horn, and had allowed four ships stocked with munitions and supplies to get through to the city. Mehmet sent waves of troops to their deaths to prevent the victuals getting through and had his admiral whipped and threatened to impale him for his failure.

A VOYAGE OVERLAND

An Italian in the sultan's service is thought to have provided the answer to his woes, by suggesting a bold plan to transport a fleet overland from the Bosphorus to the Golden Horn and to attack the boom from the rear. Mehmet's engineers duly set to work building a road 60 metres (200 ft) above sea level then down to the harbour, a distance of some 10 miles (16 km) through the scrub. Then a track of timbers greased with mutton and ox fat was laid, capable of carrying metal-wheeled cradles. The

ships were raised from the water with pulleys and hauled overland by oxen.

As they passed the city, the sails were hoisted, to the astonishment of the defenders, who saw a fleet proceeding overland down the hill to the harbour. This remarkable feat culminated in about 70 Turkish ships being launched on the Golden Horn, robbing the Greeks of their supremacy there and leaving the Genoese isolated in Pera on the far side. The Turks also built a pontoon bridge to improve communications and erected a floating battery to pulverize the soft underbelly of the city.

Morale and supplies were low within the walls. Some people tried to convince the emperor to flee. He refused, saying: 'It is impossible for me to go away: how would I leave the churches of our Lord, and his servants the clergy, and the throne, and my people in such a plight? ... I pray you, my friends, in future do not say to me anything else but "Nay, Sire, do not leave us." Never will I leave you.'

NO HOLDS BARRED

When after seven weeks there was still no breach in the walls, the grand vizier persuaded the sultan to send another embassy to the emperor proposing an annual payment or the abandonment of the city with a free passage for its citizens and goods. The emperor was to be granted a kingdom on the Peloponnese. Constantine refused. Now the sultan announced that the choice was between death by the sword or conversion to Islam.

An all-out attack was planned for 29 May. Mehmet consulted his astrologers. who told him that this would be an auspicious date. The previous Sunday, the 27th, he rode among his men promising them three days of pillage. The Turks prepared all night for the attack, filling in the moats to the sound of pipes and trumpets. The beleaguered inhabitants could hear their joyful shouts of: 'There is no God but Allah and Mohammed is his prophet.'

Within the city the church bells tolled and icons were carried around in procession. On the night of the 28th, the sultan rallied his troops, while on the far side of the walls the emperor told his followers that it was a man's duty to die either for his faith, his country, his family or his sovereign. Now they must be prepared to die for all four. He spoke of the city's tradition and the perfidy of the sultan. In Gibbon's words, this fine speech was 'the funeral oration of the Roman empire'.

Those present 'wept, they embraced: regardless of their families and fortunes, they devoted their lives; and each commander, departing to his station, maintained all night a vigilant and anxious watch on the rampart'. The citizens woke the next morning to an indescribable din signalling the assault. The men ran to their posts followed by women carrying stones and beams to repair the walls. The attack came in three waves: a force of *bashi-bazouks* (Ottoman irregular troops), driven forward by beatings to stop them from wavering. Their job was to wear down the enemy. They were followed by Anatolian regiments, who fought their way up to Giustiniani's stockade, built to plug a gap made by a previous bombardment. They were greeted by volleys of stones and the defenders fought with their hands to drive them back. The Anatolians sustained heavy losses, but Orban's cannon destroyed the stockade before dawn and 300 Turks stormed through the gap. They were met by a Greek detachment led by the emperor in person armed with an iron mace. They killed many of the sultan's men and forced the rest back through the walls.

Mehmet fumed at this reverse and sent in his Janissaries, personally urging them on to the moat. Yet the Christians still managed to withstand the onslaught, even though they had been fighting for four hours without respite.

THE CITY FALLS

Ultimately, though, the Greeks were doomed by two fatal mishaps: they had undertaken a sortie against the Turkish flank from the Kerkoporta Gate (a small postern near the Palace of Blachernae), but had failed to secure it on their return. A group of Turks now penetrated the gate and scaled the tower above. The second was the wounding of Giustiniani at close quarters, who begged to leave the battlefield. The emperor pleaded with him to stay, but the Italian insisted. He was carried to a Genoese vessel in the harbour. The sight of him leaving the fight told the Genoese that the day was lost.

Morale quickly collapsed. The sultan ordered an attack on the Gate of St Romanus. An Anatolian of enormous height called Hassan scaled the stockade to the very summit. He was killed, but

'God forbid that I should live an emperor without an empire! As my city falls, I will fall with it.'

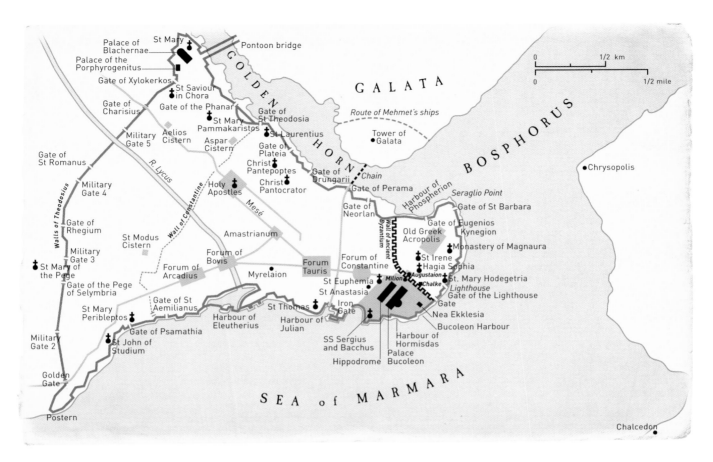

Map of the siege of Constantinople, showing the seaward and landward defences that the Byzantine Greeks used to defend the city against Mehmet II's attack.

those following him overwhelmed the Greeks, then ran on until they reached the city's inner wall, which they scaled unopposed. On reaching the heart of Constantinople, the cry went up 'The city is taken!'

Turks were pouring through the postern gate. Constantine galloped back to the Gate of St Romanus and made a last attempt to rally the Greeks. When he saw the city was lost he tore off his insignia 'and plunged headlong into the mêlée of the oncoming Janissaries, and was never seen again, alive or dead' (Lord Kinross).

An orgy of slaughter ensued. Hoping for deliverance by an angel, the Greeks fled to the Church of Hagia Sophia. There they were rounded up and taken to the soldiers' tents to be divided among them.

ENTER THE CONQUEROR
The emperor had been slain, and some 30,000 Christians enslaved or deported, while thousands more became 'food for the sword'. Sultan Mehmet entered Constantinople on 29 May 1453 riding a white horse. All around him the city was being sacked by a triumphant Ottoman army. (A Venetian observer was doubtless exaggerating when he said blood flowed through the streets like rainwater after a sudden storm and corpses floated out to sea like melons along a canal.) The swag taken by the soldiers included gold, silver and precious stones. Mehmet rode on to Hagia Sophia, built by the emperor Justinian, dismounted and picked up a handful of dust 'which he poured over his turban as an act of humility before God' (Philip Mansel). He entered the church, gave thanks to Allah and ordered that the grand building be turned into a mosque.

For this feat of arms, Mehmet was dubbed *Fatih* ('Conqueror'). His victory paved the way for even greater glory under his successors. 'To Rome! To Rome!' was the constant cry of Mehmet's great-grandson Suleyman the Magnificent, under whom the Ottoman empire reached its zenith. Yet while the Ottomans never got to Rome, they did make it to the walls of Vienna – twice (in 1529 and 1683).

NIEUPORT

Maurice of Nassau *v.* Albrecht of Austria
2 July **1600**

THE SAME PERIOD OF INTELLECTUAL FERMENT that brought a root-and-branch re-evaluation of humanity's place in the universe also presided over a renaissance of interest in the theory of warfare. Just as science, art and literature sought inspiration in classical models, so statesmen and generals now began to draw lessons from the military strategists and practitioners of ancient civilizations, notably Greece and Rome.

Warfare, however, presented a set of problems unknown to the arts and sciences. Where Greek and Roman practice could teach modern strategists some things, in others contemporary armies had already far surpassed the ancients. Artillery was a prime example. When Charles VIII of France invaded Italy in 1494, he was able to use his bronze cannon to level Spanish and Habsburg fortresses in a way the Romans never could without the benefit of artillery or gunpowder. Castles were rendered obsolete until new designs (by the French marquis de Vauban in particular) made them proof against heavy guns.

Artillery pieces, then, were the prime mover behind the seismic shift in military strategy during this period. But the advent of mobile heavy guns brought home with renewed force the great advantage of good roads for moving troops to fight wars (a lesson well understood in Roman times, but since neglected).

As muskets became lighter, more reliable, and more portable, they found increasing use as battlefield weapons. Musketeers took up their positions on the flanks of battle formations, like the archers of the Black Prince or Henry V.

Even so, the pike remained the preferred weapon of the infantryman.

The year 1568 saw the beginning of protracted struggle by the Protestant northern Netherlands to gain its independence from Catholic Spain. This conflict went on for nearly three generations (the Dutch refer to it as the Eighty Years' War) until finally resolved within the wider peace settlement that ended the Thirty Years' War (the Treaty of Westphalia, 1648).

A MODERN COMMANDER

Prince Maurice of Nassau (1575–1625) was the son of William the Silent, the governor (*stadhouder*) of Holland, who proclaimed independence from Spain and who was assassinated in 1584. A master tactician and the most celebrated European commander of his generation, Maurice may be credited with organizing the uprising against Spain into a coherent war of liberation and finally ridding the Dutch Republic of the threat from its former colonial master. First and foremost, he grasped that new techniques were required both to attack and defend a city under siege in this new age of increasingly mobile artillery.

The Princes Battel:

The Arch D

Maurice began by schooling himself in the siege techniques developed by his father's great adversaries, the Spanish dukes of Alba and Parma. The historian John Childs has given a definitive account of their methods: first, the town or city was blockaded and then enclosed: 'within a double ring of redoubts (contravallation and circumvallation) which protect the besieger's camp. First trenches, then zigzagged saps (mines) were excavated towards the "front" selected for attack, and the artillery installed in the batteries. Lighter cannon destroyed breastworks and countered the garrison's artillery whilst the heavier guns concentrated on breaching the fortifications. When the defending line had been substantially subdued, the besiegers sapped up the glacis (sloping earthwork rampart) to capture the counterscarp (the other slope of the ditch in front of the main wall or scarp). The artillery was then advanced to begin battering the main ramparts, while the attacking infantry built a bridge or causeway over the wet ditch ready to assault the breach.'

MILITARY REFORMS

Maurice was an intellectually minded military reformer who understood that his army had to be turned into a professional force if it was to achieve its objectives. As befitted a Renaissance prince eager to rediscover classical models, he steeped himself in the works of ancient military theorists. Yet he also learned a great deal from modern strategists. One of these,

In this 17th-century print of the Battle of Nieuport, the small and manoeuvrable units of Dutch troops (top left) stand in clear contrast to the larger Spanish *tercios* ranged against them. Maurice was a master tactician who mostly avoided pitched battles against a numerically superior opponent.

Justus Lipsius, his tutor at the University of Leiden, had written treatises not only on the Roman army, but also on siege warfare and was in a perfect position to instruct the young prince. Maurice sent his officers to study at Leiden, while his cousin John established the military academy at Siegen.

Maurice did not have the manpower to create a citizen army. As a result, the majority of his army was made up of mercenaries, mainly from the Protestant countries of northern Europe: England, Scotland, Germany, Switzerland and Denmark. Nevertheless, he was careful to offer them the sort of terms that bred loyalty to him.

Maurice was keenest of all to reform the infantry. For the first time soldiers were to be regularly and properly paid. Also, following the advice of the Roman strategist Aelianus Tacticus (Aelian), much emphasis was placed on drill. This was a crucial discipline for efficient pikemanship and for the loading and reloading of the still-cumbersome muskets. The pikemen and the musketeers were synchronized

and the infantry were able to improve their rates of fire.

The regimental structure was only just evolving into something resembling what we know today. Over the course of the 16th century, the Spanish had developed a highly efficient military unit of 1,500 men known as the *tercio*. Maurice further refined this arrangement, making it into an oblong configuration of five ranks of pikemen flanked by platoons of musketeers. Subsequently he divided these into battalions of 800, and later still into formations of 580 men arranged in a chessboard pattern, in imitation of Roman legions. Indeed, it was said of Maurice that he waged war as if he were playing a game of chess. These smaller units were far more manoeuvrable than the Spanish *tercios*. The junior officers were Dutch, and Maurice was an early believer in rewarding talent irrespective of class – a radical step at a time when most commissions were the preserve of the aristocracy. He was ably supported in his reforms by the attorney general Johan van Oldenbarneveldt and his cousins William Louis and John VII, count of Nassau-Siegen.

He also scrapped the old artillery, introducing new weapons of standard calibre well suited to the sort of sieges that were his speciality. A small force of some 12,000 was kept as a standing army with six field guns and 42 cannon. A foundry had existed in The Hague since 1589. Two treatises by the contemporary Dutch mathematician Simon Stevin provided a theoretical basis for Dutch fortress design.

STRATEGY AND FORTUNE

As the revolt developed, it became clear that the Low Countries had divided along religious lines. The southern part (which did not secede) remained Catholic, while the northern part was Calvinist. Maurice therefore concentrated his efforts on the seven northern provinces. His power base

The siege of Bergen-op-Zoom by Alexander Farnese, duke of Parma, in 1588. Both Parma and the Spanish commander Spinola (in 1622) failed in their attempts to capture this town.

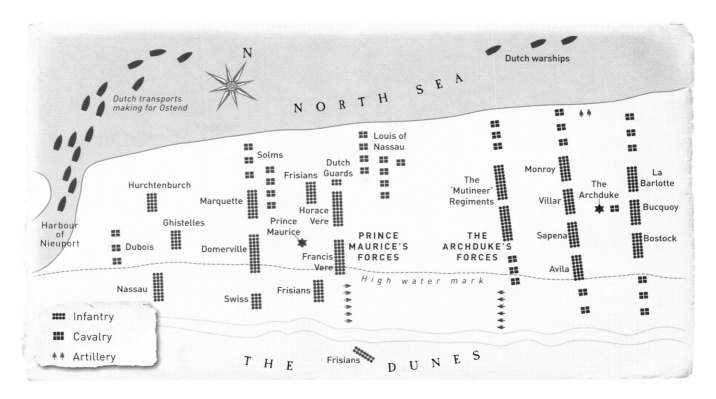

The map shows the disposition of forces at the Battle of Nieuport.

North Sea

Dutch warships

Dutch transports making for Ostend

N

Louis of Nassau

Solms

Frisians

Dutch Guards

Hurchtenburch

Marquette

Horace Vere

The 'Mutineer' Regiments

Monroy

Villar

The Archduke

La Barlotte

Bucquoy

Ghistelles

Prince Maurice

PRINCE MAURICE'S FORCES

THE ARCHDUKE'S FORCES

Sapena

Bostock

Harbour of Nieuport

Dubois

Domerville

Francis Vere

Avila

Nassau

Swiss

Frisians

High water mark

Infantry

Cavalry

Artillery

Frisians

THE DUNES

---

lay in the provinces of Holland, Zeeland and Utrecht, from which he steadily extended his control over Groningen, Overijssel, Friesland and Gelderland. In consultation with the Dutch parliament, the States General, Maurice identified a number of key cities to besiege. Between 1589 and 1609, no fewer than 29 fortresses were retaken, reversing the successes that the duke of Parma had enjoyed after 1587.

Maurice's chance came when Parma's work was interrupted by the sailing of the Glorious Armada in 1588. But after foul weather and Sir Francis Drake's fleet had put paid to Spanish designs on England, Parma was redirected to support the Catholic cause against the Protestants in France. Maurice exploited Parma's absence to take Breda. Soon Zutphen, Hulst and Nijmegen were under his control; then Steenwijk and Coevorden, followed by Gertruidenberg and Groningen. The strategic balance was altered by peace between France and Spain in 1598. However, Maurice's army was soon in the ascendant again, thanks to mutiny in the Spanish forces and a new and inexperienced governor of the Spanish Netherlands, Archduke Albrecht of Austria.

KEY VICTORIES

Where possible, Maurice avoided open battle, a lesson most likely learned from the Roman general Fabius Maximus in his war of attrition against Hannibal. In 1597, at the Battle of Turnhout, he won an exemplary victory over a Spanish force under Varas, who lost 2,500 men to only 100 Dutch. In 1599, Maurice advanced down the Flemish coast towards Ostend. The Channel port was under the control of an isolated Dutch garrison, and he intended using it as a base for operations against Dunkirk and Nieuport. On 2 July 1600, he defeated a slightly smaller Spanish force in the dunes outside Nieuport. Victory in a closely fought engagement was clinched by the co-ordination of the different units of Maurice's army and his skilful deployment of artillery. However, Maurice was unable to capitalize on his victory, as his army was not strong enough to besiege Niueport or Dunkirk.

At the behest of a new Spanish commander, Ambrogio Spinola, a 12-year truce was concluded in 1609. When fighting resumed in the region in 1621, it was more or less a sideshow to the Thirty Years' War.

Dutch and Spanish forces at the Battle of Nieuport. The Dutch field army of 14,000 foot and 1,600 horse faced a Spanish force of 10,000 foot and 2,000 horse.

LUTTER-AM-BARENBERG

Johannes von Tilly *v.* Christian IV of Denmark
27 August **1626**

FERDINAND II, WHO BECAME HOLY ROMAN EMPEROR in 1619, was intent on extending Habsburg domination. Jesuit-educated, he saw himself as the sword of the Counter-Reformation that would rid his empire once and for all of the Protestant menace. His first target was Austria, where as many as nine-tenths of the population had embraced Protestantism, including virtually all the nobility.

On 23 May 1618, the Thirty Years' War began with the 'Defenestration of Prague', when a band of Protestants flung the Catholic regents appointed by the emperor out of an upper window of Hradschin Castle onto a dungheap below. Led by Graf Heinrich Thurn, Protestant nobles challenged Catholic authority in Bohemia and Moravia by choosing a new king: Frederick, Elector Palatine (who was married to James I of England's daughter Elizabeth Stuart). The ensuing conflict devastated Central Europe. Germany, in particular, would not recover culturally or economically for another 150 years.

Rising to the Protestant challenge, Ferdinand's allies invaded Frederick's new realm: Spanish troops occupied the south, while in the north Bavarian forces led the way. At the Battle of the White Mountain outside Prague on 8 November 1620, Frederick's army of 15,000 was defeated by 25,000 imperial troops under Graf Johannes Tserclaes von Tilly and Charles de Longueval, comte de Bucquoy. The imperial army went on to ravage Bohemia and snuff out Czech independence.

Frederick fled; a king without a country, he went into exile in The Hague. History recalls his brief, doomed reign in the epithet 'the Winter King'.

THE 'MONK IN ARMOUR'
The fragile resolution of the empire's religious divisions reached at the Diet of Augsburg in 1548 now broke down. Tilly was a Walloon who had served under the duke of Parma in his suppression of the Protestant Dutch republic until the latter's death in 1592. He was unswerving in his loyalty to the Catholic Habsburgs. In his youth, he had seen his homeland ravaged by Calvinists and was bitterly opposed to their cause. A period in a Jesuit seminary in Cologne did nothing to moderate his views. Although he did not find his vocation in the church, his devout past lived on with the nickname the 'Monk in Armour'.

After Parma's death, he continued to serve the Habsburgs, fighting the Turks in Hungary from 1594 onwards and winning promotion to field marshal in 1605. On leaving the imperial army, he served Duke

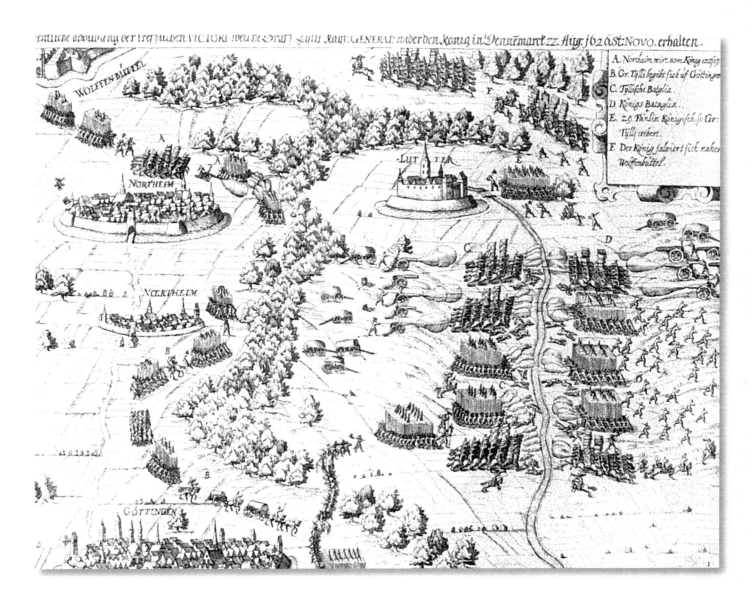

A. Northeim wirt vom König entsetz
B. Gr. Tylli begibt sich uf Göttingen
C. Tyllische Bataglia
D. Königs Bataglia
E. z.o. Fändlin Königisch: so Ger: Tylli erobert
F. Der König salwiert sich nahen Wolfenbüttel

Maximilian of Bavaria, and in 1610 he was made commander of the army of the newly formed Catholic League of German princes.

In alliance with the Spanish army of Flanders under Gonzalo Fernández de Córdoba, Tilly proceeded to crush the Protestant armies of the margrave of Baden-Durlach, Graf Ernst von Mansfeld and Prince Christian of Brunswick, so bringing the 'Palatinate phase' of the war to a victorious conclusion for the empire. Tilly's army laid waste the lands through which it passed: Heidelberg was reduced to rubble after an 11-week siege. In 1623, Tilly was made a count in recognition of his achievements.

The Spanish general Don Ambrogio Spinola also played a major part in the Protestant reversal in the early phase of the war. He had cut their supply line through the Rhineland and captured the important Dutch fortress at Breda. Meanwhile, Tilly's League army had borne the brunt of the campaign in the Palatinate. The emperor's own Austrian forces were tied down countering the threat posed by Prince Bethlen Gabór of Transylvania. In the winter of 1624–25, Bavaria asked for assistance and the emperor reorganized the army. Tilly continued to lead the forces of the Catholic League, but now a new, separate imperial German army entered the fray

Contemporary topographical map showing the progress and aftermath of the Battle of Lutter-am-Barenberg. The key in the top right-hand corner details the various phases of the engagement. The final item reads 'F: The king takes refuge in Wolfenbüttel'.

The Defenestration of Prague in 1618, which marked the start of the uprising of Bohemian Protestants against Catholic rule, had far-reaching consequences for the peace and security of 17th-century Europe. Engraving by Swiss engraver Mattäus Merian, subsequently coloured.

Christian's miraculous survival was interpreted by his men as a good omen.

At first, Tilly was able to check the progress of Christian's army, but powerful forces were rallying to the Protestant cause. On 9 November 1625, in The Hague, the English and Dutch agreed to throw their (principally financial) weight behind a grand anti-Catholic coalition that brought together the strange bedfellows of Denmark, France (which was still backing the Winter King), and the Ottoman sultan Murad IV (who supported Bethlen Gabór).

Graf Ernst von Mansfeld was given the task of leading the Protestant army. His mission was to attack Wallenstein and march along the Elbe to meet up with Bethlen Gabór and attack Austria from the rear.

under the command of the brilliant but mercurial Moravian mercenary Albrecht von Wallenstein.

A RASH ADVENTURE

From the summer of 1625 onwards, the Protestant armies were led by Christian IV of Denmark. Christian was not motivated by faith alone: to fund his dissolute lifestyle he coveted the rich bishoprics of Verden, Bremen and Osnabrück. Also, despite his undoubted personal bravery, he lacked good counsellors and placed too great a hope in British and Dutch assistance. His decision to enter the war was rash, and only served to spread the conflict, and the misery it brought, beyond the borders of Germany.

In July 1625, Christian's 17,000-strong army crossed the Elbe and made for Hamelin. During this advance, the king was thrown from his horse and fell 25 metres (82 ft) down a steep slope, but emerged almost unscathed. In an age much given to portents and soothsaying,

DEADLY TRAP AT LUTTER

This was no easy task. Mansfeld was bloodied by Wallenstein at Dessau Bridge, losing a third of his army. A small force under Brunswick was largely ineffectual; Brunswick died in June. Meanwhile, in the belief that Tilly had been seriously weakened by having to quell a peasant revolt in Upper Austria, Christian set off in hot pursuit of his main adversary. The Danish king marched from Wolfenbüttel in Brunswick with an army of 21,000 men. His route took him down the valleys of the Innerste and the Neile and between the forests of the Hainberg and the Oderwald. Tilly had been reinforced with 8,000 of Wallenstein's men and a further 4,300 under Count Nicholas Desfurs. Skirmishing with Christian's vanguard, Tilly lured the Danish king into a trap.

Historian John Childs calls Lutter: 'Tilly's greatest and most professional battle.' Too late, on 24 August, Christian realized that Tilly's strengthened army of 24,500 was larger than his own and began to fall back on Wolfenbüttel. Pouring rain

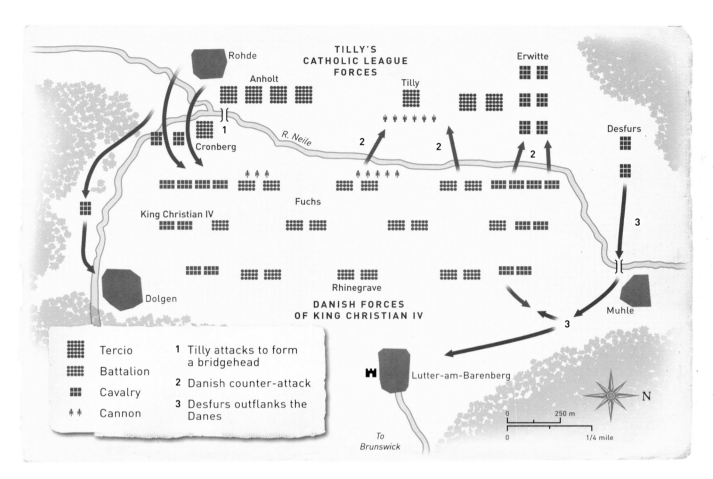

Tercio

Battalion

Cavalry

Cannon

1 Tilly attacks to form a bridgehead

2 Danish counter-attack

3 Desfurs outflanks the Danes

Rohde

Anholt

TILLY'S CATHOLIC LEAGUE FORCES

Tilly

Erwitte

Desfurs

Cronberg

R. Neile

1

2

2

2

3

King Christian IV

Fuchs

Dolgen

Rhinegrave

DANISH FORCES OF KING CHRISTIAN IV

3

Muhle

3

Lutter-am-Barenberg

To Brunswick

N

0   250 m

0   1/4 mile

and the densely wooded terrain hampered his retreat. All the while, he was harassed by elements of Tilly's army. At Lutter-am-Barenberg he was caught in a snare as the narrow road was blocked by a baggage train. Christian had no choice but to take up position behind the Neile.

Christian's tactics harked back to Maurice of Nassau. The men were formed up into battalions of 1,200 soldiers in three echeloned lines with the cavalry at either flank. Tilly had arranged his men in five old-fashioned *tercios* with his cavalry also on the wings.

Tilly tried to establish a bridgehead on the south side of the Neile at Rohde, but was driven back by Christian's cavalry. This emboldened the Danes to launch a disorganized attack across the Neile, taking on his main positions. They were cut to ribbons by musket and artillery fire, while the imperial cavalry under Desfurs

crossed the bridge at Muhle and outflanked the Danes. A rout ensued, in which Christian lost some 8,000 men. Tilly's casualties amounted to just 700. The Danish king had his horse shot from under him.

Germany was now at the mercy of the combined armies of Tilly and Wallenstein, who swept the Danes from Schleswig-Holstein and the Jutland Peninsula, forcing them to take refuge in the islands. Germany had been reconquered for Catholicism. At the Peace of Lübeck of 22 May 1629, Christian was allowed his lands back provided he supported the imperial cause and created a navy at Wismar. Despite the humilitaing defeat in his rash military adventure, Christian accepted these peace terms with equanimity. He reasoned that his new navy would at least be directed against his arch-rival across the Baltic, the Swedish king Gustavus Adolphus.

Deployment of forces at Lutter-am-Barenberg in Lower Saxony. The decisive moment came when Desfurs's cavalry got behind the Danish lines. Eventually, Christian's artillery positions fell into enemy hands, causing a rout.

BREITENFELD

Gustavus II Adolphus *v.* Johannes von Tilly
17 September **1631**

BY 1629, THE FORCES OF THE CATHOLIC Holy Roman Emperor seemed to have gained a decisive upper hand in the Thirty Years' War. Things looked bleak for the Protestant cause in Germany, all the more so since two of Lutheranism's principal champions – Christian IV of Denmark and Gustavus II Adolphus, king of Sweden (1594–1632) – were sworn enemies. However, the empire's star general Wallenstein overstretched himself in trying to secure an outlet to the Baltic. This drew Gustavus Adolphus, the ablest military commander of the age, into the conflict in 1630, turning the tables in the Protestants' favour.

Gustavus Adolphus was a formidable adversary. Like his mentor Maurice of Nassau he employed mercenaries – often from England and Scotland. He also introduced conscription, creating a regular army that was: 'The most homogenous and closely-knit infantry in Europe.' Like Maurice, he paid his troops to prevent looting and desertion. When they reached 50, they were granted tracts of land.

A MILITARY INNOVATOR

Another matter in which he followed his mentor was his attention to manoeuvres, drill and sound equipment. He began by upgrading Swedish weaponry, fitting iron tips to pikes to prevent them from being lopped off by the enemy. He also introduced lighter muskets (though the musketeer was still encumbered by the fork-rest). His battalions were made up of 500 or so men – arranged six ranks in three or four squadrons to make a T-shaped brigade of 1,500–2,000 men, plus officers and NCOs. Swedish formations were a good deal less cumbersome than the bulky *tercios* favoured by the imperial armies. Gustavus Adolphus arranged his

brigades in wedge- or arrow-shaped formations. Their line was just six men deep: one-fifth the depth of their opponents. Each squadron was protected by two or three 3-pounder guns firing canister shot.

He had also learned the efficacy of the cavalry charge from his former enemies, the Poles. Other armies still employed the 'caracole', in which the cavalryman halted his horse and fired his pistol then peeled off to reload. Gustavus saw this as slow and suicidal. His reforms created an army that was 'decisive in attack, unwavering in defence and capable of great mobility'.

Most armies of the period relied on musketeers protected by pikemen, but Gustavus Adolphus was the first to deploy this basic combination as an offensive force. Swedish musketeers fired salvoes into the enemy line and the pikemen tumbled into the breaches they had caused and wrought carnage. This tactic would prove fatal to the cumbersome *tercios*.

INTO THE FRAY

Since 1620, Gustavus Adolphus had been embroiled in a long and costly war with Poland. A truce was concluded in 1629,

Panoramic view of the battlefield at Breitenfeld, from a copper engraving (1637) by Matthäus Merian the Elder. The unwieldy imperial formations (top) were two companies deep, while the Swedish were deployed just one company deep, permitting greater manoeuvrability.

freeing his battle-hardened armies to intervene in the Thirty Years' War. Despite being a Catholic power, France under Louis XIII (and more importantly Cardinal Richelieu) was so hostile to the Habsburg Holy Roman Empire that it was prepared to sanction and even fund the Swedish king's venture provided he left Bavaria, France's potential ally, in peace. Gustavus Adolphus's personal interest in the conflict was as a devout Lutheran, but he also had a personal score to settle with Emperor Ferdinand, who had backed Poland against Sweden. Furthermore, he feared for Sweden's security in the face of a powerful empire.

A key moment in the Thirty Years' War came in May 1631, when the strategically important city of Magdeburg on the River Elbe fell to imperial forces under Johannes Tserclaes von Tilly, who had been besieging it since the previous November. Tilly's troops, plus those of his subordinate, the Catholic convert Graf Gottfried zu Pappenheim, ran amok, massacring five-sixths of Magdeburg's 30,000 inhabitants. This terrible atrocity was a propaganda disaster for the empire and added fuel to the Protestant cause.

In September 1631, a shortage of supplies drove both the Swedes and the imperial armies into Saxony. The elector of Saxony, John George I, refused Tilly permission to enter his realm, but Tilly ignored him, storming Merseburg and Leipzig. The elector rallied to Gustavus adding his 18,000 men to the 23,000-strong Swedish army.

Initial dispositions of the armies at the Battle of Breitenfeld. This, the first significant Protestant victory in the Thirty Years' War, was vital in persuading wavering countries to throw their weight behind the Lutheran cause.

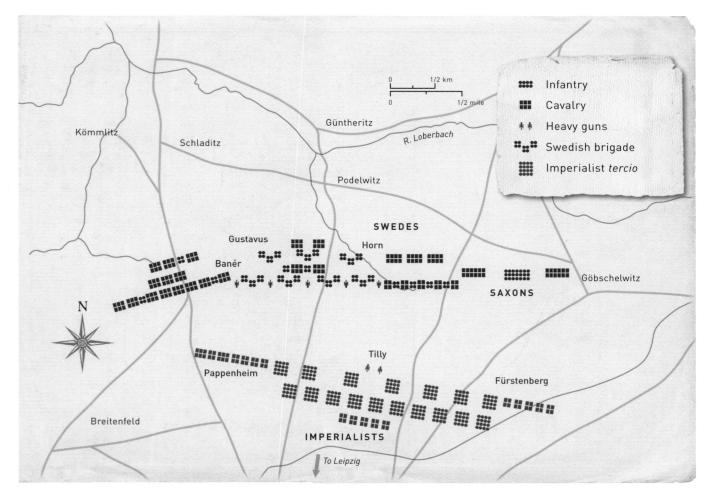

SQUARING UP FOR BATTLE

Breitenfeld, Gustavus Adolphus's first and greatest battle of the Thirty Years' War, was fought in rolling hill country 5 miles (8 km) north of Leipzig on 17 September 1631. Facing him was a combined imperial army of 32,000 men, now under the 71-year-old Tilly's sole command after Wallenstein's dismissal by the emperor for insubordination.

The cavalry commander Pappenheim overcame Tilly's initial caution about giving battle. The action began with an artillery duel. Gustavus Adolphus had 51 heavy field guns, Tilly just 27: he was outnumbered and outgunned. Pappenheim tried to outflank the Swedes, but his feared cuirassiers in their black armour failed to make any inroads against the unorthodox Swedish line, who unleashed lethal musket salvoes and cavalry charges. Pappenheim's men broke and fled. They later re-formed under his orders and redeemed themselves by covering Tilly's retreat.

Gustavus Adolphus followed Maurice of Nassau's teachings to great effect. Tilly was effectively facing two armies – the Swedes, and the Saxons under Hans Georg von Arnim, each one flanked by its own cavalry units. Tilly's cavalry on the right wing, commanded by Egon von Fürstenberg, quickly saw off the Saxon horse on the right, while Tilly's *tercios* made short work of the elector's infantry. It looked as though Tilly was about to clinch another famous victory.

The Swedish left under Gustav Horn was dangerously exposed, but Tilly failed to rout them when he attacked their exposed flank with 20,000 infantry and 2,000 horse. The flexible Swedes managed to form a new front against the imperial assault and drew up their reserves. But as Tilly's 17 *tercios*, 50 files wide and 30 deep, laboriously tried to regroup after their failed attack, the Swedes fell upon them. Musketeers, pikemen, cavalry and

Gustavus Adolphus at the Battle of Breitenfeld (contemporary painting by J. Walter). The Swedish king personally led the charge of the Finnish light cavalry brigade (*Hakkapelittas*) against the imperial line.

field guns stormed the lines and worked their way into the gaps. As Tilly's troops were reeling in confusion, they were hit in the flank by Gustavus Adolphus's Finnish cavalry, which captured the imperial guns and began raining artillery fire down on the imperial army. It was a complete reverse. Tilly lost 7,600 dead and 9,000 wounded or prisoners; another 4,000 deserted. The Swedes lost a total of 1,500 men, the Saxons twice that number.

Tilly was professional enough to regroup his forces, but he was beaten once again by Gustavus Adolphus at the Battle of the River Lech in Bavaria and mortally wounded. He died at Ingolstadt on 20 April 1632. His adversary Gustavus lived only a little while longer: while on the brink of victory at the Battle of Lützen on 16 November of that year, he was fatally shot in the back.

MARSTON MOOR

Parliamentarians *v.* Royalists
2 July 1644

THE CIVIL WARS OF 1638–52 were the costliest conflicts ever fought on British soil, resulting in the deaths of over 10 percent of the population. The wars began when King Charles I sought to impose his own brand of religion on the Scots, a cause parliament rejected. With the king and parliament at loggerheads, in October 1642 Charles raised an army of 12,500. Opposing him were 14,000 troops under the earl of Essex. As the conflict spread, the Puritan Oliver Cromwell emerged as parliament's coming leader of men.

Oliver Cromwell was not a professional soldier, and did not fight his first battle until he was over 40. He trained to become a lawyer before entering parliament, as MP first for Huntingdon and then for his *alma mater*, Cambridge. A passionate horseman, in 1643 he raised a troop of cavalry to join the earl of Manchester's 'Eastern Association'. Having embraced Puritanism in his youth, he sought 'Godly discipline' on and off the field of battle. Cromwell not only possessed faith, he had an adamantine will. Indeed, historian Christopher Hill called him 'God's Englishman'. Not for his soldiers the licence afforded to those of Tilly and Pappenheim: there was to be no swearing, whoring or pillaging. Godliness,

though, was not always a match for the skill of the royalist cavalry. Moreover, the far wealthier royalists were able to arm themselves with swords, breastplates and pistols at their own expense.

Cromwell's troopers were called 'Ironsides', from his nickname 'Old Ironsides', first conferred on him at Marston Moor by his adversary, the royalist cavalry commander Prince Rupert of the Rhine. Like Gustavus Augustus, Cromwell rejected the 'caracole' and subscribed instead to the cold steel and shock of the full-blooded cavalry charge.

The first battle of the English Civil War was fought at Edgehill near Banbury in 1642. Neither side could claim victory and even if Essex controlled the field at the

The largest battle ever fought in Britain, Marston Moor pitted 27,000 parliamentarians against 18,000 royalists. Until Cromwell's decisive leadership carried the day, the battle was a confused mêlée, as shown in this painting of the engagement by the 19th-century artist John Barker.

The queen brought Charles 3,000 reinforcements to Oxford. His army was now numerically superior to that of Essex. Meanwhile, Prince Rupert took Bristol. Handsome and bold, Rupert – who was the son of the 'Winter King' Frederick V and Charles I's sister Elizabeth – cut a dashing figure and gained a reputation for invinciblity before Marston Moor. The king failed to take London, but laid siege to Gloucester instead. Essex relieved the city, but Charles barred his way home and the two armies engaged at Newbury, a battle that claimed the lives of many royalist horsemen.

In January 1644, the earl of Leven crossed the River Tweed with 21,500 Scots to reinforce the parliamentary army. Charles countered by wooing Irish support through turning a blind eye both to Catholicism and nascent Irish nationalism. This ploy enabled him to recruit substantial Irish reinforcements, chiefly infantry.

Frontispiece of an anti-royalist pamphlet, depicting Prince Rupert of the Rhine and his famous white poodle 'Boy'. This tract attacked Rupert for his 'barbarous cruelty against the towne of Brumingham', where his troops had carried out harsh reprisals and set fire to 80 houses in April 1643.

end, he had neglected to prevent Charles from marching on London. Charles dithered, however, and by the time he reached Turnham Green, parliament had an army of 24,000 waiting for him. He turned tail and went to Oxford to spend the winter.

Meanwhile, the royalists Sir Ralph Hopton and Lord Wilmot raised armies in the west and routed parliamentary forces under Sir William Waller. Parliament lost control of the Severn Valley, leaving Bristol and Gloucester in danger of falling to the king.

In the north, Charles's commanders William Cavendish, marquess of Newcastle, Sir Marmaduke Langdale and George Goring were also victorious. The 6,000-strong parliamentary army under Lord Fairfax and his son Sir Thomas Fairfax were beaten at Adwalton Moor in June 1643 and driven back to Hull.

MASSING FOR BATTLE

Marston Moor was the largest and most important battle of the English Civil War. Leven's Scots had travelled south and met up with Fairfax's northern army, which in turn united with Essex's force from East Anglia. Lord Manchester had brought a large body of cavalry. The marquess of Newcastle, commanding the king's forces in the north, fell back on York. Charles ordered Prince Rupert to relieve York at all costs. Rupert crossed the Pennines and outmanoeuvred the parliamentary army to join Newcastle.

The parliamentary forces resolved to stop the king's men from marching south. On 2 July, a day punctuated by repeated heavy summer rain showers, their rearguard was on Marston Moor, southwest of York. The royalists sallied forth from York to give battle. Newcastle, though, dragged his heels: he was reluctant to fight and Rupert could not engage the enemy before the royalists had assembled their line. It was the afternoon before both armies had taken up position: foot in the centre and cavalry on the flanks – including the dragoons, who acted as mounted artillery. Between them lay the road from Long Marston to Tockwith. The parliamentarian front was a mile and a half (2.4 km) long, the royalist one a little longer. In front of the royalists lay some farmland and a ditch. The parliamentarians were on slightly rising ground overlooking the moor. The royalist armies, 18,000 in total, were heavily outnumbered by the allied Scots/parliamentarian force, which comprised around 27,000 men including 2,000 cavalry under Fairfax and a Scottish reserve, plus 3,000 under Cromwell. Facing Fairfax was the cavalry under Goring, while Lord Byron commanded the horse opposite Cromwell.

The artillery began a cannonade at around 2 p.m. Yet as the afternoon wore on, it seemed increasingly unlikely that battle would be joined that day. Newcastle retired to his coach and called for a pipe of tobacco. Around 6 p.m., most royalist commanders retired for dinner, followed shortly after by Prince Rupert. The two sides traded insults: as the allies sang psalms and yelled their battle cry 'God with us', the royalists paraded caricatures of John Pym, the parliamentary leader who had died in December after securing the Scottish alliance. Both sides kept their matches burning in readiness.

CONFUSION REIGNS

Royalist musketeers had occupied the ditch, when at around 7 p.m. rain began to fall. This provided the ideal screen for the parliamentarians to surge forward, though it is not clear who gave the order to attack. As a chaplain present at the scene recalled, they moved down the hill 'like so many thick clouds'. On the left of the line Cromwell's Ironsides charged Rupert's cavalry, the two leaders meeting in combat for the first time. Rupert had wisely placed groups of musketeers between his cavalry, who succeeded in breaking up Cromwell's charge. When he saw that Cromwell was in trouble, the Scottish second-in-command David Leslie charged Rupert's flank. In his *Life of Oliver Cromwell*, the writer and statesmen John Morley stressed how vital this intervention was: 'The diversion enabled Oliver, who had been wounded in the neck, to order his retreating men to face about… With Leslie's aid they put Rupert and his cavalry to rout.'

However, the royalist infantry now began to put up a fierce fight, and might

'Both armies were mixed up together, both horse and foot, no side keeping their own posts. Here …[a royalist witness] met a shoal of Scots, loud in lamentation as if the day of doom had overtaken them. Elsewhere he saw a ragged troop reduced to four and a cornet, then an officer of foot, hatless, breathless and with only so much tongue as to ask the way to the next garrison.'

VISCOUNT MORLEY OF BLACKBURN, *LIFE OF OLIVER CROMWELL* (1900)

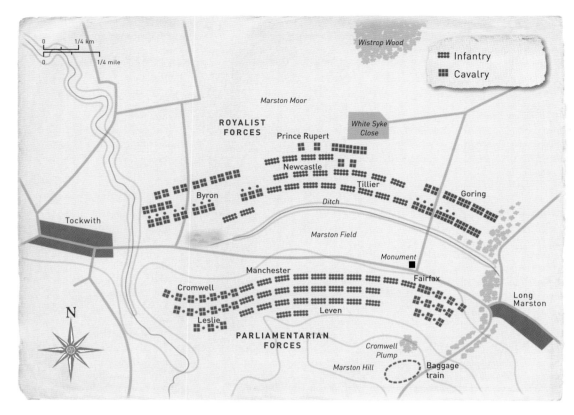

On 2 July, 1644 the two armies squared up to one another between the villages of Long Marston and Tockwith, southwest of York. Two actions were decisive to the outcome: the dogged resistance of the Scots infantry in holding the centre of the allied line, and Cromwell and Fairfax's outflanking of the royalist infantry.

well have gained the upper hand had it not been for dogged resistance by two Scots regiments. After two hours of fighting, Fairfax had been wounded and it looked as though the parliamentarians might be routed. Thinking all was lost, Leven and Lord Fairfax and many of their men left the field: 'Both armies were mixed up together, both horse and foot, no side keeping their own posts. Here … [a royalist witness] met a shoal of Scots, loud in lamentation as if the day of doom had overtaken them. Elsewhere he saw a ragged troop reduced to four and a cornet, then an officer of foot, hatless, breathless and with only so much tongue as to ask the way to the next garrison' (Morley).

Back on the battlefield, however, fighting continued long into the night. Cromwell coolly regrouped and riding at a trot delivered a decisive blow to a body of Goring's royalist cavalry that had succeeded in scattering Sir Thomas Fairfax's horse on the right and had left the field in search of plunder.

'STUBBLE TO OUR SWORDS'

Cromwell had been joined by a wounded Fairfax and the cavalry now attacked the royalist infantry from the rear taking them completely by surprise. Military historians liken this remarkable coup to Seydlitz's charge at Zorndorf during the Seven Years' War. Victory was plucked out of the enemy's hands.

The royalists struggled bravely: one of Newcastle's regiments, the 'Whitecoats', fought to the bitter end in the Hatterwith enclosures on the northeastern edge of the battlefield. An allied captain admitted he had 'never in all the fights he was in, met with such resolute brave fellows'. Some units of Rupert's cavalry also carried on fighting long after the battle was lost.

Prince Rupert is said to have hidden in a beanfield while Cromwell passed; parliament's propagandists later made much of this ignominious turn of events. Rupert's white poodle 'Boy', which had accompanied him into battle on all his previous campaigns, was among the dead.

The royalists lost at least 4,000 killed and 1,500 captured: as Cromwell put it: 'God made them stubble to our swords.' Some 2,000 parliamentarians and Scots died. The marquess of Newcastle went into exile and Rupert escaped with 6,000 men. York capitulated on 16 July.

COUNTDOWN TO REGICIDE

While defeat at Marston Moor effectively broke royalist power in the north, the situation was very different in the south. Essex foundered in his attempts to wipe out royalist forces under Prince Maurice and Sir Ralph Hopton in Cornwall. In August, the royalists closed the net around Essex; though he himself escaped from Lostwithiel, 6,000 of his infantry surrendered, handing the royalists their greatest victory of the war.

Disappointed by Essex's performance, Cromwell now called for the creation of the New Model Army under the command of Sir Thomas Fairfax. The 'Self-denying Ordinance' of December 1644 should have meant that he had to resign his military office like the aristocrats and Presbyterians in the House, but he was granted a temporary commission as Lieutenant-General of Horse. Cromwell's

intervention was also decisive at Naseby in 1645, but the battle was less close run. The seizure of Charles I's letters was a crucial propaganda victory, since they demonstrated that he had attempted to foment rebellion in Ireland.

After Naseby, the parliamentarians mopped up pockets of resistance, culminating in the capture of the king by the Scots at Newark in 1646. A Second Civil War broke out in 1648. A royalist force brought down from Scotland by the duke of Hamilton was destroyed by Cromwell at Preston. The king's continuing duplicity and stubborn unwillingness to compromise now led inexorably to his trial and execution.

Cromwell's first wholly independent command was in Ireland. His reputation was indelibly sullied by the massacres his troops committed at Drogheda and Wexford. He was made captain-general after the Irish campaign: head of the parliamentary army.

The Battle of Marston Moor is commemorated by an obelisk on the Tockwith–Long Marston road. After the battle, Cromwell stated: 'Truly England and the Church of God hath had a great favour from the Lord in this victory given unto us.'

BLENHEIM

The Confederacy *v.* Franco-Bavarian armies
13 August **1704**

THE 17TH CENTURY IN EUROPE was a period of almost constant war. This was due in large part to the expansionist aims of Louis XIV of France and his rivals' determination to thwart him. From 1688–97, the League of Augsburg War pitted most of Europe against the French monarch. England was antagonized by France's patronage of the Catholic James II, who had been deposed in favour of his daughter Mary and her husband William of Orange during the Glorious Revolution. Louis's recognition of James II's son James Stuart – 'the Old Pretender' – as rightful king of Great Britain and Ireland forced England to act against him.

The League of Augsburg War witnessed the emergence of an outstanding English military commander in John Churchill, duke of Marlborough. Born in 1650, the young Churchill first distinguished himself in military service during a brief period of alliance between England and France (the Third Anglo-Dutch War of 1672–75). He commanded an English regiment fighting under the great French marshal the vicomte de Turenne at the Battle of Ensheim in Alsace in 1674.

Created earl of Marlborough in 1689 for his part in aiding the Glorious Revolution, Churchill bloodied the French at the Battle of Walcourt in Flanders on 25 August 1689, charging at the head of his men and inflicting 2,000 casualties at the cost of just 300 on the allied side.

The Battle of Blenheim, painted in 1705 by the artist Jan van Huchtenburgh. This Dutch painter accompanied armies on campaign, and was commissioned by Prince Eugène and other commanders to record the chief incidents of the battles they fought.

ALLIED AGAINST LOUIS

Close on the heels of the League of Augsburg War came the War of the Spanish Succession, which broke out in September 1701. England, the Habsburg empire, the United Provinces (Netherlands), Brandenburg-Prussia and most of the smaller German states joined forces in the so-called 'Confederacy' to oppose the

accession of Louis's grandson to the throne of Spain after the death of the last of the Spanish Habsburgs, Charles II, in 1700. Louis was supported by Savoy, Spain and Bavaria, as well as Mantua and the archbishop of Cologne.

The first campaigns of this conflict were played out in Italy and Alsace, where the outstanding Allied commander was Prince Eugène of Savoy. Refused a commission in the French army, he had volunteered for service under the Habsburg emperor Leopold I. Prince Eugène was a fearsome warrior, who became the scourge of the Turks in their attempts to overrun Western Europe (notably at the Battle of Zenta in 1697). His partnership with the duke of Marlborough was one of the most dynamic alliances in the history of warfare.

In early 1702, Louis's invasion of the Spanish Netherlands posed a grave threat to the neighbouring United Provinces and galvanized the Anglo-Dutch-led Confederacy into action. Marlborough was instrumental in capturing the French fortresses on the River Meuse (Maas) later that year, actions that led to his elevation to a dukedom.

In the spring of 1703, the main theatre of war suddenly shifted south when the

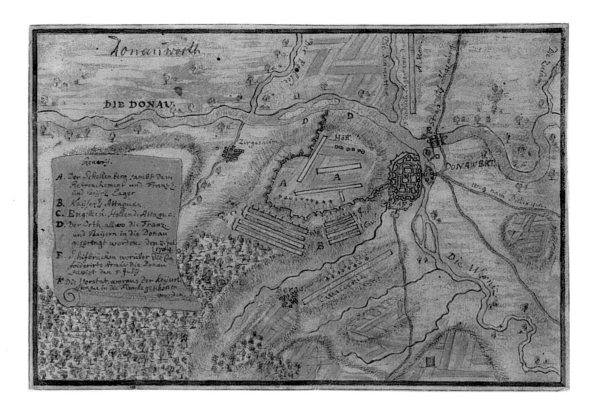

Contemporary map of the Battle of the Schellenberg, the prelude to the main engagement at Blenheim. A French survivor later recalled the bitter hand-to-hand fighting there: 'Rage, fury and desperation were manifested by both sides, with all the more obstinacy as the assailants and assailed were perhaps the bravest soldiers in the world.'

French, in alliance with Bavaria, moved to capture Vienna. Maximilian of Bavaria, however, was diverted to the Tyrol, while the French commander Maréchal de Villars remained kicking his heels and fending off allied forces in the Danube Valley as he tried to bring Maximilian back to the task in hand. When Franco-Bavarian forces finally reunited at the beginning of 1704, they had around 85,000 men under arms and were ready to advance on Vienna.

MAN OF THE MOMENT

Now was the moment for Marlborough to show his mettle. As the English seized control of the Rock of Gibraltar, Marlborough endeavoured to lure the French away from the road to Vienna and face him in battle. After misleading the French into believing that he was going to attack them on the Moselle, he left his base camp in Holland and marched his men 250 miles (400 km) in pursuit of his enemy in Bavaria. Marlborough's troops had to cover a lot of ground quickly, but under generous conditions that allowed

them liberal periods of rest. At Frankfurt they were all given new boots. Marlborough linked up with the other Allied commanders, Margrave Louis of Baden and Prince Eugène, at Mondelsheim on 10 June. Eugène's force of 10,000 was assigned the task of distracting the French under the Maréchal de Villeroi from intervening in Bavaria, while Baden's army of 30,000 men merged with Marlborough's 35,000.

Marlborough employed a mix of old and new tactics. While his cavalry charges harked back 70 years to Gustavus Adolphus, almost all his army was equipped with new bayonets, which made pikemen redundant. The grenadiers, each of whom carried three grenades, were armed with the modern flintlock fusil. Meanwhile, the artillery fired not only balls but cartridge, a devastating anti-personnel munition.

The allied army won its first costly victory storming the Schellenberg at Donauwörth on 2 July to establish a bridgehead on the south side of the Danube. The artillery under Colonel Blood played an important part in blunting the attacking forces from the murderous 'death-angle' in the town's fortifications. Marlborough had had his eye on the town for weeks, as he intended to site a magazine for his army there. He and Prince Eugène set about burning local villages to try and lure the Franco-Bavarians out to fight.

On 12 August, Prince Eugène joined up with Marlborough's army at Blindheim (Blenheim) about 10 miles (16 km) southwest of Donauwörth. They had around 56,000 men between them. In the Prussian ranks was a young lieutenant named Kurt-Christoph von Schwerin, who would later win fame by securing victory for Frederick the Great at the Battle of Mollwitz in 1741, and who was killed at the Battle of Prague in 1757.

The French army, outnumbering the allies with its 60,000 men, was led by the Maréchal de Tallard, former ambassador to the court of St James's.

Marlborough and Prince Eugène caught the French napping on the morning of the 13th. Tallard was forced to deploy his men rapidly on a position between Blenheim on the Danube and Lutzingen on his left. In the centre was the village of Oberglau. Tallard had fortified the three villages in his line.

Marlborough was short of foot soldiers, but he had a clear advantage in cavalry, and was pleased to see that Tallard had unusually concentrated his horsemen in ideal cavalry terrain between Blenheim and Oberglau. His coup was to bottle up a large part of the French forces within the village of Blenheim.

DIFFICULT TERRAIN
Eugène faced the comte de Marsin and the elector across a tricky bog with 74 squadrons of Imperial horse together with 18 battalions of infantry (two-thirds Prussian, one-third Danish), while Marlborough was on the left in front of

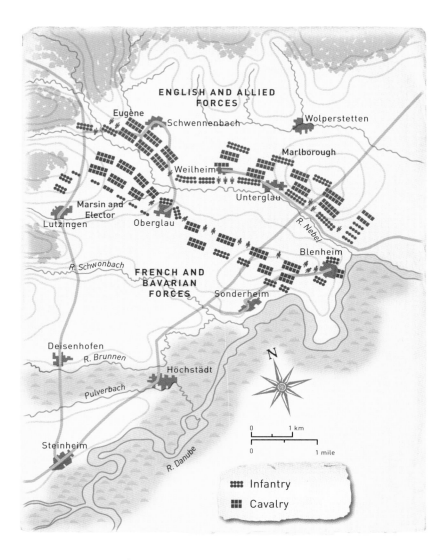

Tallard. Eugène's forces made repeated attacks across the morass, but the agitation had the effect of preventing the elector or Marsin from being able to help Tallard, who was in desperate need of reinforcements. But if Eugène had problems negotiating the swamp, it was also true that Marsin's cavalry was of little use there either.

Eugène's cavalry (commanded by the duke of Württemberg) succeeded in crossing the Nebel – the stream that separated the two armies, flowing through boggy ground into the Danube – and breaking through Marcin's horse, but

Disposition of the armies at the Battle of Blenheim. On the right wing of the allied army, Prince Eugène repeatedly led his imperial infantry and cavalry forward despite several repulses.

encountered a second line and were driven back across the stream. The Prussian infantry advanced next, but took a pasting from the artillery and lost ten colours. Eugène's army was back where it started. He now launched a second cavalry attack, which likewise failed. The second infantry attack was the one that struck home. Aided by a barrage from his 14 guns, Eugène unleashed his Prussians on the village of Lutzingen while the Danes finally overran the Franco-Bavarian guns. However, with no cavalry support, they were forced to beat a retreat.

Marlborough was as keen as ever to seek a place where he could bring numerical superiority to bear on the enemy, and favoured diversionary attacks if he did not enjoy this advantage. Once the enemy had redeployed their troops to deal with these attacks, he was able to concentrate his own to deliver a crushing blow. Oberglau was held by 14 battalions of French infantry including Irish émigrés under de Blainville. The Dutch, commanded by Prince Holstein-Beck, attempted to storm the village, but were faced by superior numbers of French. The prince himself was killed in this action. At this stage in the fight it seemed as if the French would gain the upper hand and succeed in splitting the Confederates in two.

Marlborough rallied the Dutch and brought out Count Fugger's Imperial Cuirassiers, who caught the French in the flank.

COMING TO A HEAD

The battle began in earnest when Lord Cutts attacked Blenheim twice with his 9th Confederate Column. The first wave under Brigadier Rowe was badly mauled and the French captured his colours before being driven off. Cutts's reserves commanded by Colonel Wilkes attacked next, defeating the élite Gendarmes and recovering the colours. Tallard was now so alarmed that he brought out the French reserves, packing his line. His front was so congested that the men could not even fire their guns. To make matters worse, the French had set fire to the villages, so their own soldiers were being grilled as they fought.

Similarly, a Dutch attack on the centre of the French line at Oberglau was driven back by Marsin's cavalry. Marlborough ordered the Imperial Cuirassiers to charge Marsin's flank to confine them and keep Oberglau isolated. Then Eugène stormed the French artillery with their powerful battery of 16 guns, but was forced to withdraw once again. While Tallard was distracted by what was happening on his left, Marlborough resorted to siege techniques: he used his pioneers to lay fascines – bundles of wood – and erect five bridges made of tin pontoons while repairing the old stone bridge destroyed by the French. Now the English foot guard commanded by the duke's brother General Charles Churchill was able to advance across the Nebel. It was then, at about midday, that Eugène began to launch his diversionary attacks on Marsin and the elector on the Franco-Bavarian left, pinning them down and preventing them from coming to Tallard's assistance.

The French Gendarmes saw action against three squadrons of English horse commanded by Colonel Frances Palmes, who braved the enemy's pistol fire and advanced on them sword in hand, putting them to flight before wheeling round and attacking the original group of Gendarmes in the flank. This was improvisational thinking on Palmes's part; officially, the English cavalry was forbidden from using pistols in this way and could only fire them when pursuing a defeated enemy. Fresh squadrons were sent to deal with Palmes, but he ordered Majors Oldfield and Creed to wheel outward and charge them. This time Tallard had weakened

the centre in response to the attacks on Blenheim. Using a unique formation of two lines of infantry between two of cavalry, Marlborough was able to ward off the French cavalry charges. The infantry was to move first to cover the advance of the cavalry. Tallard boasted that the more men who crossed the Nebel, the more would be killed, but he seems to have missed his moment to attack. Marlborough deemed the process was going too slowly and moved all his cavalry across as quickly as he could, the troopers leading their horses across the two branches of the stream by their bridles.

THE BREAKTHROUGH

The first French attack was effective, but Marlborough's horse regrouped and the Gendarmes were driven off. Marlborough was able to get 8,000 cavalry and 14,000 infantry over the Nebel in this way. The 54-year old English generalissimo personally led a charge and by 5.30 that afternoon, he had breached the weary horsemen at Tallard's centre and his forces poured through the gap. The French infantry was cut down by volley fire, artillery and cartridge. Tallard's cavalry turned and fled with Marlborough's horse in hot pursuit. The French ran all the way to the Danube, many of them plunging over the deep ravine to their deaths.

The other half of Marlborough's horse, under General Hompesch, rode into Marsin's flank while Prince Eugène attacked head on.

Charles Churchill surrounded the smouldering village of Blenheim, where 27 battalions surrendered to him at 11 p.m. The French garrisons at Oberglau and Lutzingen were able to withdraw in good

order covered by the Franco-Bavarian cavalry, but at the cost of their guns. Tallard's men were not so lucky: his army was annihilated. All in all, 28 French and Bavarian regiments laid down their arms. Tallard himself was held prisoner at Nottingham until 1711. Once his victory was secured, Marlborough jotted down a note to Queen Anne on a tavern bill. Anne was naturally ecstatic when she received the news eight days later.

BROTHERS IN ARMS

The two allied armies had been perfectly co-ordinated – no mean feat when strong-willed generals share a common stage. Marlborough and Prince Eugène worked so well together that after the battle medals were struck portraying them as the twin brothers Castor and Pollux from Roman mythology. It had been a crushing defeat, with Franco-Bavarian casualties totalling 38,000, while the allies lost 12,000. Vienna was now secure and the French were driven from Germany. Maximilian went into exile and Bavaria was annexed by Austria. Blenheim was Louis XIV's first defeat.

John Churchill, duke of Marlborough, was distinguished by his bravery and readiness to give battle in an age when many generals preferred to maintain a defensive posture. This portrayal of the duke at Blenheim is from a tapestry in Blenheim Palace, the grand country seat in Oxfordshire granted to Marlborough by Queen Anne in recognition of his victories.

RAMILLIES

Duke of Marlborough v. French and Bavarian forces
23 May 1706

'CASTOR AND POLLUX' – Marlborough and Prince Eugène – continued to win battles against the combined might of France and Bavaria. Some, like Oudenarde and the Pyrrhic victory at Malplaquet, were a joint effort, while others Marlborough fought on his own. One of the English commander's solo triumphs was Ramillies, where his defeat of Villeroi and the elector of Bavaria opened the way for the allies to take Antwerp, Ghent, Ostend and Bruges.

By 1706, the fifth year of the War of the Spanish Succession, the Confederates had failed to wrest the Netherlands from the French. The allies – the Dutch in particular – were running short of money and the mercenary princes were refusing to fight until they had received payment in full.

Louis XIV wanted peace, but on his own terms. In order to dictate these, he was determined to show the allies that he could still beat them. He therefore ordered his commander Maréchal de Villeroi to give battle. For his part, Marlborough had penetrated the French defensive system on the Lines of Brabant, destroying one entire section between Zoutleew and Merdorp.

Marlborough was anxious to tempt the Maréchal de Villeroi into fighting before he could receive the reinforcements being brought over by Marsin.

Villeroi raised the siege of Zoutleew and advanced to meet his adversary. He thought that he would be facing only the Dutch, as neither the Prussians nor the Danes had agreed to fight. In the event, Marlborough had been able to persuade the Danes to deliver their cavalry, who arrived the day before the battle. He missed only the Prussian infantry, who had shored up his right flank at Blenheim.

On Whit Sunday, 23 May 1706, Marlborough sought out his chosen

Contemporary painting of the allied victory at the Battle of Ramillies. This momentous victory effectively destroyed Louis XIV's ambitions in the Spanish Netherlands, ensuring that the territory remained in Habsburg hands for over a century.

field of combat. The French positioned themselves well in open country behind the marshes of Little Geete north of the town of Namur, with their right wing on the River Mehaigne and their centre at the village of Ramillies. Their left terminated at the village of Autreglise. Marsin's cavalry had joined them, but not his infantry. The French positions looked remarkably similar to those they had adopted two years earlier at Blenheim, with the Mehaigne replacing the Danube, and the villages of Ramillies, Oberglau and Taviers, replacing Blenheim. The big difference, however, was that they did not have the Nebel and its marshes. In addition, even though on the French left there was the River Geete to hold the allies back, on the French right there was nothing but wide-open country.

Both armies numbered roughly 50,000 men, but in terms of morale, the mood was better among the allied troops. The morning was wet and foggy. When the mist lifted, Marlborough saw what he had hoped to find: the French front, 4 miles (6.4 km) in length, resplendent in new uniforms. Marlborough had more artillery, but Louis had equipped his armies with several new three-bore field guns, which were carefully concealed from the enemy.

The duke pitted the Dutch and Danish cavalry against the French *Maison du Roy* – the French Household Cavalry. Marlborough opened up with an artillery barrage across the Geete at 1 p.m. He pushed back the French right while Lord Orkney and the English regiments crossed

the Geete. They made progress on the left flank, entering the villages of Autreglise and Offuz. Villeroi was alarmed and reinforced his line from the centre, while leaving enough troops to keep the centre strong.

AN EFFECTIVE RUSE

The attack on the French left was merely a feint. The assault on Autreglise and Offuz was called off. In mid-afternoon, he cunningly disguised the fact he was removing the troops from his right and sent them over to the left. The French right was pushed back while Villeroi was still manning his left in the illusion he was facing the main body of Marlborough's troops. It was, however, just a thin red line. The cavalry was redeployed between Ramillies and Taviers. The French right was weakening, while the allied length was being reinforced.

On the southern half of the battlefield, more than half Marlborough's men were Dutch commanded by Overkirk. Others came from Protestant Europe: Scots, Swiss and Scandinavians. Taviers was only weakly defended, and while Villeroi was away in Offuz it quickly fell to the allies. A force that came to relieve it was driven off by the Danish horse. Now the Danish cavalry was able to attack the French flank at Ramillies and positioned themselves behind the French line.

The *Maison du Roy* managed to break through the lines of Dutch cavalry opposite them between Taviers and Ramillies, but their attack was checked by

'A terrible blow had been dealt at Blenheim to the arms of France. But her military prestige had made a partial recovery, owing to the failure of the allies to profit by their great opportunities in 1705.'

HISTORIAN G. M. TREVELYAN

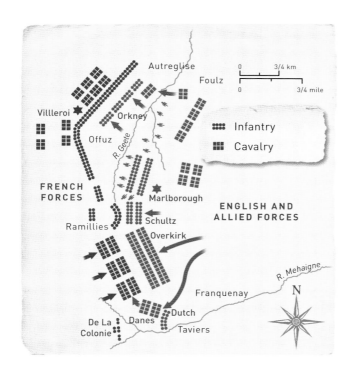

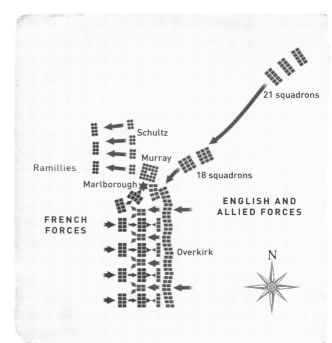

The general
engagement at
Ramillies (left) and the
duke of Marlborough's
decisive intervention
(right).

platoon firing from four regiments of foot. Marlborough had been in the greatest danger at the time of the attack. He was thrown from his horse and had to run for safety 'encumbered by his heavy wig and jackboots' (Trevelyan). General Murray brought up some Swiss infantry to save the general, and as the French cavalry pursued their quarry they were impaled on the Swiss bayonets. While Marlborough was mounting a fresh horse, Colonel Bringfield, who was holding the stirrup, had his head blown off by cannon fire.

At 6.30 p.m., Ramillies fell after heavy fighting. It was staffed by 20 French and Swiss battalions and a dozen cannon. It capitulated to a force under the Dutch general Schultz, including Scottish and English battalions, with Marlborough bringing in more and more troops from his right. His attempt to form a second line was swept away by Marlborough's cavalry. The French fled, only to find that the Danes were drawn up behind them. The Danes gave chase, cutting down the fugitives. The elector of Bavaria and Villeroi only narrowly escaped capture. Offuz and Autreglise yielded without a fight, the infantry of the *Maison du Roi* throwing down their arms.

By the next morning, the French had only half their army left: they had suffered 8,000 dead and wounded and 7,000 taken prisoner. Marlborough had lost 4,000. All the French guns had been captured, along with 80 standards. The Spanish Netherlands would remain part of the Habsburg empire until the French Revolution. The French were driven all the way back to their borders, with key ports such as Antwerp and Ostend falling without so much as a shot being fired.

DESPAIR IN DEFEAT

Louis was in utter despair over the defeat at Ramillies. On 26 May, the king was informed of it at his *levée* (the morning audience of ministers held in the French king's bedchamber in the royal palace at Versailles). The duc de Saint-Simon was present, and reported his monarch's dark mood: 'Never did I see him so troubled or in such a state of consternation. Worst of all, knowing no more than the gist of the matter, he was without news for six days, as the post had been halted. The days ticked by like years, and he was tortured by knowing neither the details nor the consequences of the unfortunate battle and what had become of his family and friends. The king was reduced to asking news from everyone he met without encountering anyone who could put him in the picture.'

LAUFELDT

EUROPE WAS WRACKED BY DISPUTED ROYAL CLAIMS in the 17th and 18th centuries. In 1740, it was the turn of the Habsburg empire, where no male heir could be found to succeed Charles VI. The emperor had settled the succession on his daughter Maria Theresa and secured the consent of the empire's constituent nations through the 'Pragmatic Sanction' of 1713. Over time, the main European powers recognized the Sanction. Salic Law, however, dictated that Maria Theresa could not become Holy Roman Emperor, and Charles hoped that the other German states would agree to elect her husband in her place.

Even the Habsburg family itself was divided over the succession: the two daughters of Emperor Joseph I (Charles's brother and predecessor) refused to recognize Maria Theresa's claim. They were married to the electors of Saxony and Bavaria and repudiated the Sanction when it was ratified by the Imperial Diet in 1732. When Charles died in 1740, a number of German princes reneged on their promises, notably Frederick II ('the Great'), the new Prussian king, who had inherited his father's rancour over the disputed succession in the principalities of Jülich and Cleves and intended to redress Prussia's losses by claiming the rich imperial province of Silesia.

His decision to annexe Silesia sent Europe tumbling into war. Once Frederick had achieved his aim, he withdrew from the field of combat, leaving the English and the Habsburgs facing the French again. Once more, French support for a Jacobite pretender, Charles Edward Stuart ('Bonnie Prince Charlie'), fanned the flames.

Most of the action in the second half of the War of the Austrian Succession took place in Flanders. The French armies were commanded by Marshal Maurice de Saxe, the illegitimate son of the elector of Saxony. He saw action in the Saxon army at Malplaquet as an adolescent, but finding his ambitions thwarted in his homeland, he won his spurs instead in the French army.

THE BATTLING IRISH

Saxe was not the only foreigner to serve France. The Irish Brigades played decisive roles in the conflicts of the period. Their decisive intervention ensured that the French won the Battle of Fontenoy on 11 May 1745. When the French lines wavered under an English assault, Saxe moved the Irish Brigade forward. It consisted of six infantry regiments, commanded by Bulkeley, Clare, Berwick, Rothe, Dillon and Lally plus the FitzJames cavalry regiment. They totalled 3,870 infantry and 250 cavalry, including some 40 MacDonaghs under the command of Charles O'Brien, Lord Clare, who went on to become a marshal of France.

They turned an imminent defeat into victory by driving the English Brigade of Guards from the field. It is said that a Captain Antony MacDonagh of Dillon's Regiment was the first to engage the enemy, urging his men on with the stirring

battle-cry: '*Cuimhnidh ar Luimneach agus ar feall na Sasanach!*' ('Remember Limerick! Remember English perfidy!'). The brigade lost 750 killed and wounded. All are now commemorated by the Celtic high cross on the field of Fontenoy.

The English retreated in disorder, leaving behind 60 major pieces of artillery, along with the regimental colours of the 2nd Regiment of Foot Guards (Coldstream Guards) and other regimental standards. Colonel Francis Bulkeley's regiment captured the colours. The English lost 7,500 killed or wounded, while total French casualties numbered 7,200.

Saxe was riding high. Flanders fell to his forces in February 1746. He took Mons in July and Namur in September. On 11 October he defeated Prince Charles of Lorraine at Rocoux, where 120,000 French faced an allied force of 80,000. At the start of 1747, he was made *Maréchal-général des camps et armées*, a rank only previously held by Turenne and Villars.

The opposing armies were increasingly vast. In 1747, as the Protestant Netherlands

Surveying the battlefield at Laufeldt, Marshal Maurice de Saxe (centre right) consults with King Louis XV. This contemporary painting by Pierre L'Enfant hangs in the palace at Versailles.

faced a greater threat than at any time since 1672, the allies mustered a force of 180,000 British, Austrians and Dutch.

SAXE'S DOUBLE BLUFF

Saxe's most famous, yet also most controversial, victory came at Laufeldt near Maastricht in 1747. Prince William, duke of Cumberland, the younger son of George II of England, was again in charge of the Pragmatic Army. He began by shadowing Saxe's forces and playing cat-and-mouse with him. For most of the time, the two armies were in sight of one another across the River Demeer. Louis XV, who was accompanying the French army, urged Maurice to take the formidable nearby fortress of Maastricht, but his commander was intent on securing victory before capturing the town. He exercised two brilliant deceptions. The first was to make Cumberland shadow the wrong army, while he moved the bulk of his forces into a position west of Maastricht. His next ruse was to make Cumberland believe that most of his forces were on the heights of Herderen when in fact the position was occupied by just 12,000 men. By 12 July, Maurice had positioned his troops entirely to his liking.

Almost 250,000 men (136,000 French and 100,000-plus Allies) now found themselves hemmed into a confined space for the impending battle. The French faced north on a 5-mile (8-km) front from Elderen to Herderen and Montenaken to the outskirts of Wilre. The allies faced south, with their right composed of Austrians left of Grote-Spaeven, cut off from the main army by a small ravine. The Dutch occupied the centre from Grote Spaeven to Vlijtingen. The left flank, comprising the British, Hanoverians and Hessians, ran east from Laufeldt, leaving a narrow gap between there and the fortress of Maastricht.

Maurice focused his attention on this gap: he proposed to crash into the left centre at Laufeldt while letting his cavalry and infantry attack the flank on the western River Jaar to cut the allies off from Maastricht. Despite sodden ground and rain he gave the order to attack. An opening artillery barrage set Laufeldt ablaze. Maurice assumed that the Pragmatic Army had abandoned the village and formed up behind it. But Sir John Ligonier – a French Huguenot commander serving in the British army – proposed a strategy to Cumberland that he had learned at the Battle of Fontenoy, where the French had hidden their troops in the ruined town. Cumberland dithered, but eventually occupied the hamlets. When the French grenadiers assaulted Laufeldt they found it bristling with guns: no fewer than five French attacks failed.

Cumberland reinforced his positions. At 2 p.m., Maurice decided to launch an attack on the right of the line. After four hours, he was able to gain footholds in Laufeldt and Vlijtingen. When Saxe charged Vlijtingen with his cavalry, Cumberland ordered the Dutch horse to take them in the flank. The Dutch charge was shambolic, however, enabling the French infantry to press home their attack.

Once again it was Ligonier who saved the day, at least temporarily. Maurice ordered the French cavalry to turn the allied flank at Wilre. He sent in 140 squadrons commanded by the comte d'Estrées, but Sir John, acting on his own initiative, led out the allied cavalry. The plain above the Jaar was excellent cavalry country and there was a tremendous battle in which the allies beat back the French and prevented them from filling the gap

'Sire, I present to your Majesty a man who has defeated all my plans by a single glorious action.'

Marshal Saxe on Sir John Ligonier

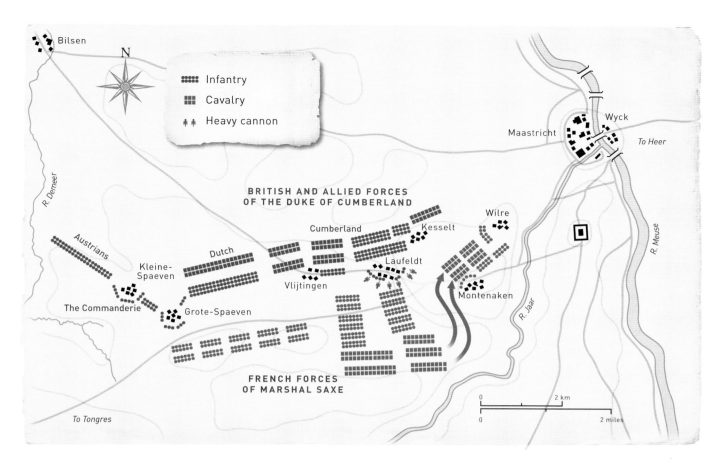

Bilsen

N

:::: Infantry
■■ Cavalry
♠♠ Heavy cannon

R. Demeer

Austrians

Kleine-Spaeven

Dutch

The Commanderie

Grote-Spaeven

Vlijtingen

BRITISH AND ALLIED FORCES
OF THE DUKE OF CUMBERLAND

Cumberland

Kesselt

Wilre

Laufeldt

Montenaken

FRENCH FORCES
OF MARSHAL SAXE

Wyck

Maastricht

To Heer

R. Meuse

R. Jaar

To Tongres

0   2 km
0   2 miles

between Maastricht and the allied army. Elsewhere, though, French forces were prevailing and Cumberland now ordered Ligonier to charge again, this time to cover a general allied retreat. While Ligonier's charge was successful, cutting straight through the French cavalry, he and his men found themselves trapped on the other side by the French infantry. In an attempt to escape, Ligonier tried to pass himself off as a French officer, but the Order of the Bath gave him away and he was taken prisoner. Meanwhile the Austrian cavalry had been moved up to cover the withdrawal of the Pragmatic Army.

After the battle, Saxe graciously presented Ligonier to his king with the following words: 'Sire, I present to your Majesty a man who has defeated all my plans by a single glorious action.' Subsequently, the French used the Huguenot as a peace envoy.

A PYRRHIC VICTORY?

Saxe's victory at Laufeldt was by no means resounding. At 10,000, French losses were grievous, and exceeded (possibly by a considerable margin) those suffered by the allies. Appalled at the carnage, Louis XV now made moves to secure peace. Saxe's skill in marshalling his huge force had been impressive, but criticism of him, once unthinkable, now began to make itself heard. With hindsight, it is also true to say that he often had the advantage of poor generals as adversaries. Yet, Frederick II greatly admired the French commander, a compliment Saxe would later return.

Saxe's immediate objective after Laufeldt went unfulfilled; evading capture, the duke of Cumberland managed to escape and secure Maastricht. But on 16 September, Saxe succeeded in taking the strategic city of Bergen-op-Zoom by storm, amid scenes of pillage and destruction.

The following year, at the Treaty of Aix-la-Chapelle, war-weary Europe agreed to a cessation of hostilities: France consented to evacuate the Netherlands and recognize Maria Theresa's husband Francis Stephen, duke of Lorraine, as emperor.

French and allied forces at the Battle of Laufeldt. Though technically victorious, Maurice de Saxe failed to take Maastricht or to destroy the 'Pragmatic Army' of British, Hanoverian, Austrian and Dutch troops.

PLASSEY

Robert Clive *v.* Siraj-ud-Daula
24 June **1757**

THE BATTLE OF PLASSEY demonstrates that the most titanic clashes on the field of battle do not necessarily have the most momentous political consequences. Plassey was little more than a skirmish, yet it resulted in the British gaining control of India's richest province, Bengal. From there, they proceeded to establish their *Raj* (rule) over the entire subcontinent.

The victory at Plassey was the work of one obscure but ambitious man: Robert Clive. Clive entered service with the British East India Company as a 19-year-old clerk in 1744. That year, following his first journey to Madras, he found himself so depressed and impoverished that he attempted suicide. His pistol failed twice to discharge. Not long after, growing French supremacy in southern India under Joseph-François Dupleix resulted in the occupation of Madras in 1746. Clive and three companions escaped from the city disguised as Indians. He became an ensign in the company's army and distinguished himself in an attack on the French garrison at Pondicherry.

A TASTE FOR ACTION

Clive had found his true vocation in the army, Despite having had only scant military training, he proved a model officer and an inspiration to those who served under him, including the sepoys (Indian native troops), who gave him the honorific title *sabit jang* ('steady in battle').

Since the early 1700s, the East India Company had been locked in a bitter rivalry with its French counterpart over trading rights in India. By mid-century, the French were gaining the upper hand. In 1751, they and their ally Chanda Sahib, ruler of the Carnatic (Karnatika),

laid siege to the important British base at Trichinopoly. Clive was part of the British relief force, but persuaded his commander that the best strategy would be to seize the fortress at Arcot, Chanda's capital farther to the north, so forcing the Carnatic ruler to lift his siege of Trichinopoly. Clive then had to withstand Chanda's ensuing siege of Arcot. Although he commanded only 80 Europeans and 150 sepoys, he managed to beat off attacks both by the besieging force of 10,000 and by a hostile populace within the city. When Chanda resorted to trying to batter down the city gates with elephants, Clive's men shot their muskets at the animals, so enraging them that they stampeded into their own forces.

The siege of Arcot was followed closely at home, becoming 'an imperial epic' and the French threat was repulsed. More victories followed and the ultimate relief of Trichinopoly by Clive and his superior, Colonel Stringer Lawrence ('The Old Cock') spelt the end for Chanda Sahib. Clive was invalided home aged just 28 in October 1753, allegedly £40,000 the richer for his exploits.

A NEW ADVERSARY

Clive returned to India as a lieutenant-colonel in 1755, at a time when the new nawab of Bengal, the 21-year-old Siraj-ud Daula, was flexing his muscles in a bid to

Robert Clive leading his men against the forces of Siraj-ud-Daula, nawab of Bengal, at the Battle of Plassey. Detail from a 19th-century print.

make himself master of his own house. Siraj had succeeded his grandfather, Alivardi Khan, who had snatched the title of *nawab* (viceroy) from the Mughal emperor by force of arms. Alivardi Khan's chief concern was to stop the French and British from fortifying their trading counters in his domain, as he feared Bengal would be embroiled in the fighting that was ravaging the Carnatic. In the summer of 1756, Siraj occupied Calcutta and the British base at Fort William, which had been abandoned by its governor, and incarcerated a number of Europeans in its 'Black Hole' – a lock-up in Fort William used for European prisoners. Estimates of the number who perished in a single, dreadful night of summer swelter vary from 23 to 140.

A force of 600 Europeans and 900 sepoys was raised and despatched to Calcutta in five warships commanded by Admiral Charles Watson. On New Year's Day 1757, Clive retook Calcutta, as well as the town of Hooghly-Chinsura

Against overwhelming odds, Robert Clive's small expeditionary force triumphed at Plassey. He was greatly aided by bad weather and treachery in the enemy camp.

upstream, thereby regaining control of the River Hooghly. He was now convinced that Siraj would have to be deposed and replaced by a compliant puppet ruler.

DUPLICITOUS DEALINGS
Clive's main weapons in this strategy were duplicity and subterfuge. Through the agency of the merchant élite of Calcutta, he approached Mir Jafar Khan, a nobleman and Siraj's senior commander who was favoured by the money-men and Hindu Bengali dissidents. He convinced Mir to break ranks with Siraj in return for being appointed nawab in his place. Bribes were liberally handed out to secure the loyalty of Mir and his men.

Clive now needed a battle to see off Siraj and install Mir in his place. In February 1757, he carried out a pre-emptive strike on Dum-Dum, Siraj's camp outside Calcutta. The nawab retreated up the River Hooghly and allied himself with the French trading counter at Chandernagore. Clive bombarded and took the settlement, but Siraj escaped.

After marching from Kasimbazar and crossing the River Bhagirathi, a tributary of the Hooghly, Clive finally confronted Siraj at Plassey on 23 June. It was the monsoon season and the rivers were swollen. Clive had effectively cut off his only chance of retreat. He had 3,200 troops, a third of them Europeans, and ten guns to face an enemy of 50,000 with 53 guns operated by the French. The Europeans travelled by boat to protect them from the effects of the midsummer heat.

A MOMENTOUS VICTORY
The British commander hid his men in a mango grove and positioned his cannon on either side. The Europeans were in the middle, the sepoys on the flanks. The battle began at 8 a.m. with a cannonade from the French guns. The British replied, their fire ripping through Siraj's men. The

Clive and Mir Jafar
after the Battle of Plassey, in a painting by the 18th-century British artist Francis Hayman. Long presented as a great imperial feat of arms, Plassey was largely won through underhand dealings on Clive's part to ensure that Mir Jafar betrayed his former master.

heavens broke, soaking both sides and forcing the British to throw tarpaulins over their ammunition. Yet the enemy failed to do this, and presently their guns fell silent.

Although Siraj tried to outflank Clive, the battle was no more than a messy skirmish. Much of it was taken up with an exchange of cannon fire in which the Indians took a pasting. Their 24- and 32-pounders were mounted on platforms transported by 50 yoked bullocks and pushed into place by elephants. These beasts once again came to Clive's aid. When three elephants fell victim to the British barrage, the survivors became terrified and broke ranks, followed by the oxen, which also stampeded. Even some of the Indian gunners unwittingly acted in Clive's favour by setting fire to their powder. Mir Jafar witnessed the rout and sent word to Clive that he was ready to defect. However, because he was uncertain

of the position of Mir's men, Clive ended up bombarding them as well. As it was, this was of no great moment, because Siraj's men presently followed the example of the elephants and the oxen and fled, with the nawab at their head, seated on his camel.

Clive lost just 23 Europeans and 500 sepoys killed and gained Bengal. Siraj was stabbed to death at Murshidabad and Mir Jafar was duly installed as nawab. In 1769, Clive sailed home, where he was elected MP for Shrewsbury and created Baron Clive in the Irish peerage. In 1765, he returned to India as governor of Bengal. He went back to England for the final time in 1766. By this time, his health was deteriorating and he was addicted to opium. In 1774, he was found dead at his London home in mysterious circumstances, having succumbed either to an accidental drug overdose or a final, successful suicide attempt.

LEUTHEN

Frederick the Great *v.* Austrian and Saxon forces
5 December **1757**

FREDERICK THE GREAT OF PRUSSIA emerged as a major beneficiary of the War of the Austrian Succession, when his seizure of the province of Silesia was legitimized by the Treaty of Aix-la-Chapelle. On the death of Charles VI in October 1740, and just a few months after his own accession, he challenged the Pragmatic Sanction and embarked on a *Blitzkrieg* that saw him achieve all his objectives by 1745. Thereafter, he enjoyed 11 years of peace before Prussia – along with most of the rest of Europe – became embroiled in the Seven Years' War.

This decade and more of peace gave Frederick the chance to reflect on strategy and the mistakes he had made in Silesia. These reflections are contained in a privately printed book, *Les principes généraux de la guerre* of 1748. In it, he expounded on the idea of the 'oblique order', a tactic that would allow him to concentrate the bulk of his troops on one of his enemy's flanks, spreading his troops all along it. Once he had prevailed upon the point of attack, his armies could 'roll up' the enemy from the chosen flank. These tactics were first deployed at the Battle of Hohenfriedberg in January 1745.

The *Principes généraux* also offer the insight – famously reiterated in Carl von Clausewitz's *Vom Kriege* ('On War', 1832) – that war has an important political motive.

SURROUNDED BY FOES

The Third Battalion Guard Storm the Graveyard at Leuthen by the painter Carl Röchling vividly conveys the courage under fire and martial discipline that Prussian troops were already renowned for by the reign of Frederick the Great.

Frederick was convinced that he had not heard the last of Habsburg claims to Silesia, and so signed a pact with his cousin George II of Great Britain in 1756, known as the Convention of Westminster. The result was to drive the French into an alliance with Austria. The Austrian chancellor Wenzel von Kaunitz had also managed to secure Russian help by

promising them East Prussia if they would aid in the recovery of Silesia.

Frederick was keenly aware that he would have to carry out a pre-emptive strike if he was to avoid being surrounded and carved up by his powerful enemies.

The Prussian ruler decided to eliminate his enemies one by one, and to this end divided his army into three. He led the army that was to face the Austrians, but the very first nation in his sights was Saxony, which although outwardly neutral had also struck a deal with Kaunitz. In addition, Frederick had his eyes on Saxon territories. After swiftly despatching the Saxon army, the Prussians pursued the Austrians to Prague. The battle that took place outside Prague on 6 May 1757 confirmed Frederick's reputation as a general, but was strategically insignificant as it turned Frederick's campaign into a defensive one.

On 18 June, the Battle of Kolin was a bitter experience. Frederick engaged a numerically superior enemy with an advantage in altitude and was badly mauled. Frederick rallied, however, in the next two battles in the campaign: Rossbach and Leuthen. On 5 November 1757, at Rossbach, a Prussian army of

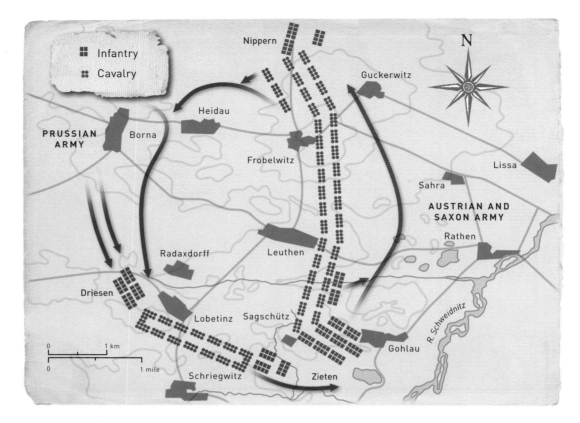

At Leuthen, Frederick used his favourite tactic of the 'oblique order', attacking the Austrian left after a feint towards the right, which the enemy mistook for a retreat.

21,000 faced a combined French and Imperial force nearly twice that size. Frederick routed his enemy, with more than 5,000 killed and the same number captured. In the process, he lost only 169 dead and 379 wounded.

The Battle of Leuthen took place just a month later in Silesia. Prince Charles of Lorraine and Field Marshal Leopold Daun had overrun much of Silesia, and Frederick stood to lose his hard-won prize. By the end of November, they had taken Breslau, the capital of the province. Frederick's army began its march from Thuringia on 13 November. He sent the great cavalry general Joachim von Zieten on ahead to bolster the remnants of his Silesian army.

STIRRING SPEECH

On 3 December, Frederick summoned his commanders to a meeting at Parchwitz. Abandoning the French in which he customarily addressed his officers, he told them in German: 'We must beat the enemy, or bury ourselves before his guns. Bear in mind, gentlemen, that we shall be fighting for our glory, the preservation of our homes, and for our wives and children... Those who stand with me can rest assured I will look after their families if they are killed. Anyone wishing to retire can go now, but will have no further claim to my benevolence...' His army of 39,000 faced Austrian and Saxon forces of 66,000 men.

The Austrians accepted Frederick's challenge and took up position before the village of Leuthen. The enemy front was some four and a half miles (7.2 km) long, with its left flank outside the village of Gohlau and the right at Nippern. The Austrians and Saxons controlled the high ground and had 210 guns whereas Frederick had 170. Their cavalry was placed in the centre, between the villages of Leuthen and Frobelwitz.

Frederick's armies were on the march from 5 a.m. When a trooper complained of the bitter cold, the king told him to have patience, things would get warm soon enough. At Borna, the vanguard encountered some Austrian and Saxon cavalry and scattered them, taking around 200 prisoners. Frederick studied the

Austrian line from high ground and noted that they had failed to anchor the left in a series of ponds and marshes. He exercised a successful feint on the right wing between Frobelwitz and Nippern, which the enemy interpreted as a suicide attack and brought up reinforcements: nine regiments of his reserve. It was an hour's march from the main point of impact south of Sagschütz. Later they decided that it was in fact a retreat: 'Our friends are leaving', said Charles of Lorraine, 'let them go in peace.'

MASTERPIECE OF MOVEMENT

Frederick knew the terrain well and was shielded by his cavalry and a small chain of hills and was able to move his infantry and outflank the Austrians using a complicated pattern of halts and advances. When they established their new line the Austrians watched in amazement, dubbing it the *Potsdamer Wachtparade* ('the changing of the guard at Potsdam'). Now Frederick brought his trademark oblique hammer blow to bear on the left wing, backed up by Zieten's cavalry of 53 squadrons and three battalions of infantry. The Protestant Württembergers in the allied front line turned and fled. Prince Moritz of Anhalt-Dessau, commanding the Pomeranian 26th, apparently told his regiment they had done well enough and could fall back. The soldiers would not hear of it, proclaiming: 'We'd have to be yellow-bellies to fall back now! Cartridges! Cartridges!' They kept up a withering volley of fire as they advanced.

It was at that moment that Ziethen's squadrons struck. The Austrians were obliged to turn their front, negating their numerical superiority. The whole army performed a left turn. This clumsy manoeuvre allowed Frederick to penetrate the village of Leuthen while the Austrians and Saxons were bombarded with cannon fire. The final Prussian advance began at around 3.30 p.m. The Austrians mounted a fierce cavalry attack, but were in turn cut up by 40 squadrons of Bayreuth Dragoons commanded by Wilhelm von Driesen.

In three hours, the Austrians lost 10,000 dead and wounded and another 12,000 taken prisoner. Frederick's casualties amounted to 8,000 men. After the battle, Frederick took shelter from the snow in nearby Lissa Castle, which he found occupied by Austrian officers. His cool greeting was: 'Good evening gentlemen; no doubt you weren't expecting to see me here.'

The injured men littering the battlefield began to sing *Nun danket alle Gott!* ('Now thank we all our God') quietly at first, but rising to a rousing chorus. Thereafter, the hymn has become known as the Leuthen Chorale.

Napoleon called Leuthen 'a masterpiece of movement, manoeuvre and resolve', but politically Rossbach was the greater victory because it knocked the French out of the European war. Frederick had begun the Seven Years' War with the hope of annihilating his enemies, but had failed to do so; Leuthen became just one battle in a long war of attrition in which Fabian tactics would ultimately win the day.

'We must beat the enemy, or bury ourselves before his guns. Bear in mind, gentlemen, that we shall be fighting for our glory, the preservation of our homes, and for our wives and children....'

FREDERICK THE GREAT BEFORE THE BATTLE OF LEUTHEN

QUEBEC

General James Wolfe *v.* Marquis de Montcalm
13 April **1759**

THE SON, GRANDSON and great-grandson of army officers, James Wolfe joined the army at 14. At 16, he underwent his baptism of fire as an adjutant at the Battle of Dettingen. By 18, he was fighting the Jacobites under the Young Pretender. At the age of 22 – and by now a major – he was wounded at Laufeldt. The following year, he was made a colonel.

Wolfe was to achieve lasting fame during the Seven Years' War and particularly in the North American campaigns (known as the French and Indian War), in which France and Britain vied to protect and expand their colonial holdings. In 1755, the French lost control of most of Nova Scotia and the native French there – the

Acadians (hence the term 'Cajuns' for the refugees who subsequently settled in French Louisiana) – were brutally expelled. Presently, however, France and her Huron allies gained ground, capturing Fort William Henry in 1757. The next year, 3,800 French beat off an Anglo-American force nearly four times larger at

Fort Ticonderoga. Fort Duquesne south of Lake Erie also repulsed a British attack.

HERO OF LOUISBOURG

Despite his involvement in a failed raid on the French Atlantic port of Rochefort in September 1757, Wolfe's reputation was untarnished and he was attached to the far more significant Louisbourg Expedition of 1758. The last French stronghold on Nova Scotia, Louisbourg was known as 'the Gibraltar of the North', thanks to its supposed impregnability. The British had in fact already seized it in 1745, but were forced to trade it for Madras at the peace conference at Aix-la-Chapelle three years later.

At Louisbourg, Wolfe demonstrated an early understanding of the sort of shock tactics associated today with commandos. Leading a hand-picked force of 1,220 men, he seized Lighthouse Point and brought its guns to bear against the port's redoubtable fortifications. As a result of the resounding success of this mission, during which he also destroyed the French fishing settlement at Gaspé Bay and continued with the expulsion of the Acadians, he was promoted to brigadier. By this stage, the tide was beginning to turn against the French in Canada. Prime minister William Pitt the Elder secured Wolfe's promotion to major-general and entrusted him with command of the expedition against French Quebec in 1759.

Wolfe landed back at Louisbourg in May 1759. His force was less impressive than he might have hoped: he had fewer than 8,000 men and 49 ships commanded by Vice Admiral Charles Saunders. The French had numerical superiority and the ships were to prove largely useless in this operation. The force travelled up the St Lawrence River, landing at the Ile d'Orléans on 28 June. The French greeted the British arrival by sending fire ships

Contemporary print showing the various stages in the assault on Quebec – the disembarking of Wolfe's force, the scaling of the heights of Abraham and finally 'the signal victory obtained over the French regulars, Canadians and Indians, which produced the surrender of Quebec'.

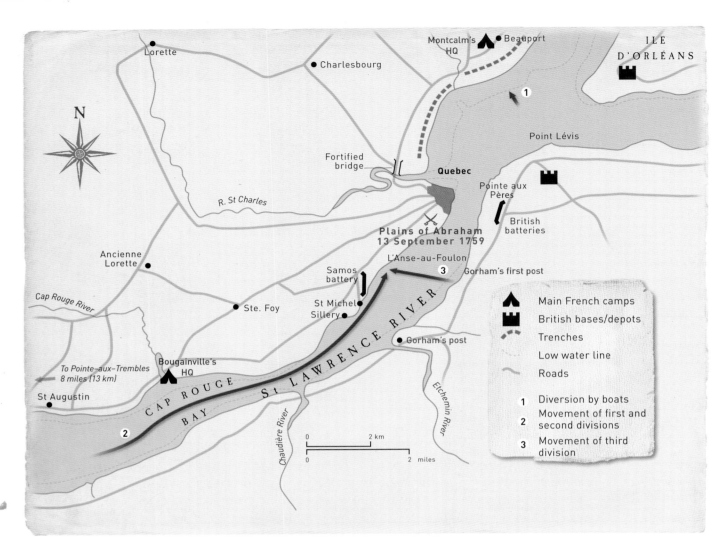

Wolfe's assault on the cove at L'Anse-au-Foulon was a meticulously planned and executed military operation. Within four hours, a force of 4,500 British redcoats was assembled in full battle order, with artillery, on the Plains of Abraham.

downstream, but British sailors in longboats grappled the craft and shoved them out of harm's way. Wolfe was able to establish a battery at Point Lévis and raze large parts of the lower town with his cannon.

For months Wolfe's army and fleet lay at anchor off Quebec City. The explorer James Cook surveyed the river for possible points of attack. It is interesting to note that on the French side as well, their most famous 18th-century explorer, Louis-Antoine de Bougainville, was one of the main protagonists in the ensuing battle.

The French were defending 5.6 miles (9 km) of redoubts from the St Charles River to the Montmorency Falls. The town's garrison consisted of 12,000 troops under the command of Louis-Joseph, marquis de Montcalm. Wolfe's first attempt to breach the city walls with a force of 5,000 men, the Battle of

Beauport, ended in abject failure. The British attackers were severely mauled by French musket fire. Fortunately a thunderstorm intervened, allowing Wolfe to recall his battered units. He had suffered 450 casualties to Montcalm's 60.

DARING COMMANDO RAID

Wolfe now tried a scorched-earth policy, flushing local inhabitants from their farmhouses and burning their homes in the hope of luring Montcalm out to fight. He was working on plans to land upriver, thereby cutting Quebec's garrison off from Montreal. The original plan proposed by his brigadiers was to land far away from the city and its batteries, but Wolfe changed his mind, writing: 'I have fixed the spot where we can act with most force and are most likely to succeed.' He had spotted a cove that seemed ideal for an

'Now God be praised, I will die in peace.'

GENERAL JAMES WOLFE, MORTALLY WOUNDED, LEARNS OF HIS VICTORY AT QUEBEC

amphibious landing. From there, he could send a small party scrambling up a supposedly unscalable cliff and seize the road before deploying on the plateau and taking the French by surprise on the Plains of Abraham. On 12 September, British troops in landing ships rowed to L'Anse-au-Foulon, a cove southwest of the city at the foot of a 52-metre (170-ft) cliff.

Boats ferried the men across the river from 2 a.m., returning to take on fresh troops until two divisions plus artillery and stores had been landed by 4 a.m. A force led by Colonl William Howe scaled the Heights of Abraham; presently, he stood on the plains and surveyed the city. The French had dismissed the idea of an assault on L'Anse-au-Foulon and the small watch was misled by a British officer speaking fluent French and shouting 'vive le roi!' in lieu of a password. Howe with 124 volunteers was able to overpower the picket and capture the camp of Captain Louis Du Pont Duchambon de Vergor. Wolfe followed an hour later, coming up by the road. By dawn, he had deployed his troops on the Plains of Abraham.

The French failed to heed the warnings, and were fooled by a diversionary attack mounted by Admiral Saunders. Only 10,000 troops were involved in the battle, which lasted under an hour. Montcalm's tactics left much to be desired. He should have waited for Bougainville, who was at hand with reinforcements, but was foolish enough to be lured out of his citadel onto the Plains of Abraham. Wolfe had managed to bring up fewer than 5,000 men while the French had more than 13,000 at their disposal. Wolfe arranged his soldiers in a horseshoe formation two deep anchored in a gristmill. The left wing

had to clear the French militia from the scrub. The intense firing generated clouds of smoke that confused the French.

Wolfe ordered his men to lie down in the high grass of the plains while volleys of French gunfire sang about their ears. Montcalm ordered an immediate attack in columns. Preceded by Indians and French-Canadian sharpshooters, he sallied forth on horseback at the head of his force, waving his sword. Wolfe's advantage was that Montcalm was descending from higher ground, but with a slight rise at the centre which impeded his movement. He gave instructions to his men to fire just twice. They waited until the French were 27 metres (30 yds) away before letting rip. The first volley caused the French to reel back, while the second scattered them.

A HEAVY PRICE

Both Montcalm and Wolfe died in the course of the battle. Wolfe was hit by two bullets, one in the base of his stomach and another, which proved fatal, in his chest. He survived just long enough to learn that he had clinched victory. Montcalm was hit by canister shot, and died the next day. The Highlanders pursued the retreating French with their swords while Bougainville's reinforcements were driven off. The French had lost 644 men killed or injured, the British slightly more: 658.

William Howe went on to take Montreal in 1760 and 'New France' became the British colony of Lower Canada. At the end of the Seven Years' War, concluded by the Treaty of Paris in 1763, Britain gained the Canadian territories from the French and controlled virtually all of North America until the American War of Independence.

AUSTERLITZ

Napoleon Bonaparte *v.* Field Marshal Kutuzov
2 December **1805**

EVEN THE TIMING WAS BOLD in this, Napoleon's greatest victory. Historically, military campaigning had its season and it was rare to fight battles late in the year. Winter weather made the land impassable and the logistics of transporting food impossible. Morale was understandably low in the cold months, and soldiers fought badly. By the 20th century, metalled roads and tanks enabled armies to fight all year round. Yet even in 1941, the Russian winter effectively doomed Operation Barbarossa, Hitler's invasion of the Soviet Union.

Austerlitz is sometimes called the Battle of the Three Emperors: Napoleon, the newly (self-) crowned emperor of France fought Francis II of Austria and Tsar Alexander I of Russia. The allied armies were under the command of the 60-year-old, one-eyed Field Marshal Mikhail Illarionovich Kutuzov: a warhorse who had been blooded in a dozen battles.

CHALLENGING THE ALLIES
Learning of the newly forged alliance between Alexander and Francis, Napoleon abandoned his plans to invade Britain (mooted since 1803), struck camp at Boulogne and marched on Germany. He arrived just in time to prevent Kutuzov from rescuing General Mack's beleaguered Austrian army. By 20 October, Napoleon and his Bavarian allies had encircled Mack at Ulm, forcing the surrender of 27,000 Austrian troops. To avoid a pitched battle, Kutuzov prudently withdrew and marched north into Moravia, leaving Vienna open to Napoleon's armies (a prize too tempting to resist). The Third Coalition had been formed against Napoleon on 24 May 1804, but Prussia had refused to join, opting for a defensive alliance with Russia instead. Yet Prussia had also

Despite ultimate defeat, many allied units acquitted themselves well at the Battle of Austerlitz. Right: *Capture of a French regiment's eagle by the cavalry of the Russian guard,* by the Russian artist Bogdan Willevalde (1818–1903).

refused to make common cause with France. Finally, Tsar Alexander had convinced the Prussian king that he must enter the coalition before 15 December.

Eager to do battle before Prussia joined the allies, Napoleon sought out Kutuzov. The 73,000-man *Grande Armée* tracked down its quarry at Austerlitz about 15 miles (24 km) east Brünn (Brno) in southern Moravia. The allies had around 86,000 men. The speed of Napoleon's march is the stuff of legend. Davout, in the van of the French forces, covered 70 miles (113 km) in 46 hours. Napoleon chose his ground well, in the words of the historian Alistair Horne displaying 'his extraordinary *coup d'oeil* for topography, his instinctive understanding of what the enemy was going to do, and his ability to act with total decisiveness'.

AN EFFECTIVE FEINT
He picked out the natural bastion of Santon Hill and the Pratzen Heights at the centre of the field. South of the Pratzen were two shallow lakes. Just before the allies reached the battlefield, Napoleon abandoned the heights, giving the impression that he had made an error of judgement: he had lost the high ground

by the allied armies at Austerlitz, Napoleon took a calculated risk, relying on his own masterly generalship and the imminent arrival of reinforcements. The maps right show the progression of the battle, carefully choreographed by 'Europe's master of manoeuvres', Napoleon.

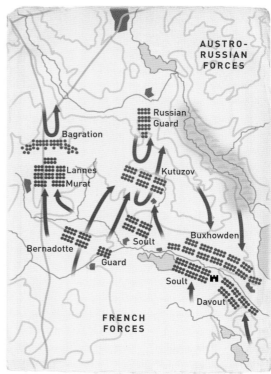

and he was outnumbered. He placed his right wing in such a position that it would prove irresistible to the allies. Meanwhile, in a ploy reminiscent of Caesar at Pharsalus, he had hidden the mainstay of his cavalry in his left together with Oudinot's Grenadiers, the Imperial Guard and Bernadotte's corps. He had observed that the Moravian mist was thick in the morning, but was dispersed by lunchtime.

In a further boost to the confident French emperor's morale, it was also an auspicious date, the first anniversary of his coronation. The allies fell for Napoleon's feint. They planned to use five columns, totalling 59,000 men, to break Napoleon's right wing, and cut the French off from Vienna. That meant coming down off the Heights. Prince Bagration would hit the

other flank commanded by Marshals Lannes and Murat. When the French line buckled, another thrust would strike the centre. But like so many before and since, the plan went wrong in execution.

Lannes and Murat were both products of the equal opportunities offered by the French Revolutionary Wars: Jean Lannes had begun life as a dyer's apprentice, while Murat was an innkeeper's son originally destined for a career in the Church.

THE SUN OF AUSTERLITZ
The attack on the right foundered first, when the wing was reinforced by a division under Louis Friant, Davout arriving with his army later. The allies transferred their thrust to the centre, abandoning the Heights in the process.

'...one of history's most remarkable victories... it showed Napoleon's genius at its best.'

HISTORIAN ALISTAIR HORNE ON THE FRENCH VICTORY AT AUSTERLITZ

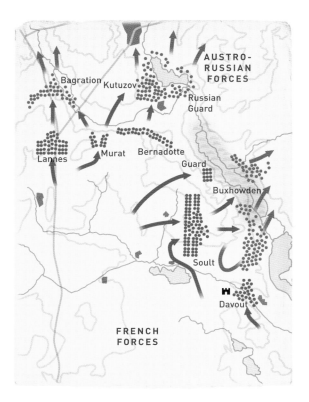

At this juncture Napoleon ordered his centre and left to attack. Visibility was poor and the troops became confused. But as Napoleon had hoped, the mist began to lift to reveal the allies split in two and with their flank exposed. He ordered Marshal Soult up on to the Pratzen at 9.00 a.m., just as the sun broke through the mist. They secured the plateau by 11.00, the decisive moment in the battle.

The rising sun clinched victory and Napoleon often paid homage to the *beau soleil d'Austerlitz*. Kutuzov realized there was a danger of his losing the fight and committed the best troops he had: the Russian Imperial Guard commanded by Grand Duke Constantine. The force of the attack caused Napoleon's men to waver, so the French emperor threw in his reserves, who succeeded in ousting the Russians. By 3.30 p.m. Napoleon's

troops were in possession of the Heights and were firing on the enemy below. It was a battle of annihilation, a Cannae. The Russians broke and Soult came down on their flank, turning their retreat into a rout. Many tried to escape across the frozen Satschan Lakes, but the artillery broke through the ice. About 16,000 were killed or wounded, while a further 2,000 perished in the lakes. Around 11,000 more were taken prisoner by the French. Kutuzov escaped at the cost of another battlefield injury.

Napoleon had broken the Third Coalition. The Russians retreated all the way to East Prussia. The Holy Roman Empire, in existence since the ninth century, came to an end. In the Treaty of Pressburg (1805), the Austrian empire lost territory in Italy and Germany. Politically it meant a redrawing of the map of central Europe, a process that was continued after the Prussian defeat at Jena the following year.

The peace memorial on the Pratzen (Prace) Heights near Brno was erected in 1910–12 to commemorate the Battle of Austerlitz. At its base stand four female figures representing France, Austria, Russia and Moravia.

AUERSTÄDT AND JENA

Napoleon Bonaparte *v.* Duke of Brunswick
14 October 1806

NAPOLEON'S MILITARY PROWESS was at its height in the early years of the 19th century. In 1806, it was the turn of Prussia to suffer a catastrophic defeat at his hands. This was made all the more painful in that it occurred only 20 years after the death of the national hero and master strategist Frederick the Great.

After Austerlitz, Napoleon became increasingly tyrannical in his dealings with King Frederick William III of Prussia. His prime concern was to coerce him into signing a treaty involving the forfeit of various lands in exchange for others that had not previously been holdings of the Prussian crown. One of the territories on offer was Hanover, which would inevitably provoke a clash with Hanoverian Britain. Frederick William's pusillanimity in agreeing to the treaty brought the roof down on his head.

Prussia was now at war with its old ally Britain and lost its merchant fleet as a result. Secretly the Prussians turned to Russia to sign a reinsurance treaty before insisting that Napoleon withdraw his armies from their borders on 6 August. Napoleon demanded that Prussia stop mobilizing, and the wheels of war began to grind.

By October 1806, Napoleon's army in Germany had doubled in size, and could now boast 160,000 men. Much has been made of the antiquated tactics of the Prussians and the inadequacies of their generals. Prussia had failed to keep abreast of the changes that had been brought about by the Revolutionary Wars (1792–1802): the campaigns that brought Napoleon to power. Artillery now played a crucial role. The great Prussian general

The field of battle
at Jena on 14 October 1806, from a lithograph by the French artists Charles Horace Vernet and Jacques François Swebach. Napoleon's crushing defeat of an obsolete Prussian army led to the occupation of Prussia and a reduction of the kingdom to half its former size.

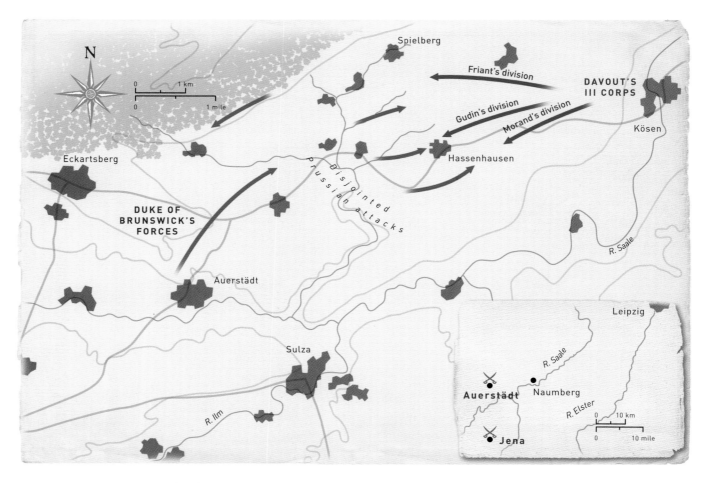

Map of the Battle of Auerstädt. The lack of any battle formations indicates that this engagement was an 'encounter battle', at which both sides unexpectedly came upon one another and began fighting. After his victory, Napoleon led the *Grande Armée* into Berlin on 25 October.

Gerhard von Scharnhorst, who was acting as chief of staff to the duke of Brunswick, wrote before the battle: 'We have been too slow about everything ... we must embrace our destiny and not give up in any way.'

The army that fought Napoleon was actually a combined Prussian and Saxon force. Yet two of its principal commanders, the duke of Brunswick and Prince Friedrich Ludwig von Hohenlohe-Ingelfingen, were at loggerheads with one another.

CHANCE ENCOUNTER

Napoleon pushed up from southern Germany through the Thuringian Forest to an area between Leipzig and Dresden, where there was a chance of outflanking the Prussians or pushing them up against a river. The Prussians began to retreat. On 8 October, the French emperor crossed into Saxony with 180,000 men. Prince Louis Ferdinand of Prussia, one of the most literate and civilized princes of the

period, was caught and killed at a skirmish at Saalfeld on the 10th.

On 13 October, French forces reached Jena in Thuringia, where Marshal Lannes, one of Napoleon's ablest commanders, reported that the whole Prussian army was encamped on the Landgrafenberg, defending the sector between the River Saale and the Thuringian Forest. It was foggy, and Lannes was confident that he could beat them. He set about securing the Windknollen, the highest point of the Landgrafenberg. Napoleon attacked on the 14th. The Prussian commander Hohenlohe committed errors that were exploited by the French. When 20,000 Prussians advanced on the village of Vierzehnheiligen, they came under withering French fire and were driven from the field.

At this stage, Napoleon was unaware that the duke of Brunswick had 63,500 more men at Auerstädt 12 miles (19 km) to the north. Two French corps commanded by marshals Davout and Bernadotte ran into him in dense fog as they came down on Hohenlohe's rear on the 14th. Bernadotte refused to help his brother marshal and narrowly avoided being court-martialled as a result. Yet Davout fought a brilliant battle on his own with 26,000 men against overwhelming odds. He sent in each of his three infantry divisions in turn between 7 and 10.30 a.m. The Prussians responded well, but they were poorly led. The 71-year-old Brunswick was mortally wounded and the king dithered over taking command. Finally, Davout launched an all-out offensive and the retreating army was routed.

Davout lost a quarter of his men in this action. Bernadotte made amends by pursuing units of the Prussian army to the Baltic and taking cavalry general Gebhard von Blücher prisoner at Ratekau in early November. Blücher – later to become the scourge of Napoleon at Leipzig and Waterloo – was one the few senior Prussian commanders to acquit himself well at Auerstädt–Jena.

A BLOW TO PRUSSIAN PRIDE

In the two battles, Prussia lost a total of 25,000 prisoners and 200 guns. Napoleon's victory was comprehensive, but he had had to rely on Davout's brilliance to save him.

Hohenlohe directed the retreat of the army across the Oder before capitulating. In Berlin, the governor, General Friedrich Wilhelm von der Schulenburg posted a bill: 'The King has lost a battle: calm is the citizen's first duty.' The shock to Prussian self-esteem was immeasurable. As usual, Napoleon proceeded to carve up the conquered territory, slimming it down to its ancient core. The double defeat gave rise to a reform movement within Prussia, which overhauled civil and military society and allowed Prussia its last moments of glory before it merged into Germany in 1871. Even Napoleon acknowledged how much the Spartans of the North had lost their former lustre in war: visiting Frederick the Great's tomb in the Garrison Church in Potsdam he said: 'Gentlemen, if he were still alive, we would not be here.'

The site of the battle at Jena is marked by a simple pillar indicating the distance to other significant battlefields and places in Napoleon's career. The final location, Longwood, is the house on the island of St Helena, where the French emperor was exiled after his defeat at Waterloo, and where he died in May 1821.

BORODINO

Napoleon Bonaparte *v.* Field Marshal Kutuzov
7 September **1812**

BY 1812, NAPOLEON'S DOMINATION OF CONTINENTAL EUROPE was almost complete. There remained just one nut to crack: Mother Russia. While she lived she could always rally opposition to France. On 23–24 June 1812, over half a million French troops – along with Poles, Prussians, Austrians, Dutch, Swiss and Italians pressed into service by Napoleon – crossed the Russian border. Many of the men who met their deaths in the ensuing months had never set eyes on France. At first, the *Grande Armée* met with little resistance, but at the onset of autumn Tsar Alexander I ordered his generals to halt Napoleon's advance. At the village of Borodino, 77 miles (124 km) west of Moscow, Field Marshal Mikhail Kutuzov planned to take his revenge for Austerlitz.

The Battle of Borodino (1913), by the Russian artist Franz Roubaud, conveys the confusion and carnage of this huge set-piece engagement, which involved a quarter of a million men on both sides.

Kutuzov must have cut an unlikely figure on his horse: he was now 67 years old and in poor health, obese and crippled with rheumatism. But his appointment to lead the army was popular with everyone but the tsar. He had 120,000 troops under his command and an impressive tally of 640 guns. Opposing him, Napoleon's *Grande Armée* had between 130,000 and 150,000 men and 587 guns. The din of their combined firepower was famously orchestrated by the composer Tchaikovsky in his *1812 Overture*.

On 3 September, Kutuzov dug in across a 5-mile (8-km) front covering the two approaches to Moscow: the old and the new Smolensk roads. His right was anchored in the Kolocha, a tributary of the River Moskva and his left by the dense Utitsa Forest. The line included four villages: Borodino on the left bank of the Kolocha and Gorki on the right, together with Semenovskoye and Utitsa. A stream (the Semenovka) and woods concealed his reserves. The great Raevsky Redoubt was constructed on Kurgan Hill in the centre

of his front, complete with trenches and a battery of ten guns.

The right was commanded by General Mikhail Miloradovich and the left by Prince Pyotr Bagration, while General Barclay de Tolly – minister of war and the descendant of an émigré Scot – was dug in on the steep south bank of the Kolocha covering Gorki. He took charge of the centre with most of the guns. Fortified flèches (defensive fieldworks) were dug between two branches of the Semenovka. The Russian position could not be outflanked because of the forest and the river; moreover, the topography of the region, with its dense copses and woods, made it useless for Napoleon's cavalry.

SUICIDE MISSION

Only a madman would have attacked such a position, but Kutuzov knew that Napoleon was desperate to deliver a *coup de grâce*. His army was bleeding to death, with soldiers succumbing to the effects of the long battle, disease or the summer heat, or simply deserting. As they

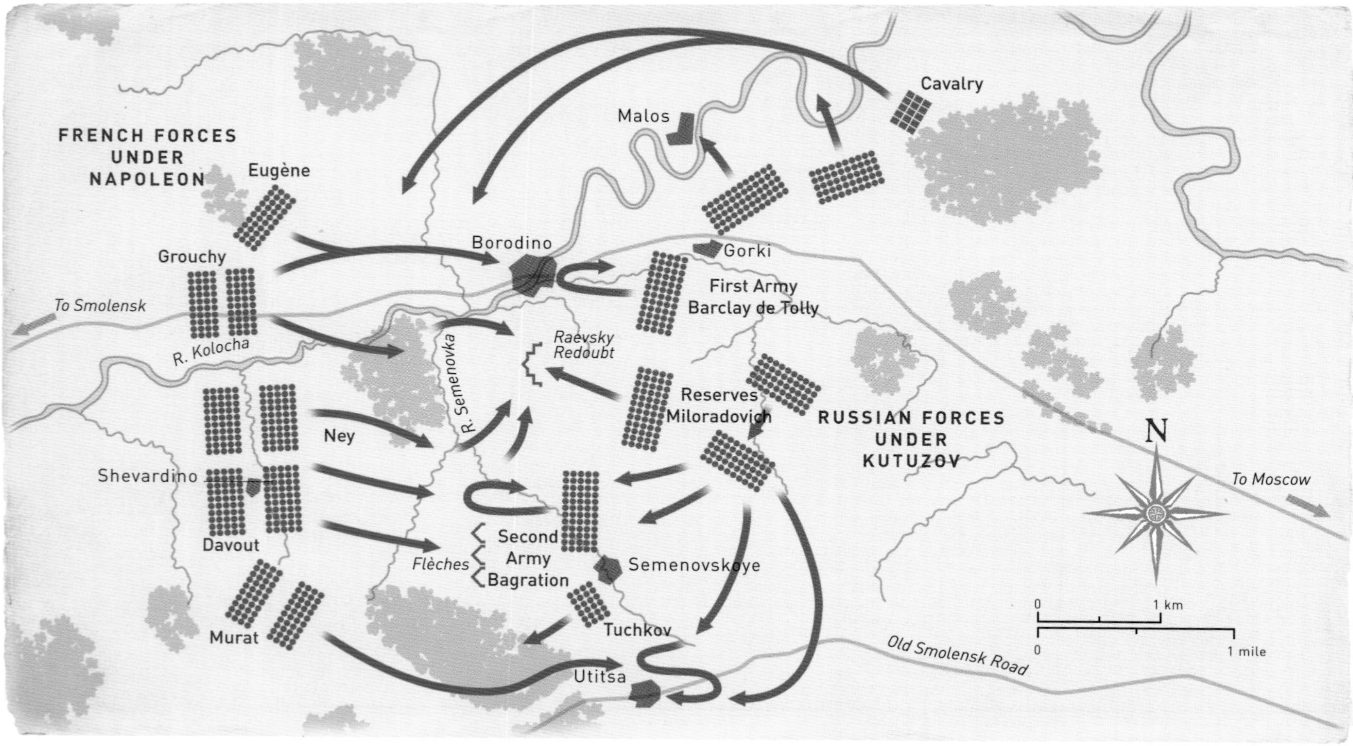
FRENCH FORCES UNDER NAPOLEON
Eugène
Grouchy
To Smolensk
R. Kolocha
Ney
Shevardino
Davout
Murat
Borodino
R. Semenovka
Raevsky Redoubt
Flèches
Second Army Bagration
Semenovskoye
Tuchkov
Utitsa
Malos
Cavalry
Gorki
First Army Barclay de Tolly
Reserves Miloradovich
RUSSIAN FORCES UNDER KUTUZOV
N
To Moscow
0
1 km
0
1 mile
Old Smolensk Road

The Pyrrhic victory at Borodino cost Napoleon one-third of his already heavily depleted army. It paved the way for the disastrous French retreat from Russia, in which 'General Winter' claimed the lives of hundreds of thousands of starving, poorly clad soldiers.

retreated, the Russians had pursued a scorched-earth policy to deny Napoleon provisions, forcing him to rely on extensive foraging to supply his forces. The French emperor had all his top corps commanders with him: the redheaded, hot-tempered Ney, Murat, Davout, Junot, and Prince Eugène de Beauharnais, as well as the Young and Old Guards.

Napoleon's plan was for Eugène to attack the village of Borodino to give the impression that the main thrust was to the Russian right, while he would deliver the body blow to the centre and left. Davout was to attack Bagration, while the Polish cavalry commander Prince Poniatowski would try to outflank him and attack him from the rear. On 5 September, 40,000 French chanced upon 12,000 Russians at Shevardino, but were repulsed.

Kutuzov now knew where the French were coming from, and strengthened his position yet further. He backed up Bagration's line too, and this was where Napoleon struck at 5.00 a.m. on 7 September. Now 100 French cannon were unleashed on the centre. According to plan, Eugène de Beauharnais captured Borodino, while Poniatowski took Utitsa to the south. Over three hours, seven Russian assaults were driven back, but the eighth hit home. Fire from 300 Russian cannon halted the French advance against Semenovskoye. Murat went on to attack the Three Flèches redoubt to the south of the Russian line. Davout sustained a wound to the stomach after being blown from his horse by grapeshot and knocked unconscious. Rapp took command until he too fell and was replaced by Desaix, who was also hit.

FALL OF THE REDOUBTS

Ney managed to seize the southernmost gun emplacement and hold onto it despite three Russian counter-attacks. Napoleon sent Murat to relieve him. Eugène eventually took Borodino and put guns in position to pound the great redoubt.

Ney wanted the Imperial Guard brought to bear on the Three Flèches, where Pyotr Bagration lay mortally wounded, sapping the morale of his men. Beauharnais threw three divisions against the Raevsky Redoubt. Napoleon got cold feet and held back the Guard, providing 400 new cannon instead.

In his epic novel *War and Peace* (1869), Tolstoy paints an unsympathetic picture of Napoleon, showing him vacillating about pouring his reserves into the withering fire of the redoubt: 'Napoleon was in the grip of the depression which descends on the gambler, who after a long run of luck during which he recklessly flung his money about and won every time, suddenly finds, just when he has carefully calculated all the chances of the game, that the more he considers his play the more surely he loses.'

At around 6 p.m., the exhausted soldiers began to give up the fight. By this stage, the guns had been roaring for ten hours. The Russians were still encamped to the east, and capable of renewing the battle the next day. There were mounds of dead all around the Raevsky Redoubt, with its 27 cannon, where French soldiers had broken through the embrasures and engaged in hand-to-hand combat with the gun crews. It finally fell in the late afternoon in a combined assault by Eugène, Ney and Murat.

THE LONG RETREAT

Around one-third of each army was lost at this engagement. Borodino is traditionally portrayed as a French victory, but it was at best a Pyrrhic one. The Russians at first claimed the laurels; it is certainly the case that their stand at Borodino delivered a mortal blow to the *Grande Armée*. After the battle, to keep his army intact, Kutuzov abandoned Moscow, set it ablaze and withdrew. Napoleon was seriously depleted by the loss of 50,000 men dead or wounded. In terms of bloodshed, it was (after the Battle of Nations at Leipzig the following year) the second most costly engagement of the Napoleonic Wars.

As winter set in and Napoleon began the long march back to the west, Kutuzov was in a strong position to harry the retreating enemy. During this terrible ordeal, 400,000 of Napoleon's soldiers perished (only a quarter of them died in battle), while just 50,000 survived. At a stroke, the *Grande Armée* had been obliterated, and the Austrians and Prussians were given fresh momentum to rise up against France.

'*Napoleon was in the grip of the depression which descends on the gambler, who after a long run of luck during which he recklessly flung his money about and won every time, suddenly finds, just when he has carefully calculated all the chances of the game, that the more he considers his play the more surely he loses.*'

LEO TOLSTOY'S ASSESSMENT OF NAPOLEON IN THE NOVEL *WAR AND PEACE*

WATERLOO

Napoleon Bonaparte *v.* Duke of Wellington
18 June 1815

BETWEEN HIS DEFEAT AT THE BATTLE OF THE NATIONS, fought outside Leipzig on 16–19 October 1813, and his abdication on 6 April 1814, Napoleon fought like a tiger to maintain his empire. He secured several victories before Blücher and the Austrian Prince Schwarzenberg chased him home. Napoleon was badly bruised on 9 March and then defeated outside Paris in the battles of Arcis-sur-Aube and La Fère-Champenoise. Sensing that his marshals were on the point of deserting him, he agreed to go into exile as the monarch of the little island of Elba off the Italian coast.

A year later, on 1 March 1815, Bonaparte tossed aside Elba's crown and returned to France: for the brief period known as the 'Hundred Days', the pike was back in the pond. The men who were busy drawing the map of the new Europe at the Congress of Vienna hastily departed to their separate lands. On 19 March, Louis XVIII, hearing that Napoleon was being received in triumph on his journey north, fled to the Low Countries. Again, the allied armies were called in to check Bonaparte, once and for all.

In March, the allies mustered vast armies in the Netherlands, with the intention of marching on Paris. The Austrians assembled 200,000 troops, the Russians 150,000 and the Prussians over 100,000. Adding in Dutch and British forces, Napoleon found himself heavily outnumbered by his enemies. Accordingly, his only possible strategy was to try and keep them divided and finish them off one by one. Their lines of communication meant that they would retreat in different directions: the Anglo-Dutch towards the sea and the Prussians to the Rhineland.

Leaving Paris on 12 June, Napoleon inflicted blows on both sections of the allied forces. On the 16th, Prussian commander Gebhard von Blücher was first to face the French emperor's 120,000-man army in battle, at Ligny in modern Belgium. With only two-thirds the strength of the French forces, Blücher was forced to retreat. After being knocked off

The Battle of Waterloo (1874) by the painter Félix Philippoteaux. Wellington famously called this momentous 14-hour battle, which finally broke Napoleon's power, 'the nearest run thing you ever saw in your life'.

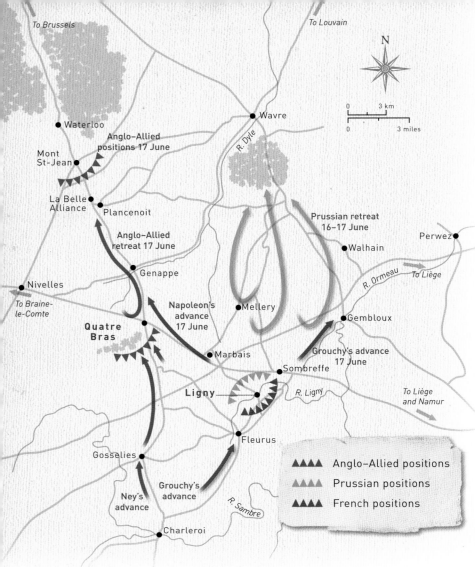

To Brussels
To Louvain
N
0 ___ 3 km
0 ___ 3 miles

To Waterloo
Anglo–Allied positions 17 June
Mont St-Jean
La Belle Alliance
Plancenoit
Anglo–Allied retreat 17 June
Nivelles
To Braine-le-Comte
Genappe
Quatre Bras
Napoleon's advance 17 June
Marbais
Ligny
Fleurus
Gosselies
Ney's advance
Grouchy's advance
Charleroi
R. Sambre
R. Ligny
Sombreffe
To Liège and Namur
Grouchy's advance 17 June
Gembloux
Mellery
R. Ormeau
To Liège
Walhain
Perwez
Prussian retreat 16–17 June
Wavre
R. Dyle

▲▲▲▲ Anglo–Allied positions
▲▲▲▲ Prussian positions
▲▲▲▲ French positions

End of the 'Hundred Days'. The final flourish of the Napoleonic army, from its last-ever victory at Ligny on 16 June to the fateful encounter at Waterloo two days later.

his horse, Blücher still evaded capture. Even so, he refused to return to Germany and instead carried out a perilous flanking manoeuvre towards Wavre and Waterloo.

Napoleon failed to exploit this victory, an error most historians have attributed to his chief-of-staff Nicolas Jean-de-Dieu Soult. Meanwhile, also on the 16th, Arthur Wellesley, the duke of Wellington, ran into the *Armée du Nord* under Marshal Michel Ney at nearby Quatre Bras. Ney made the mistake of vacillating and not launching his attack until the afternoon, by which time Wellington had brought up reinforcements.

THE MUSTERING SQUADRON

Wellington did not meet the full force of Napoleon's army until the 18th, when Napoleon cornered him on the field of

Waterloo, a village a few miles south of Brussels. By the time Napoleon caught up with Wellington, the British general had had time to choose his position.

The poet Lord Byron, who visited the battlefield less than a year after the event, imagined the deployment of Wellington's troops:

> And there was mounting in hot haste:
>   the steed,
> The mustering squadron, and the
>   clattering car,
> Went pouring forward with impetuous
>   speed,
> And swiftly forming in the ranks of
>   war;
> And the deep thunder peal on peal
>   afar;
> And near, the beat of the alarming
>   drum
> Roused up the soldier ere the morning
>   star ... ('Childe Harold', III, XXV)

Thinking that the British had been abandoned by the Prussians, Napoleon believed they would be easy meat. Wellington, however, had reached a firm understanding with Blücher, who was to play a decisive role later that day. Blücher's return to the field of battle was essentially an envelopment that Napoleon completely failed to anticipate, despite the fact it was one of his favourite tactics. Indeed, when his brother Jérôme mentioned the possibility that it might happen, Napoleon brusquely dismissed it. Wellington was commanding an Anglo-German-Dutch army comprising 68,000 men and 156 guns – just over a third of them British – while Napoleon had 72,000 men and 346 guns.

Wellington had drawn up his men in his favourite 'reverse slope' position along the Mont St Jean Ridge to block the road to Brussels. To his rear was the thick Forest of Soignes. He was Napoleon's equal in assessing battlefield terrain and had chosen his position with impeccable judgement. He had created two fortified positions: Hougoumont and La Haie Sainte.

AN EPIC STRUGGLE

The French army contained many campaign veterans who worshipped their commander and morale was high. Napoleon established his headquarters at Le Caillou, near a farmhouse with the sonorous name of La Belle Alliance. He entrusted his left wing to Ney, who was brave but also ill-disciplined and also had no discernable plan of action. Ney was later to take charge of the whole battle. Napoleon's performance was blighted by piles and cystitis, while Wellington was in peak physical form for the epic 14-hour struggle that would ensue.

Heavy rain overnight had made the ground unsuitable both for Napoleon's planned cavalry attacks and for moving up his artillery. It was not until 11.30 a.m.

that the ground had dried up sufficiently for him to deploy his grand battery of 84 guns. He decided to strike fear into his enemy instead by stretching out his front. Between him and the allies was a long, shallow valley. It was late morning when Jerôme Bonaparte attacked the farmhouse at Hougoumont where Wellington had elected to anchor his right wing, including the Foot Guards. Wellington was aware that Hougoumont stood in the way of Napoleon executing one of his flamboyant flanking movements. The battle went on all day, drawing in some 9,000 men. The 3,000 defenders held out to the very end, despite the fact that their defences were pierced momentarily by the French.

Napoleon calculated that Wellington would take his reserves from the centre and reposition them at Hougoumont. It was at the centre that he planned to slam into the allied army, but Wellington failed to release them despite seven French

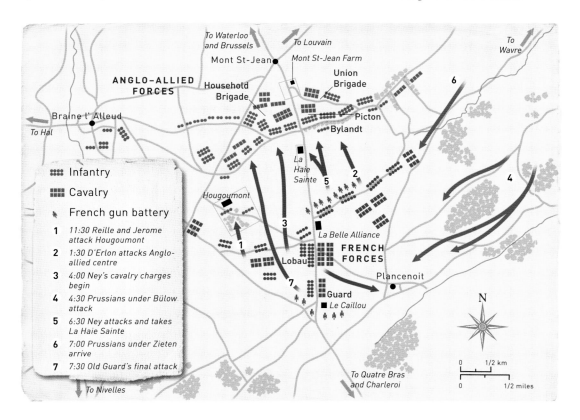

The battlefield at Waterloo; the key position of the fortified farmhouse at Hougoumont, which blocked any flanking movement by Napoleon's forces, indicates how vital it was that the British held it. A mixed garrison of English, Scots and German troops beat off all French attempts to capture the position.

The charge of the Scots Greys at Waterloo. Famously shouting 'Scotland Forever!', this heavy cavalry regiment cut through rank after rank of the French. Yet after overreaching their advance, they were isolated and slaughtered by French cuirassiers and lancers.

assaults between 11.30 a.m. and 7.30 p.m. Napoleon ended up using his reserves in a desperate attempt to take the farmhouse.

At 1 p.m., Napoleon's main battery began pounding Wellington's centre, but in their positions on the reverse slope they were in little danger from the French barrage. Two huge French columns totalling 16,000 men and led by the comte d'Erlon now came under fire from the top of the ridge from the 95th Rifles and the King's German Legion as they proceeded east on the Brussels–Charleroi road. The idea was to punch a hole in Wellington's centre-left and then roll up both sides of his front. They did succeed in taking two important points: Papelotte and the Sandpit on the allied left.

A FUTILE GESTURE

Meanwhile, the pressure on the centre had not abated even if it eventually came to a halt through the allies' point-blank firing. Some Dutch Catholics fled. General Sir

Thomas Picton, already wounded at Quatre Bras, was killed, but the British cavalry – the Union and Heavy Brigades (including the famous Scots Greys) – under Lord Uxbridge and led by General Sir Frederick Ponsonby and Lord Edward Somerset drove the French back and broke d'Erlon's divisions, turning their attack into a rout. Two standards were taken.

The Scots Greys pursued their quarry to the other side of the valley, only to be cut down by Ney's cuirassiers and lancers. In a show of bravado, however, the survivors rode on, seeking to take the great battery. They were met by a fierce French counter-attack. Ponsonby was caught and killed on the spot and the decimated cavalry rode back to the lines, of no further use to the battle.

Wellington later rebuked Uxbridge for this. It was cold comfort to Napoleon who had lost 5,000 men in the attack. Napoleon moved his position forward to La Belle Alliance.

Now Ney attacked a different stretch of the Anglo-Dutch centre. He had misinterpreted some troop movements and led his cavalry charges from 4 p.m. because Ney had believed the allies were retreating, having seen some ammunition carts moving back. He thought he could turn the perceived retreat into a rout and Napoleon fed in the Guard, but the attack was launched without the artillery and infantry support that might have ensured success. The allies were prepared and Wellington ordered his infantry to form up into 13 squares. The French cavalry rode round them over and over again, churning up the ground, but found themselves facing a porcupine of bayonets.

When he found the British squares intact, Ney carried on regardless, still failing to bring up artillery or to spike the British guns. Four horses were shot from under him. When he finally asked for infantry to be brought up, Napoleon refused.

BLÜCHER'S COUP

Napoleon was facing another threat: he had expected relief from Marshal Grouchy, but in his place, at 4.30 p.m., came Blücher's Prussians under the command of General von Bülow, whom Grouchy had been detailed to shadow. General Georges Lobau and the Young Guard cleared the Prussians out of the village of Plancenoit, which delayed the joining of Wellington and Blücher's armies until 7.30 p.m. Meanwhile La Haie Sainte was under siege and its garrison running out of ammunition. The Prince of Orange despatched the King's German Legion to relieve them, but it was cut down by

French cavalry. The farm complex fell at 6.30 p.m., when the ammunition finally gave out and the defenders surrendered. Yet Napoleon failed to take advantage of this to put further pressure on Wellington's centre. The farmhouse was later retaken by the allies.

Blücher's attack, however, deprived Napoleon of vital reserves: henceforth he would be fighting on two fronts. When that took place Napoleon advanced through the debris of Ney's cavalry with the infantry of the Old and Middle Guards at around 7 p.m. Napoleon led three furious assaults that almost reached Wellington's line. Wellington had hidden his men in the ripe corn, and with the cry 'Up Guards, ready!' he ordered the men from Sir Peregrine Maitland's brigade to rise up and fire at almost point-blank range. Napoleon's Guards were halted in their tracks. Together with a brilliant flanking movement by Sir John Colborne's Light Infantry, the French were cut down by withering fire.

Informed that the Prussians had arrived in strength, Wellington raised his hat to signal the forward march: 'Go forward boys and secure your victory!' The hussars rode out and Napoleon's forces broke. The business of pursuing the enemy was left to Blücher's men, who cut them down without mercy. Wellington and Blücher finally met at La Belle Alliance at 9.30 p.m. that evening: in Germany, the Battle of Waterloo is known as the Battle of Belle-Alliance.

Napoleon had lost 25,000 men and 16,000 prisoners, Wellington almost 15,000 and Blücher 7,000.

'As the wind carries off a flaming straw,
You heard the noise of this Grande Armée *no more.'*

Victor Hugo – 'Les Châtiments' (1853)

CALATAFIMI

Giuseppe Garibaldi *v.* Bourbon forces
15 May **1860**

DESPITE A DEATH SENTENCE HANGING OVER HIS HEAD, Italian nationalist leader Giuseppe Garibaldi returned from exile in the revolutionary year of 1848, schooled in the novel techniques of guerrilla warfare. Having commanded armies in the service of the nascent states of South America, he now offered his services to the king of Piedmont, Charles Albert to rid northeastern Italy of the Austrians who had occupied the region since the 17th century. The king turned down his offer.

Italian unification (the *Risorgimento*, or 'resurrection') had been a burning issue ever since the 1820s, and it became a popular cause in educated European circles, particularly in Britain. Undeterred by Charles Albert's snub, Garibaldi raised an army of 3,000 volunteers and marched on Rome in April 1849 in defence of the newly proclaimed Roman Republic. There, he scored some notable victories over the French forces who were supporting the pope, before being forced into exile once more. Yet his campaigns had been a great propaganda success. He returned to South America and it was 1854 before he set foot on Italian soil again.

TIRELESS REVOLUTIONARY

In 1859, Garibaldi took part in the war that broke out between Piedmont (aided by France) and Austria. Placed in command of the Alpine troops of King Victor Emmanuel II of Piedmont (who had succeeded his father in 1849), he beat the Austrians at Casale. Yet in the compromise that followed defeat, Austria was allowed to keep control of the province of Venetia. This concession infuriated the nationalists. In addition, Piedmont was required to cede Savoy and

Nice to France in reward for the services it had rendered. This was particularly galling to Garibaldi, who was born in Nice.

In April 1860, Garibaldi found a new focus for his revolutionary nationalism, when uprisings broke out in Naples and Sicily against the rule of the Bourbon king of the Two Sicilies, the timid 23-year-old Francis II. In support of the insurrection, Garibaldi launched an invasion of Sicily with 1,000 volunteers. His troops soon became popularly known as 'Redshirts', from the garb they wore in homage to the French Revolution.

The expedition set sail from Quarto near Genoa on 5 May 1860 aboard two ships, the *Lombardo* and the smaller *Piemonte*, which carried Garibaldi. He had a Piedmontese general's uniform in his baggage and a very limited number of Enfield rifles plus a couple of cannon and other antiquated guns he had commandeered from the castle at Talamone. His intention was to travel fast and light and take the enemy by surprise. His men had been arranged into seven companies and a staff of sorts formed under Nino Bixio. A small number of men were detached and sent to the Papal States in an attempt to invade them too.

Lacking even a map, Garibaldi had not decided where he was to make his triumphant landfall, and so cast about for a suitable location. Six days after setting sail, he spotted two British warships in the harbour at Marsala on the westernmost tip of the island. He calculated that their presence would prevent the Bourbons from interfering. As it was, the landing was a stroke of huge good fortune: Marsala was completely undefended. The garrison had decamped to the regional capital, Trapani. The Redshirts quickly disembarked. Eventually, one Bourbon warship did put

in an appearance; as Garibaldi had hoped, the British intervened on his behalf by firing a salvo at the vessel, which allegedly killed a dog and wounded one man in the shoulder.

The *Garibaldini* cut the telegraph wires to Trapani. The mayor and town council were persuaded to proclaim an end to Bourbon rule and make Garibaldi dictator of Sicily. They did this only reluctantly, as they were intensely suspicious of the Piedmontese, northerners who spoke an entirely alien dialect of Italian. Contrary to the way the scene has

Garibaldi's 'Redshirts' storming the Bourbon army's position on the Pianto dei Romani at the Batttle of Calatafimi. This gallant action was to lead within just five months to the overthrow of the Kingdom of the Two Sicilies and Garibaldi's triumphant entry into Naples.

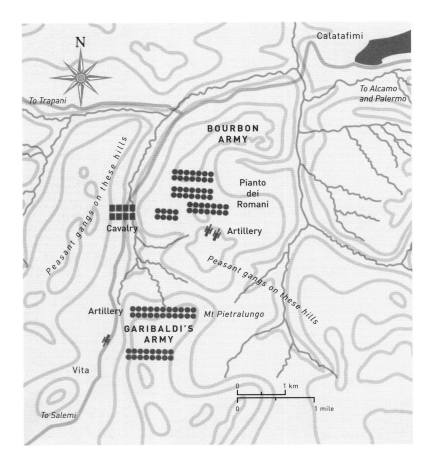

N

Calatafimi

To Alcamo
and Palermo

To Trapani

Peasant gangs on these hills

**BOURBON
ARMY**

Pianto
dei
Romani

Cavalry

Artillery

Peasant gangs on these hills

Artillery

Mt Pietralungo

**GARIBALDI'S
ARMY**

Vita

To Salemi

0   1 km

0   1 mile

**Disposition of the
opposing armies** at
Calatafimi on 15 May
1860. Despite their
commanding position,
the Bourbon army
lacked the will to fight
against Garibaldi's highly
motivated revolutionary
volunteers.

been portrayed (in the celebratory plaques
that adorn the city of Marsala, for
example) there was no great enthusiasm
on either side.

On 13 May, the Redshirts arrived at
Salemi brandishing sabres, but little else.
There, they met up with some peasant
irregulars, or *picciotti*. In his new role as
dictator, Garibaldi decreed that all men
aged between the ages of 17 and 50 had
to join the colours. He was effectively able
to double the size of his force. Presently,
he learned that the Bourbons had sent
3,000 men under General Landi to
confront him and that they had cut off
the road to Palermo at Calatafimi.

FEARLESS LEADER

Garibaldi clashed with the Bourbon
troops at Calatafimi on 15 May. He was
outnumbered, and the king's men had
chosen a good defensive position on top
of a terraced hill called il Pianto dei

Romani outside the town. They had two
cannon to his one; he had only a handful
of rifles, while they had many more, plus
plenty of ammunition. But leading from
the front with his sword drawn, Garibaldi
urged his troops up the hill by stages,
taking shelter behind the terraces cut into
the mountainside. One member of the
expedition wrote: 'We thousand attacked,
with the General in the lead: every last
soldier was used without pause, without
care, and without reservation because on
that day rested the outcome of the whole
expedition.' Garibaldi was so reckless in
the face of the enemy fire that some of his
staff tried to shield him from their bullets.
Then one final charge brought them to the
uppermost terrace. Garibaldi is said to
have shouted: 'Italians, here we must die!'
With a mighty bayonet charge (Garibaldi's
favourite tactic) they pushed on to the top
of the hill. Against all odds, Garibaldi's
men put the king's men to flight, and
scattered them across the fields.

About 30 of Garibaldi's Redshirts had
been killed and over 100 wounded. But
the road to Palermo now lay open to
them. The action at Calatafimi also
greatly enhanced Garibaldi's reputation
for fearless leadership and contributed to
the myth of his invincibility. Volunteers
now flocked in droves to join his cause.

STORMING PALERMO

He pushed on to Palermo via Alcamo and
pitched camp on the high plain of Renda
overlooking the city while he and his
lieutenants worked out a plan of action.
They agreed to employ a feint: while
pretending to retreat and sending their
wounded down the road to Corleone, to
the south, they would march through the
mountains to join up with Giuseppe La
Masa's force at Misilmeri. La Masa, along
with Rosolino Pilo and Giovanni Corrao,
were the leading Sicilian revolutionaries.
These *squadre* (guerrillas) greatly aided

Garibaldi by cutting Bourbon supply lines and telegraph wires. The hope was to take the king's forces by surprise and enter the city from the southeast.

On 25 May, the exhausted *Garibaldini* linked up with La Masa. They decided to descend on Palermo by a mountain path at Gibilrossa. On the 27th, they took the garrison at Palermo completely by surprise. There was a skirmish at the Ponte dell'Ammiraglio, where Garibaldi urged his men on from his horse. They knocked down a temporary gate at the Porta Termini and raced through the city to the Piazza Fieravecchia market, arriving at 4 a.m. The objective was well-chosen: the market traders were well-known for their revolutionary sympathies.

From the market, they dashed through the narrow streets. Garibaldi took the Piazze Pretorio and Bologni and the town hall. For three days there was fighting in the streets. Garibaldi appeared fearless in the midst of commotion, bombs and naval shells fired by the warships in the harbour. The battle is brilliantly evoked in Luchino Visconti's film of Giuseppe Lampedusa's 1958 novel *Il Gattopardo* ('The Leopard').

On 30 May, after a request for a truce from the Bourbons, Garibaldi put on his Piedmontese uniform and boarded the British warship HMS *Hannibal*. On 6 June, General Lanza withdrew his 20,000 troops from the city. The disparity in sizes between the two armies was astonishing, but discontent with the Bourbons was a further factor: as recently as April there had been an insurrection in the city. In the words of historian Lucy Riall, the 'government was weak, isolated and unpopular'.

Garibaldi's landing at Marsala sparked off uprisings in Agrigento, Messina and Catania. In Messina and Catania, the local governments fled. Garibaldi and his men were able to step into a political vacuum.

ITALY UNIFIED

Further engagements at Reggio and Volturno saw him rout the Sicilian army and gain complete control of the island. On 22 August, Garibaldi crossed the Straits of Messina, again under the watchful eye of the Royal Navy. Now the political unification of Italy was just a matter of time. In September, his entry into Naples brought an end to Bourbon rule in southern Italy. King Victor Emmanuel joined him in November.

The year 1866 was a momentous date in the annals of Italian unification. Fighting on two fronts, against Italy and Prussia, Austria scored two victories against the Italians at the Second Battle of Custozza and the naval battle of Lissa in the Adriatic off Croatia. But a crushing defeat by the Prussians at Königgrätz ended the war and forced Austria to cede Venetia to Italy. Only Rome would hold out until 1870, when the last opponent to Savoyard rule, Pope Pius IX, withdrew into the Vatican.

'We thousand attacked, with the General in the lead: every last soldier was used without pause, without care, and without reservation because on that day rested the outcome of the whole expedition.'

EYEWITNESS ACCOUNT OF ONE OF GARIBALDI'S REDSHIRTS AT THE BATTLE OF CALATAFIMI

SHENANDOAH VALLEY CAMPAIGN

General Thomas 'Stonewall' Jackson *v.* Union forces March–June **1862**

THE AMERICAN CIVIL WAR was a long and bloody struggle that erupted when southern states refused to accept the election of the first Republican president, Abraham Lincoln in 1860: not one single vote had been cast in his favour in the south. The sticking-point was Lincoln's proposal to outlaw slavery. It was an increasingly live issue: John Brown had been executed in 1859 for fomenting a slave insurrection. At his execution, the future general 'Stonewall' Jackson commanded a unit of artillery meant to keep the public at bay.

Between December 1860 and February 1861, seven Southern states seceded from the Union, called up their militias and formed their own 'Confederacy', with Jefferson Davis as its president. He set up his first capital in Montgomery, Alabama. Federal institutions were occupied and one – Fort Sumter in Charleston harbour – was bombarded.

Lincoln assembled an army to deal with the rebel states, which caused four more to join the south: North Carolina, Virginia, Tennessee and Arkansas. Militarily, the South was far weaker, with a pool of just over a million men to draw on, as against the North's four million. Moreover, the North held a virtual monopoly of industrial might; the states of Massachusetts and Pennsylvania alone produced more goods than the whole of the South. Confederate communications

were also poor, with only a very limited mileage of railway tracks.

The Civil War was also the first fully mechanized conflict in history, with new military technologies in widespread use for the first time. These included repeating rifles, hand grenades, land mines, ironclads and even the submarine. As a result, the carnage was terrible. Americans had less experience of warfare than Europeans, although many of the leading players had seen action in the Mexican War of 1846–48.

By 1 July 1861, Lincoln had raised an army of 300,000 men, whereas by 1 August, Davis had only two-thirds of that figure. As 'citizen armies' they were reluctant to submit to discipline. Early on, the idea developed of a war of attrition and starving the Confederates into submission.

Richmond, the capital of Virginia, superseded Montgomery as the capital

Lithograph depicting a Union position being overrun by a Confederate cavalry charge at the First Battle of Bull Run on 21 July 1861. This engagement saw raw Northern troops pitted against well-commanded and trained Southern forces.

of the Confederate States. Its location, only 110 miles (178 km) southwest of Washington, posed a serious problem for the South's military planners. If the Unionists could capture it, it would give them a serious morale boost and sap that of the South.

STRATEGIC CORRIDOR

The Shenandoah Mountains, an outlying range of the Appalachians, are a largely impassable barrier that formerly divided British America from the French colonies. The best defence of both Richmond and Washington were the waterways that flowed roughly west to east, of which the most important were the Rivers James, Rappahannock and Potomac, and the large expanse of water in Chesapeake Bay.

The valley was a strategic corridor of the highest importance, as it led north to the Potomac and Washington. On the eastern side it is framed by the Blue Ridge Mountains while to the west it is bordered by the Shenandoah range. Running down the middle are the two branches of the Shenandoah River.

The first major battle of the Civil War was the First Battle of Bull Run (also called the Battle of Manassas) on 21 July 1861. This engagement earned Confederate commander Thomas J. Jackson his nickname 'Stonewall': when General Bernard E. Bee – who was killed in the fight – saw Jackson on top of Henry House Hill, he remarked: 'There is Jackson, standing like a stone wall. Rally behind the Virginians!' After that both the brigadier and his brigade were known by this name, and Jackson was promoted major general.

Jackson, a former professor at the Virginia Military Institute, had graduated from West Point in 1846, a year whose alumni included no fewer than 24 Civil War generals including George McClellan (commander of the Union Army of the Potomac) and the Confederate George Pickett, who won fame at Gettysburg. It is an indication of what a bitter family feud the Civil War was to be. Jackson's famous line was: 'Always mystify, mislead and surprise the enemy.' Jackson was able to use the Shenandoah terrain brilliantly.

From March 1862, the Unionists began bringing up troops for a battle. McClellan's Army of the Potomac marched on Manassas, with Nathaniel P. Banks and John C. Frémont pushing their six divisions up the Shenandoah Valley. At the sight of the Northern onslaught, the Confederate generals manning these sectors – Joseph E. Johnston, Jackson and Edward Johnson – beat a retreat.

McClellan did not pursue the Confederates. Despatching one division to reinforce Frémont, and taking one of Banks's divisions to join his own army, he conceived the idea of taking Richmond. Perhaps drawing on his experience as an observer in the Crimean War, he planned to transport his forces down the Potomac by boat to the mouth of the Rappahannock River and from there march overland to Richmond. Eventually it was decided the forces would be landed on the tip of the Virginia Peninsula, thereby stealing a march on the Confederates who were at Manassas. Meanwhile Johnston moved his men down to the peninsula to defend the city of Richmond.

While McClellan was advancing on the Confederate capital, Jackson was given the job of pinning down Federal troops in the Shenandoah Valley so that they could not come to McClellan's aid.

Faced with the concentration of Union troops in the valley and commanding only a small division, Jackson abandoned Winchester in the north. Even so, on 23 March, he attacked James Shields's division at Kernstown. He had underestimated its strength and retired hurt. Kernstown was certainly a Federal victory, but the very fact that Jackson had believed himself strong enough to pounce caused alarm in Washington. At the northern end of Shenandoah Valley was the Unionist army of Nathaniel Banks at Harper's Ferry. There was no question now of moving Banks's two divisions and they left McClellan's main corps in the Piedmont commanded by Irvin McDowell.

Jackson retreated as far as Swift Run Gap on the Blue Ridge. He brought Ewell over to join him and prevent the Yankees from occupying the valley and sent his own Stonewall Division to join Johnson on the Rappahannock. Now only 11,000 Confederates lay between McClellan and his prize at Richmond. He was able to invest the town.

BRILLIANT CAMPAIGN

Jackson now proceeded to defeat the Northerners in a series of brilliant victories: Front Royal, Winchester, Cross Keys and Port Republic. These battles have been studied by American and British army staff colleges ever since. In between, his 'foot cavalry' covered huge distances up and down the valley, often marching barefoot.

On 8 May, Jackson defeated Frémont's advance guard at the Battle of McDowell, leaving the rest of his army to retreat northwards up the valley. Jackson then took ten brigades and attacked the Federalists at Front Royal on 23 May, capturing a regiment. Two days later they routed Banks's three brigades at First Winchester. The Unionists retreated in

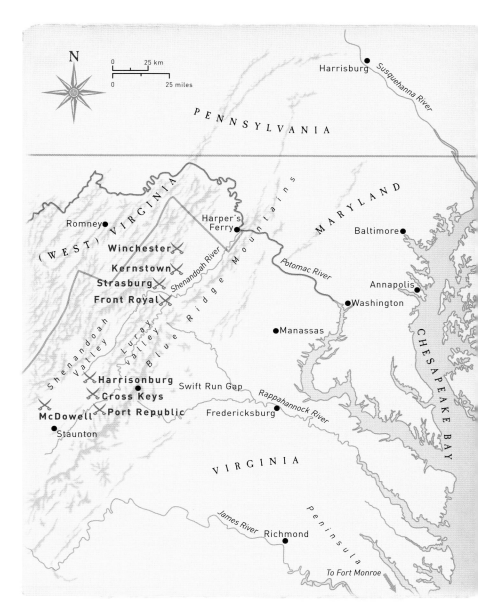

Map of the Shenandoah Valley Campaign, showing the site of the eight battles that took place between March and June 1862. Of these, all but the first, Kernstown, were Confederate victories.

disarray as the Confederates pursued them all the way to the Upper Potomac. Now Jackson threatened Harper's Ferry.

McClellan found himself with insufficient troops to defend Washington and the government panicked at the thought that the capital was in danger. Lincoln was so worried by Jackson's successes that he sent in reinforcements, drawing men away from McClellan at Richmond. Leaving Joseph E. Johnston to defend Richmond, Jackson campaigned at the head of the valley.

CAT AND MOUSE

The New York militia was called up. Its untrained troops were despatched to Harper's Ferry and Frémont entered the Shenandoah Valley with six divisions to try and cut Jackson off. The siege of Richmond was called off and McDowell was ordered to take two divisions to Front Royal to catch Jackson.

Jackson now faced the possibility of being cut off to the rear by the combined might of McDowell and Frémont. But things did not go to plan for the Union. The weather was poor, and the ground was wet in the mountains. Jackson's better trained men eluded the Unionists and dealt a sharp blow to Frémont at Strasburg on 1 June, before withdrawing up the valley with Frémont in hot pursuit.

Establishing his headquarters at Strasburg, Jackson continued to make a mockery of Banks's numerical superiority. The Unionists went north and south, but still Jackson eluded them.

On 6 June at Harrisonburg, in the course of yet another victory over Frémont's forces, Jackson suffered a reversal when he lost one of his best cavalry commanders, Turner Ashby. Just

'Always mystify, mislead and surprise the enemy.'

MOTTO OF GENERAL THOMAS 'STONEWALL' JACKSON

two days later, though, the Confederates' morale was boosted by Ewell, who routed Frémont's army at Cross Keys. If that was not enough, Jackson hammered Shields's two brigades at Port Republic, sending Frémont and Shields into retreat.

Seeking to consolidate his victories, Jackson now considered a thrust into Pennsylvania. This never came to pass, as he received a call to relieve Richmond.

Banks moved south along the valley in pursuit of Jackson, then returned to Strasburg. Shields was despatched east to Fredericksburg to reinforce McDowell's army for the advance on Richmond which was to be caught in a pincer movement, with McClellan attacking from the east.

Fresh from their victories in the Valley Campaign, Jackson's exhausted troops now performed less well in the Seven Days Battles that concluded the Peninsula Campaign around Richmond.

Two months later, on 29–30 August 1862, Jackson regained his tactical flair when he once again faced, and defeated, a Union army at Manassas Junction, in what became known as the Second Battle of Bull Run.

A GRIEVOUS LOSS

In the spring of the following year, he and Confederate commander Robert E. Lee pulled off a brilliant victory at the Battle of Chancellorsville. However, while reconnoitring with his men during this action, he was accidentally shot and died of pneumonia eight days later. The

Confederacy suffered gravely from the loss of such a talented general. Lee likened it to 'losing my right arm'.

The Shenandoah Valley Campaign was of enormous strategic significance. Jackson operated with relatively small forces, varying from four to ten brigades. Ranged against him, in its attempt to occupy not only the Shenandoah Valley but also central Virginia, the Union army fielded forces of up to 30 brigades.

Jackson's campaign has been compared to Frederick the Great's in 1760, which was singled out by no less an authority than Clausewitz for its brilliance at deceiving and wearing down the enemy. As Jackson continued to keep eight divisions tied down, McClellan's plan to take Richmond was frustrated, and commanders in Washington were left exasperated. While Jackson lived, the Confederates appeared unbeatable.

Union general George McClellan, Stonewall Jackson's adversary and fellow West Point graduate from the class of 1846, riding through Frederick, Maryland, in September 1862.

CHANCELLORSVILLE

General Robert E. Lee *v.* General Joseph Hooker
1–4 May **1863**

IN WHAT HAS BEEN CALLED 'one of the most notable displays of generalship in history' the Confederate commander of the army of Northern Virginia, Robert E. Lee – whose father had led George Washington's light cavalry in the War of Independence – defeated a far larger Union army. Yet he suffered unsustainable losses in the process.

In 1863, the Union was winning on the Mississippi, but they had failed to secure control of the heartlands of the US eastern seaboard – Virginia, Maryland and Pennsylvania. Moreover, their navy had not managed to subdue Charleston and there was no sign of a swift solution to the problems in Tennessee.

The greatest menace was the Confederate army in Fredericksburg, which was poised to strike a blow against either Maryland or Pennsylvania. Wave upon wave of Union troops had been sent against Lee's defensive network at Fredericksburg in a manner that prefigured the trench warfare of the First World War. These assaults resulted in terrible losses.

'GIVE US VICTORIES'

Lee's job was to prevent the Union from seizing the Confederate capital at Richmond. As it was, Richmond held out for three years. The Army of the Potomac was led by Joseph ('Fightin' Joe') Hooker who had previously commanded a division. Lincoln had appointed him in place of Ambrose Burnside, the man primarily responsible for squandering lives at Fredericksburg. The president's blunt message to Hooker was: 'Give us victories.'

Hooker was not a bad general, but, as military historian Sir John Keegan has written, was especially unfortunate in being charged with the responsibility of challenging Lee in a 'contest of manoeuvre warfare, an art of which Lee was already a master and perhaps the leading expert in the Western world'.

The preliminaries began with the clearing of hospitals and the provision of arms and ammunition. Horses were in want of shoes, and adequate supplies needed to be guaranteed. Hooker had to disrupt the enemy's supply lines too, and starve them out of Fredericksburg, so he despatched his cavalry against the railway that brought them in. However, this strategy failed as a result of the swollen waters of the Rappahannock, which stymied the whole advance.

Hooker had around 125,000 men to Lee's ragged, often barefoot 60,000. He divided his army, sending three corps over the Rappahannock and four westward towards Chancellorsville, a small settlement with a large house at its centre. It should have been game, set and match to Hooker, but Lee's position, between Hooker's armies, was a strong one. Hooker now inexplicably shunned the opportunity of sending his cavalry under Major George Stoneman to cut Lee off from Richmond. Instead, in the teeth of protests by his officers, he ordered his army to fall back on Chancellorsville. His complacent, and false, assumption was that

The fatal wounding of General Thomas Jackson by fire from his own side at the climax of the Battle of Chancellorsville. Lee's greatest military triumph was marred by this tragedy.

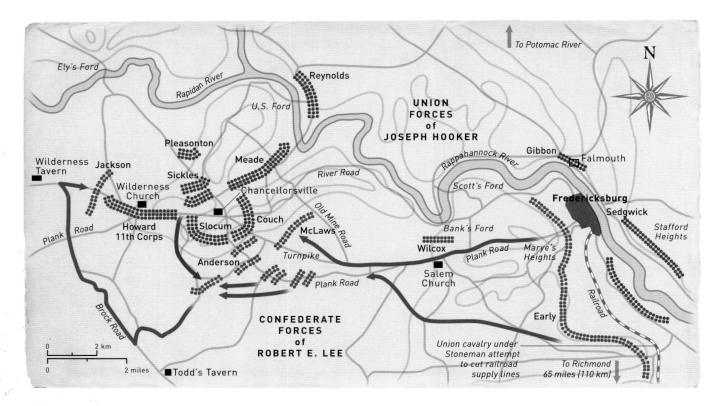

Union and Confederate forces at the Battle of Chancellorsville. This engagement has been called 'Lee's perfect battle', but for all his skill, he was aided in large measure by the incompetence of his opposite number, Joseph Hooker. Several of Hooker's subordinate generals openly questioned his decisions and refused to serve under him again.

he had the Southern commander exactly where he wanted him.

LOSING THE INITIATIVE

Worse still was Hooker's failure to take the initiative, an omission that enabled Lee to carry the fight to him. Incredibly, the Union commander allowed Lee to violate two of the cardinal rules of war – never to march an army across the enemy's front nor to divide an army in the face of the enemy – and to get away with it. Lee and Jackson were bewildered by Hooker's tactics and decided to gamble. Yet Hooker had at least chosen a site of great natural strength to make his stand, surrounded by thickets. The only flaw was that his right flank protruded from the wilderness and was vulnerable. Lee ordered Jackson to attack Hooker's flank from the rear.

Jackson set out at 7.30 a.m. on 2 May. His rearguard was attacked by two divisions commanded by General Daniel Sickles, but Sickles had no inkling of Jackson's intentions and the Confederate commander executed a feint and drew off Sickles corps in pursuit. At dusk, Jackson

reached the position of Howard's 11th Corps. Most of the soldiers were German immigrants, who were nonplussed by a sudden stampede of deer and rabbits past their position. The next they heard was the famous 'rebel yell' and Jackson's troops were upon them 'with all the fury of the wildest hailstorm'.

The Union troops somehow managed to form a line, and Jackson's men came under fire from their own men as they returned from reconnaissance, but the Confederates continued to envelop the Army of the Potomac. Hooker found himself completely outmanoeuvered.

DEMISE OF A HERO

It was then that the Confederates suffered a body blow. While out reconnoitring that evening, Jackson was hit in the arm and hand by fire from his own men, who mistook his party for Union troops. Surgeons amputated Jackson's arm. Lee mourned: 'He has lost his left hand, but I have lost my right.'

Even so, no vital organ had been hit, and the prognosis was optimistic. But just a week later, on Sunday 10 May, Jackson contracted pneumonia and died. His dying words were: 'Let us cross over the river and rest under the shade of trees.' Lee was painfully aware that the Confederacy could ill afford to lose such a great general.

A SHOCKING SETBACK

Lee now renewed the attack on Hooker, who had sent a force under John Sedgwick to take Fredericksburg. J. E. B. Stuart assumed command of Jackson's force. Hooker should have attacked, as he had the strength, but he dug in instead and shortened his line. Not only had Hooker squandered all his advantages, he recalled Sedgwick, who had been making progress at Salem Church on 3-4 May, to cover his retreat. Hooker succeeded in organizing a cavalry charge.

As they abandoned Hazel Grove, the Confederates took their place and pushed forward to take a hill called Fair View, which occasioned bitter fighting in country described as 'scraggy oaks, bushy firs, cedars and junipers, all entangled with a thick, almost impenetrable undergrowth and criss-crossed with an abundance of wild vines'.

In a murderous fight, the Confederates succeeded in taking Fair View. The rebels had brought up their artillery, which was pummelling Chancellorsville, including Chancellor House, Hooker's HQ. A shot hit one of the pillars of the house, which split in two. Hooker was leaning on it at the time and was thrown and knocked unconscious. On the 5th, he ordered his forces to fall back behind the Rappahannock, a clear admission of defeat.

Sedgwick and Hooker eventually managed to capture the heights of Fredericksburg, distracting Lee, who was

now obliged to deal with the threat to his rear. By this time, however, the Union troops were exhausted and did not press home their advantage. They lost 17,000 men to the Confederates' 13,500. But quite apart from Jackson's death, the South could not sustain such losses. Union general George Meade, who was commanding the left, saw little action and suffered only 700 casualties.

When Lincoln received news of the setback at Chancellorsville on 6 May, he paced about the White House, exclaiming: 'My God, my God. What will the country say?' Later, he held a meeting with his senior officers, but dismayed them by failing to criticize Hooker's conduct. They wanted Hooker replaced by George Meade.

Chancellorsville was a perfect Confederate victory although some credit must go to Hooker for allowing it to happen. The defeat almost brought about the downfall of Lincoln's administration.

Heavy casualties: Confederate dead piled up behind a stone defensive wall on Marye's Heights outside Fredericksburg at the Battle of Chancellorsville. Although the South emerged victorious from this fight, it did not have the manpower to sustain such major losses.

'My God, my God. What will the country say?'

US PRESIDENT ABRAHAM LINCOLN ON THE UNION DEFEAT AT CHANCELLORSVILLE

GETTYSBURG

General Robert E. Lee *v.* Major General George Meade
1–3 July **1863**

DESPITE LOSING HIS BEST MAN IN 'STONEWALL' JACKSON, Robert E. Lee was still intent on taking the war to the North by invading Pennsylvania. The last time he had tried this, he had marched into Maryland, where his progress was checked at the bloody Battle of Antietam on 17 September 1862. Lee's objectives were never wholly clear, but he may have reckoned that a victory on northern soil would persuade European nations to recognize the legitimacy of the Confederacy, or even force the Union to sue for peace.

Lee's advance up the Shenandoah Valley caused alarm in Washington. When the vacillating Union general Joseph Hooker failed to attack even after Lee had reached the Potomac River at Harper's Ferry, he was dismissed. From that moment on, Lee had a somewhat tougher nut to crack in George Meade, who had unexpectedly been given command of the Army of the Potomac on 28 June, a role he took on with reluctance. But Meade promptly seized the strategic initiative. His advance into Pennsylvania on 29–30 June threw down the gauntlet to Lee.

HALTING LEE'S INVASION

After having divided his Army of Northern Virginia, Lee reassembled it when he heard that the Army of the Potomac was approaching to try and prevent him from crossing the Susquehanna River, which runs east–west across Pennsylvania. Against his better judgement, he was forced to stand and fight at Gettysburg. He learned that Union troops were already occupying the town, which contained supplies of boots, which he badly needed. Gettysburg was a solidly built town in rolling countryside with little in the way of woodland. To the south lay two ridges: directly south was Cemetery Ridge, which

The Battle of
Gettysburg by the
American illustrator
Henry Alexander Ogden
(1856–1936). This battle
marked the turning point
of the Civil War and was
notable, even within a
conflict notorious for
heavy casualties, for the
appalling carnage it
wrought on both sides.

ended in Cemetery Hill (with a separate piece of high ground called Culp's Hill just to the east). To the southwest, Seminary Ridge ran to two hills called Round Top and Little Round Top. Before the Round Tops there was rocky land: Devil's Den, the Wheatfield and Peach Orchard.

Lee had lost his cavalry under the flamboyant General 'Jeb' Stuart, which had ridden off to pursue other quarry and not returned. In fact, Stuart had been badly bruised at the Battle of Brandy Station, the largest cavalry engagement of the entire war. Lee's army arrived from Chambersburg from the north and engaged detachments of Meade's forces outside the town. Initially, things went well for the Confederates. The Yankees were driven through Gettysburg, ending up in a concave formation with their right anchored in Culp's and Cemetery Hills and their centre on Cemetery Ridge.

A MISSED OPPORTUNITY

But the battle was fated to be another three-day event. Lee was ill, and not commanding with his usual aplomb. The Union forces retreated to assume the high ground to the south and Lee decided not to give battle that day (1 July) as the situation was too fluid.

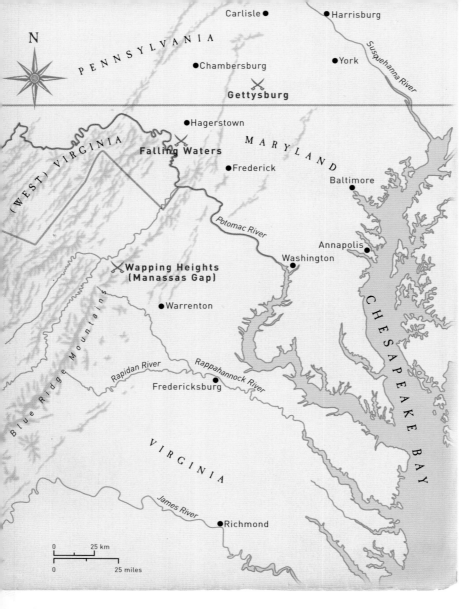

N

PENNSYLVANIA

Carlisle ●   ● Harrisburg

● Chambersburg   ● York

✕
Gettysburg

● Hagerstown   M A R Y L A N D

✕
Falling Waters   ● Frederick

(WEST) VIRGINIA   Baltimore ●

Potomac River

Annapolis ●
Washington ●

✕ **Wapping Heights
(Manassas Gap)**

● Warrenton   C H E S A P E A K E   B A Y

Blue Ridge Mountains

Rapidan River   Rappahannock River

Fredericksburg ●

V I R G I N I A

James River

● Richmond

Susquehanna River

```
0      25 km
0      25 miles
```

The retreat of Lee's forces after defeat at Gettysburg saw the Confederates fight two rearguard actions, at Falling Waters on the Potomac on 14 July and Wapping Heights nine days later. At both engagements, the Union army was held up long enough to allow the bulk of the Army of Northern Virginia to escape.

But on hearing that the bulk of Meade's forces was about to arrive, he decided to try and 'press' the Union forces southwards, and to seize Cemetery Hill before they could dig in. Lee had around 72,000 men, while the Unionists had 93,000.

The Confederate commander ordered General Richard Ewell to take Cemetery Hill 'if practicable', but the Second Corps was too disorganized and Ewell chose not to attempt the assault. Meanwhile, the Union troops consolidated their position by digging trenches. By the next morning (2 July) the opposing armies faced each other across the two parallel ridges, with a valley two-thirds of a mile (1.1 km) wide between them.

Lee lost an opportunity on the first day of the battle to capture a commanding hill.

He ordered General James Longstreet ('Lee's Old Work Horse') to launch a full-frontal attack against Cemetery Ridge. Longstreet was against the idea: he wanted to march the army south and fight in the countryside, or wait for the Unionists to attack as they had done at Fredericksburg. Longstreet maintained that they should not attack, as that was precisely what Meade wanted them to do; but Lee insisted: 'They are there in position, and I am going to whip them or they are going to whip me.'

As it was, Longstreet not only waited, he also failed to attack the sector designated by Lee. Instead of rolling up the Union positions from the south, he launched a ferocious assault on the Round Tops and the Devil's Den. Little Round Top enjoyed a commanding station over the battlefield and if artillery could be brought up it would decide the battle. It was defended by Colonel Joshua Chamberlain, and 386 men. His defence of the hill that day probably saved the Union army from defeat. After sustaining 125 casualties and running out of ammunition, he ordered his men to fix bayonets and charge, taking 300 prisoners.

Major General Daniel Sickles won his laurels when he disobeyed orders and brought his Third Corps off Cemetery Ridge to occupy the Peach Orchard–Wheatfield salient. This action doubled the Union line exactly where Lee planned to breach it.

By the end of 2 July, the Confederates had attacked north and south of the Union line. That night, at a conference with his commanders, Meade predicted that Lee would attack his centre the following day. By now, his forces were massed on the westerly left wing, strung out in a 'fishhook' formation designed to enable him to reinforce threatened sectors if need be.

PICKETT'S CHARGE

On 3 July, Lee rode along Seminary Ridge watching the Union forces opposite. He made up his mind to attack Cemetery Hill and ordered Longstreet to charge it with his own First Corps and General George Pickett's raw recruits. Longstreet openly voiced his objection to what he thought was an unworkable plan, but obediently set to work bringing up 160 guns to bombard the Union positions prior to the assault. The two-hour artillery barrage merely served to inform the Unionists of the point of attack. Pickett asked Longstreet for permission to advance, fixing on a copse of trees on Cemetery Ridge. Along with General James Pettigrew and 12,500 men, Pickett advanced in fine order across a mile (1.6 km) of ground swept by artillery and musket fire delivered by defenders safely protected by a stone wall.

'Pickett's Charge' has gone down as one of the great disasters of the battle from the Confederate point of view. General Winfield Hancock bloodily repulsed the Virginians, with Pickett losing some 85 percent of his men. The ill-fated charge has been called the 'high water mark of the Confederacy'. According to the later testimony of one of the Union soldiers defending Cemetery Hill: 'They pushed on toward the crest and merged into one crowding, rushing line, many ranks deep.' They were churned up by 'irregular, hesitating fire', shrapnel and canister. As they emerged before the Union lines they were hit by a deadly volley and appeared to melt before the defenders' eyes.

Lee's own verdict was that: 'I never saw troops behave more magnificently than Pickett's division of Virginians did today.'

AFTERMATH OF THE BATTLE

Lee's army withdrew south in pouring rain on the night of 4–5 July. Meade had won, but only two of his divisions pursued the Confederates, while his main army veered off through Maryland to try and cut off their retreat. The Confederates had been halted by the Potomac, which had burst its banks, but Meade judged them too strong to attack, and eventually they managed to slip away.

In a battle characterized by costly mistakes on both sides, nearly a third of Lee's army had been killed or wounded. Meade lost almost as many (23,000). The Union failed to press home its advantage against the Confederates, for whom the defeat at Gettysburg had been grave but not terminal, despite losing so many men. Even so, they never regained the upper hand.

Gettysburg was not Lee's finest hour. That same day Ulysses S. Grant captured Vicksburg. Modern historians tend not to give such credence to Lee's abilities as they did a century ago. Lee generally fought men of subaltern ability and without Jackson, he never again showed real brilliance.

A Union 12-pounder cannon in the National Military Park at Gettysburg, which was established to preserve the site of the famous battle.

VICKSBURG

Ulysses S. Grant *v.* Confederate forces
4 July **1863**

THE TIDE WAS TURNING AGAINST THE SOUTH. **A day after the mauling they received at Gettysburg, the key city of Vicksburg on the Mississippi fell to the army of Ulysses S. Grant. The Confederacy, now split in two, had been defeated in both the eastern and the western theatres of war and would never regain the initiative.**

Ulysses Simpson Grant did not seem like natural leadership material, graduating from West Point without great distinction and later only narrowly avoiding a court-martial for drunkenness. Yet he rose to become the Union's best general in the Civil War and went on to serve as president of the United States (1869–77). As well as being a fine battlefield commander, Grant also had a keen understanding of the wider strategy of modern warfare. He knew that it was as important to destroy an enemy's economic resources as it was to kill its men.

'VICKSBURG IS THE KEY'
For some time, the Confederacy had been losing its key fortresses. The first actions that brought Grant to the attention of both sides in the Civil War were his seizures of Forts Henry and Donelson on a tributary of the Mississippi in February 1862. By the summer of 1863, following the surrender of New Orleans over a year before, Vicksburg and Fort Hudson were the only key positions that it retained on the Mississippi.

However, a naval assault alone was not enough to take Vicksburg; it required the assistance of a large army on the river's eastern bank. Moreover, given its location at the heart of Confederate

General Ulysses S. Grant (right foreground) and his staff survey mining operations at the siege of Vicksburg. This fanciful impression of the action was produced by the Chicago printmakers Kurz and Allison in 1888.

territory in central Mississippi, Grant would first have to fight his way through to the city before he could besiege it. Its capture was vital; while Vicksburg remained in Confederate hands, all Union commerce with New Orleans was blocked. As Lincoln stated: 'Vicksburg is the key.'

A TOUGH NUT TO CRACK
The problem of Vicksburg was the site, on a high bluff on a hairpin bend on the right bank of the Mississippi just before the river forks, the left-hand side heading up to Milliken's Bend and the right becoming the Yazoo with its many bayous. This seemingly unassailable position had earned it the nickname of the 'Gibraltar of the West'. The Confederates had built huge earthworks, but the fort itself was on the steep Walnut Hills with their woods and ravines. The bottoms of the ravines were an impassable wilderness overgrown with trees some 12–15 metres (40–50 ft) high. The approaches were rendered perilous by the swamps and bayous – oxbow lakes formed after the great river changed course, which dried out in the summer but became swamps in the spring. The difficulties were compounded by the notoriously humid summer weather and huge swarms of mosquitoes.

The fort had been constructed in the tradition of Vauban with redoubts, redans, lunettes and artillery platforms. It was commanded by General John C. Pemberton. Thus far, all assaults on it had failed, including one by General William T. Sherman, under Grant's command, in late 1862. In an attempt to bypass the fort and allow gunboats to reach the main course of the Mississippi, Grant even came up with the impractical idea of excavating canals. But when he tried cutting a channel below Milliken's Bend, the spring floods all but drowned the diggers. Elsewhere the canal-builders' efforts were impeded by huge trees in their path. After months of hard labour, the project had to be abandoned.

ARMY–NAVY OPERATION

In the face of these frustrations, in April 1863 Grant conceived a new plan to take the city from the east and south, where it was only lightly defended. To move his men from their position north of Vicksburg without exposing them to the 14 miles (23 km) of Confederate gun emplacements on the right bank, Grant marched them down the west bank of the river. His idea was to rejoin the Mississippi below Vicksburg and ferry his troops to the east bank.

> '*The fall of the Confederacy was settled when Vicksburg fell.*'
>
> ULYSSES S. GRANT

Grant received intelligence that the best place to cross was at Bruinsburg below Grand Gulf. On the night of 16–17 April Union Flag Officer David Porter ran the gauntlet of the guns at Vicksburg, with his gunboats stacked with bales of cotton: three got through, one was sunk. More vessels followed and by 30 April there were enough ships down river from Vicksburg to begin transporting the Army of the Tennessee across to Bruinsburg.

Meanwhile, Colonel Benjamin Grierson mounted a cavalry raid on the South as a diversion, riding 600 miles (966 km) and devastating central Mississippi.

Once across the Mississippi, Grant sent two of his corps under generals McPherson and McClernand to face Joseph E. Johnston, who was busy assembling a new army of around 20,000 troops at the state capital, Jackson. Living off the land and moving fast with no supply line, these forces took the Confederates by surprise. On 14 May, Jackson was taken and burned. Two days later the Union struck again at Champion Hill, 20 miles (32 km) east of Vicksburg. Against Confederate president Jefferson Davis's advice, Pemberton had led his large force out of the city to confront Grant in the open field. Roundly beaten, Pemberton now fell back. After another clash at Big Black River Bridge on the 17th, he ran for Vicksburg and safety.

Having cut Vicksburg off from its hinterland, Grant invested the fort on 19 May. Anticipating a swift victory, he poured men into the assault, but after sustaining 3,000 casualties, was forced to call off the attack four days later.

The Vicksburg garrison was hoping for relief from Johnston, but he never appeared. Everything was in short supply: bread, flour, meat and vegetables. The inhabitants ate mule, peanuts and rats while Grant bombarded the town from boats and land-based cannon. On 25 May, Pemberton declared a truce to bury the dead. There was a certain amount of fraternization throughout the siege, with exchanges of coffee and tobacco.

UNDERMINING THE FORT

Now sappers were sent in to undermine the fort and dig trenches and parallels. Each time they advanced the cannon came closer. By 7 June, the closest battery to the fort was some 70 metres (75 yds) away.

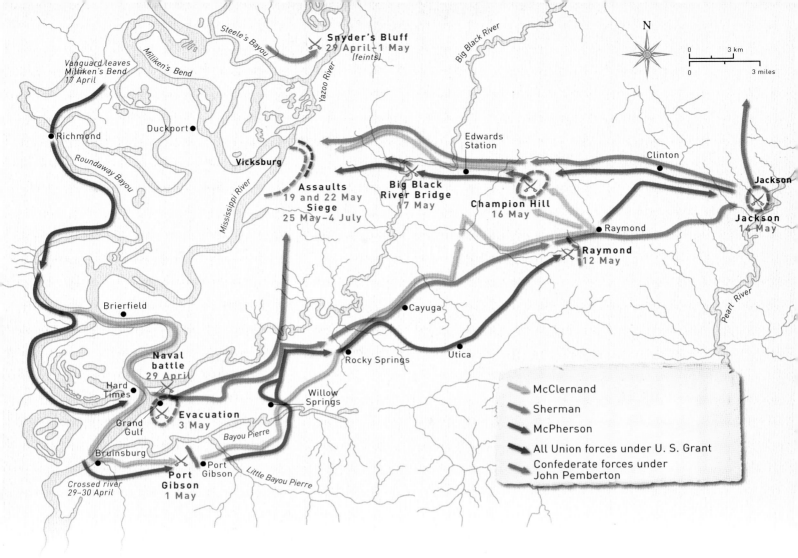

To protect them from defensive fire, the sappers worked behind cotton bales, but the Confederates set fire to them. By 22 June, the sappers had reached the base of the Fort Hill breastwork. Colonel Andrew Hickenloper, devised a way of tunnelling under the Confederate position and packing the underground chamber they created with over 900 kg (2,000 lbs) of explosive. On 25 June, it was detonated and most of Fort Hill went up with it. But, the defenders had realized the danger and erected a new parapet, from which they continued to pour fire down on the besiegers. The assault was called off.

Tunnelling resumed, and a new shaft was finished on 1 July. Another explosion blew the Third Louisiana redoubt sky high and with it the slaves who had acted as Confederate counterminers. They were all killed bar one, who was thrown through the air and landed behind Union lines.

Pemberton was building boats in the hope of escaping. His men were starving and close to mutiny. Grant sensed surrender was inevitable, and even when he heard of Johnston's approach he dismissed the idea of his small force being able to raise the siege. By 3 July, white flags began to appear on the parapet. Two Confederate officers brought a demand for a ceasefire to spare what Pemberton called 'effusion of blood'. At first Grant was inclined to accept nothing less than unconditional surrender. He relented, however, and allowed the officers to retain their swords; 31,600 paroles were written out and the Union soldiers shared their rations with the defeated Southerners. News of Vicksburg's fall led General Frank Gardner to capitulate at Port Hudson on 8 July.

Grant's Vicksburg campaign of April–July 1863. The capture of this fortified city gave the Union control of the Mississippi and effectively sliced the Confederacy in two, by cutting off Arkansas, Louisiana and Texas from the rest of the secessionist states.

KÖNIGGRÄTZ

Helmuth von Moltke *v.* Ludwig von Benedek
3 July **1866**

IN THE SEVEN WEEKS' WAR OF 1866 between Prussia and Austria, Prussian forces were nominally commanded by King William I, but he boasted a brilliant chief of staff in Helmuth von Moltke. Following his appointment in 1857, Moltke had completely reformed the General Staff, turning it into the intellectual élite of the Prussian army. Like Clausewitz, Moltke believed in the complete annihilation of the enemy. He was complemented by Prussia's 'Iron Chancellor' Otto von Bismarck, who regarded war as an adjunct to diplomacy.

The period since the demise of Napoleon had seen many new developments in the art and science of waging war. In particular, Moltke had seized upon the opportunity offered by the railways for transporting troops and bringing them fresh to battle. He was also quick to equip his infantrymen with the new breech-loading, bolt-action Dreyse needle-gun, which trebled their rate of fire. His preferred strategy was to begin a campaign by splitting his forces, following his own precept of 'march apart and strike together'. One army had the job of 'fixing' the enemy while the other two manoeuvred against its flanks. Like many military planners, Moltke longed for a Cannae – an encirclement and annihilation – but Königgrätz failed to live up to this ideal.

Prussian infantrymen in action at the Battle of Königgrätz, from a watercolour by Carl Röchling. Their Dreyse needle-guns had a far superior rate of fire to the Austrians' muzzle-loading weapons, and played a major role in deciding the outcome.

LOOMING CATASTROPHE

In the struggle for supremacy among the German-speaking states, Prussia's main rival Austria not only lacked a leader of Moltke's calibre, but theirs was a hopelessly old-fashioned army defending a moribund political system. With no divisions or clear chain of command, hidebound by rigid thinking in the upper echelons and poorly equipped, Austrian forces were no match for the Prussian war machine.

Prussia had quickly seen off Austria's allies in Hanover and Electoral Hessen. Combined Prussian strength was around 245,000 men, who faced a slightly smaller Austrian-Saxon army at the fortress of Königgrätz in Bohemia (the action is also sometimes called the Battle of Sadowa). The Austrians had one advantage in their excellent cannon, which they possessed in greater number than the Prussians. But the Austrian field marshal Ludwig von Benedek was not confident of victory, and on 30 June telegraphed his emperor, Francis Joseph, to advise him to sue for peace: 'a military catastrophe is unavoidable.'

The Prussian army was divided into three: the Army of the Elbe, under the command of General Herwath von Bittenfeld, was advancing from Torgau; the First Army commanded by Prince Frederick Charles was coming from the Lausitz; while the Second Army, led by crown prince Frederick, had departed from Neisse in Silesia.

On 29 June, Herwath rapidly disposed of the Saxons at Gitschin outside Dresden. By 1 July, the armies were within a day's

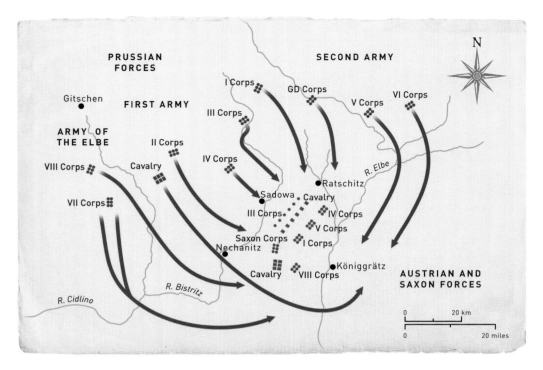

Moltke's gamble
of uniting three armies on the field of battle, made possible by the new mobility offered by the railway, paid off at Königgrätz. But it was a close-run thing, as one of his armies arrived late, thus jeopardizing the operation.

march of one another. On 2 July, Moltke attempted to telegraph the crown prince to tell him to join up with the other two elements of his force, but found the apparatus out of order. Instead riders were sent the 20 miles (32 km) to deliver the message.

Moltke's forces had marched through heavy rain, arriving at Königgrätz on 3 July. It was still raining on the morning of the battle, and one of his three armies lagged behind, giving the Prussians a total strength of 135,000. Benedek did not, however, exploit this weakness by ordering an immediate attack. He even blocked the suggestion of General von Mollinary that he should outflank the Prussian armies before the arrival of the third army.

ARTILLERY V. NEEDLE-GUN

As the Prussians took up position west of the River Bistritz, the Austrian artillery opened fire, pinning down the Prussian right. Prince Frederick Charles took the initiative to launch his 75,000 infantry against 180,000 well-entrenched Austrians. Advancing through the forest, the Prussian centre was checked by the Austrians and driven back. At this stage of the battle, the Austrian artillery was

proving so effective that the Prussian army might have been defeated by a well-managed cavalry charge. Ludwig von Benedek would not sanction this, however.

The Skoda cannon in the Austrian batteries had a better range than the Prussian guns. In contrast, once the Prussians were able to advance far enough, their needle-guns really came into their own.

By 11.00 a.m., the Prussian centre had been pushed back, but the Austrians had exposed their right flank to Prussian fire. The Second Army arrived by 2 p.m., and an hour and a half later all three Prussian armies were advancing. At 2.30 p.m., the crown prince was in position with 100,000 men and the Prussian artillery was now close enough to pound the Austrian centre. The Prussians had pushed into the Austrian flank. With the situation confused and in flux, Frederick Charles asked the crown prince commanding the Second Army to lend him assistance.

Moltke now decided that the whole of the crown prince's army should strike the Austrian flank. The chief of staff observed the battle from a hill, in the company of Bismarck and King William: emblematic of the close co-operation between Prussia's military, monarchical and political leaders. Periodically the Austrian artillery and cavalry rallied. Gifted commander though he was, Moltke was aided immeasurably in this engagement by the poor leadership of Benedek.

The Austrian North Army was now hit from all sides, and despite the bravery of both the cavalry and the excellent artillery, there was no way of averting disaster. General Hiller von Gärtringen and the First Foot reached the Austrian guns and the defenders took to their heels. At that stage, the Austrians had lost their guns and the high ground and their centre had been rolled up. Then the Second Army broke though Austrian lines and the Army of the Elbe broke the Saxons on the Austrian left as Ratschitz fell. At 3 p.m. the Austrian cavalry covered a general retreat.

PRUSSIAN SUPREMACY

With the Elbe at his rear, Benedek had no way of retreating; at this juncture the engagement might well have turned into a Cannae. Moltke confidently assured his sovereign: 'Your Majesty will win today not only a battle but a campaign.' But in the event, Moltke was slow to pursue the Austrians, as his troops became bogged down in mud. In addition, cholera and exhaustion were widespread in the Prussian ranks.

The failure to rout the enemy may also have had a political motive: Bismarck was certainly keen to impress on the Austrians their subordinate role in German politics, but, mindful of their potential usefulness as future allies, did not want them to smart from a complete humiliation.

By 6 p.m., Prussian victory was assured. The crown prince and his father greeted one another in a silent embrace and the king hung the *Pour le mérite* order around his son's neck.

The Austrians fell back across the Elbe. They lost a total of 44,000 men killed, wounded or missing, with half of these taken prisoner. The Prussians suffered 9,000 casualties, though the number of dead was comparatively light (99 officers and 1,830 men).

Now Bismarck had his chance to dictate a peace on his terms, which would leave Austria and her allies only lightly chastised yet also further his aim of excluding Austria from a Prussian-dominated 'small Germany' (*Kleindeutschland*). Reflecting on his struggle to prevail over the hawks of the General Staff, he wrote to his wife: 'I have the thankless task of pouring water into the bubbling wine and making it clear that we don't live alone in Europe but with three other powers who hate and envy us.'

The Austrian emperor agreed to an armistice on 22 July. At Prague, Austria renounced its share in Schleswig-Holstein and Prussia further expanded its portfolio of German provinces with the acquisition of Hanover and parts of Hesse and Saxony. Politically, the battle had huge consequences not just for Germany but for the whole world: not only was Austria forced out of Germany, but it was obliged to concede equal status in the empire to the Hungarians thereby initiating the final phase of the Habsburg empire. The victory Moltke clinched over the French four years later at Sedan in 1870 would lead to the creation of the Second German empire on 18 January 1871.

Commemorative medal struck in honour of the Prussian victory at Königgrätz (Sadowa). Diplomatic intervention by the French emperor Napoleon III led to peace negotiations between the Austrians and Prussians. Four years later, it was France's turn to be crushed by Prussian military might.

'I have the thankless task of pouring water into the bubbling wine and making it clear that we don't live alone in Europe but with three other powers who hate and envy us.'

OTTO VON BISMARCK ON HIS DELICATE DIPLOMACY AFTER THE SEVEN WEEKS' WAR

TEL-EL-KEBIR

Sir Garnet Wolseley *v.* Arabi Pasha
13 September 1882

THE CRIMEAN WAR OF 1853–56 exposed major flaws in the organization and provision of the British army. The practice of purchasing commissions rather than awarding them on the basis of talent produced a rash of incompetent aristocratic commanders. Moreover, the army's equipment was in a parlous state. There was clearly dire need of reform. Salvation was to come in the unlikely form of Garnet Joseph Wolseley, a Protestant grocer's son from Goldenbridge, Inchicore, County Dublin in Ireland.

Wolseley's father had in fact been a major before turning to commerce; even so, a more unexpected rise from such an obscure background to the rank of field marshal and overall command of the British army would be hard to imagine even today, let alone in the late 19th century. His progress was partly due to the faith placed in him by Edward Cardwell, the reforming minister of war in Gladstone's liberal government of 1868–74. Cardwell's improvements remained in force until they were supplemented by further reforms under Lord Haldane in 1906–10.

One of the central provisions of the Cardwell Reforms was the creation of military bases worldwide to deal with a growing number of wars and insurrections, as the British empire expanded by some 100,000 square miles (260,000 sq km) every year. Wolseley, who won his commission in the infantry in 1852, made his name in the colonies. He served in Burma, the Crimea, in India during the Mutiny and in China. Most important of all was the experience he gained over nine years' service in Canada from 1861 onwards. His suppression of Riel's Rebellion in Manitoba (1869–70) gained him a reputation as an efficient and forward-looking commander. In 1862, while stationed in North America, he visited the Confederacy and was greatly impressed by Stonewall Jackson and Robert E. Lee.

Bird's-eye view of the Battle of Tel-el-Kebir. On the left ot this contemporary illustration can be seen the Sweetwater Canal and the Cairo to Ismailia railway line, both of which Wolseley used to bring up supplies before the battle.

In 1873, Wolseley took command of the campaign against the Ashanti King Koffee in present-day Nigeria. This campaign gave rise to the notorious 'Wolseley Ring', a coterie of like-minded fellow officers that was greatly resented by those outside the charmed circle.

Lampooned by W.S. Gilbert in the libretto of *The Pirates of Penzance* as 'the very model of a modern major-general', it was Wolseley who nevertheless made good the mistakes committed by Viscount Chelmsford in the Zulu War. Chelmsford had allowed a British army to be massacred by Zulu warriors at

'... the very model of a modern major-general'

W.S. GILBERT MOCKS WOLSELEY

Isandlwana. He captured King Cetshwayo and defeated Chief Sekukuni. In 1884, Gladstone despatched Wolseley to the Sudan to rescue General Gordon. This mission was not crowned with success, however: Gordon was killed in Khartoum in 1885, two days before the relief force arrived.

TROUBLE IN EGYPT

Muhammad Tawfiq Pasha – still nominally the khedive, or Ottoman Turkish viceroy of Egypt – came to the throne there in 1879. He had long taken a pro-Western stance, notably in his support for the excavation of the Suez Canal. The canal, planned by the French engineer Ferdinand de Lesseps, had opened in 1869. It created a short-cut for shipping between Europe and Asia, obviating the long and perilous route around the Cape of Good Hope. Britain realized the vital importance of the canal in defending its empire in India, and used its financial muscle to purchase the khedive Ismail Pasha's shares in the enterprise in 1875. Both France and Britain made it clear to the khedive that there would be no interference in Egypt's affairs unless the country descended into anarchy.

But as opposition to Western involvement in Egypt grew, to which the khedive responded weakly, the British and French lobbied for Ismail Pasha's dismissal by the Ottomans, who duly obliged. Yet his son Tawfiq proved no more competent than his father. The country continued to amass a large foreign debt. Meanwhile, crop failures spread misery among Egypt's poor. All these factors, compounded by the khedive's supine attitude to the Western powers, prompted army officers under Colonel Ahmad Arabi Pasha to stage an uprising in January 1881. Arabi demanded an end to the privileges enjoyed by Europeans and Turko-Circassians and halted payments to the canal's foreign bondholders. Britain and France responded by issuing a joint note assuring the khedive that he could count on their aid in the event of internal unrest. A crisis conference was held in Istanbul, while an Anglo-French naval squadron hovered off the Egyptian coast.

Tensions ran high. Heading a nationalist administration as minister of war, Arabi insisted on upholding Egyptian autonomy. With French and British interests under threat, the Ottoman sultan saw a chance to regain his lost province. An attempt by the khedive to force Arabi to resign caused rioting in Alexandria on 11 June, directed at the European colony. Fifty Europeans were killed, including French sailors, and the British consul was severely wounded. Elsewhere, mobs attacked Greeks and Jews. The British prime minister William Gladstone came under intense pressure to act. Two of his ministers threatened to resign before he gave orders to bombard Alexandria. He did this with much reluctance, as he detested war.

The Egyptians began to fortify the harbour. On 3 July, the UK government instructed Admiral Seymour to open fire and silence the batteries if this work continued. Accordingly, at 7.10 a.m. on 11 July, HMS *Alexandra* shelled and destroyed the harbour guns. Further riots ensued; the city was set ablaze and more people killed. The khedive sought refuge on one of Seymour's vessels and Arabi seized power. On 13 July, a British naval force occupied Alexandria.

BRITAIN GOES IT ALONE

Despite being majority shareholders in the canal, the French had declined to take part in the bombardment and their fleet had sailed away. Gladstone, an ardent opponent of colonial expansion, now faced the unwelcome prospect of a full armed response to the emergency, leading inevitably to military occupation and annexation of Egypt. Queen Victoria exerted pressure on the Liberal prime minister (whom she disliked intensely) and her eldest son 'Bertie' – the future King Edward VII – volunteered to fight.

The scene was set for a full-scale invasion. Under prime minister Léon Gambetta, the French had been keen to co-operate with Britain in Egypt, but his cabinet fell in January 1882. The new administration was canvassed for their support, but declined to act. When the news broke Egyptian bonds leaped 35 percent on the stock market. A British 'expeditionary force' under Sir Garnet Wolseley was duly sent to Egypt in July.

With 35,000 men, Wolseley now found himself in command of the largest force despatched from Britain since the Crimean War. The bulk of his army came from Britain and was ferried to Malta and Cyprus, while 7,000 Indians arrived in Aden. The Prince of Wales was reined in; the royal family was represented instead by his brother,

Detailed layout of the opposing armies' deployment at the Battle of Tel-el-Kebir. Rather than risk a long, tiring outflanking movement through the hot desert, Wolseley decided to launch a surprise head-on attack on Arabi Pasha's position.

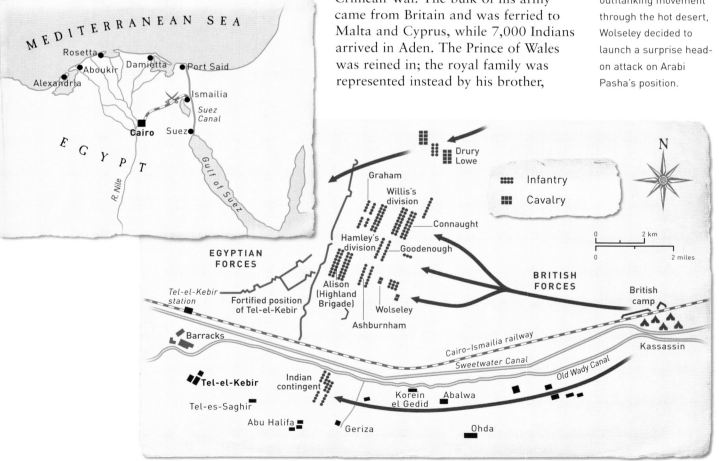

British Artillery Entering the Enemy Lines at Tel-el-Kebir, an illustration from *Huthinson's Story of the British Nation* (1923). The battle was over in an hour and Arabi's men took to their heels with Wolseley's cavalry in hot pursuit.

Prince Arthur, duke of Connaught (a godson of the duke of Wellington), commanding a Guards brigade.

PARRY AND THRUST

The British tried to march directly on Cairo, but their progress was halted for five weeks at Kafr-el-Dawwer, a well-fortified position bristling with modern artillery made by the German firm Krupp. The British deceived Arabi into thinking that they would not make the canal their objective. Once his defences were down, 40 British warships sailed into the waterway and took up defensive positions while Wolseley deployed his troops.

Wolseley used a number of feints to dupe Arabi into believing the attack would come from the west. His principal aim was to prevent the Egyptians from attempting to block the Suez Canal. Arabi

took the bait and thought that Wolseley would disembark at Aboukir, when in fact he headed for Port Said at the northern end of the canal. Marines and sailors secured key positions in the city. Meanwhile the army reached Ismailia, mid-way down the canal, on 20 August. Here a railway link allowed Wolseley to bring up supplies before the final advance. By 6 September, he was in full control of the canal.

The army marched to Kassassin on 24 August and from there to the well-fortified Egyptian positions at Tel-el-Kebir. An unexpected attack on Kassassin caused some casualties among the British forces. The Egyptians attempted a breakout on 28 August, but this was scattered by a moonlit charge by the Household Cavalry. Another advance was successfully repulsed on 8 September.

British and Egyptian forces met in a dawn engagement on 13 September after Wolseley had marched his troops across the desert by night. The ground was as flat and as hard as a parade-ground. Wolseley had worked out the distance that had to be covered before dawn broke, which was just before 5 a.m. They struck camp at 1.30 in the morning and marched in silence, guided by the stars. The Egyptians spotted the Highlanders as they came through the dawn light and there was a fierce fight, the units in the van mounting a bayonet charge. Arabi had about 20,000 men and 75 guns to Wolseley's 16,000. Arabi Pasha's army at Tel-al-Kebir was easily defeated. Around 2,000 Egyptians were killed to 57 Britons, 45 of them from major general Alison's Highland Brigade.

A BRITISH PROTECTORATE

The next day the British entered Cairo, occupied the city and restored Tawfiq as a puppet ruler. Arabi was captured in mid-October and exiled to Ceylon where he was pardoned in 1901.

Wolseley was made a full general and named Baron Wolseley of Cairo. Prince Arthur, duke of Connaught, was awarded the Order of the Bath, and the queen distributed 330 other medals after Tel-el-Kebir, including decorations for three Maltese soldiers and a number of Indians. As a memento of the campaign, Victoria was given a Turkish carpet taken from Arabi's tent, which Arthur had slept on after the battle.

In the British parliament, the Conservative leader Lord Salisbury taunted Gladstone: 'You have not held up the khedive; you have picked up the khedive. He must be sustained by that which is the only thing left upright in that land – namely, the power of Great Britain.' As a direct result of Britain's intervention, Egypt became a protectorate of the British empire, and most importantly securing safe passage for its vessels through the Suez Canal.

'You have not held up the khedive; you have picked up the khedive. He must be sustained by that which is the only thing left upright in that land – namely, the power of Great Britain.'

LORD SALISBURY TAUNTS GLADSTONE FOR HIS INTERVENTION IN EGYPT

TANNENBERG

THE SECOND BATTLE OF TANNENBERG was mythologized by German nationalists as revenge for the defeat of the Teutonic Knights by Polish, Russian and Lithuanian forces at the same site in 1410. In fact, the second battle was fought near Frögenau, over 20 miles (32 km) from Tannenberg. But leaving aside its manipulation for political ends, the battle was a remarkable feat of arms by its principal architects, the Prussian generals Paul von Hindenburg and Erich Ludendorff.

Russian machine-gunners at the Battle of Tannenberg. By the outbreak of war, both Russian and German forces were equipped with home-produced copies of the Maxim gun. Yet such weapons proved more effective in the trench warfare of the Western Front than during the mobile war in the east.

The myth of Tannenberg was compounded by events that took place before and at the end of the Second World War. When Hindenburg died in 1934, the decision was taken to bury the former president of the Weimar Republic at the place of his greatest triumph. As Nazi forces retreated through East Prussia in the spring of 1945, his monument was deliberately blown up and his body shipped to the heart of Germany to prevent the Red Army from seeking revenge on his bones or the memorial stones. Some of the stones remained, however, and were used to build a 'gift' by the Soviets to the people of Poland – the Palace of Culture in Warsaw.

MAN OF THE MOMENT

Hindenburg was a member of the General Staff that had made up the intellectual élite of the Prussian army since Moltke's reforms of the late 1850s. He was also a *Junker*, part of the Prussian nobility that once formed the backbone of the country's officer class. By contrast, his younger fellow commander Erich Ludendorff was a more typical product of his age and culture. From a middle-class background, his aggressive, Pan-German

sentiments were widely reflected in Wilhelmine Germany. By the outbreak of the First World War, the *Junkertum* represented just 13 percent of the officer caste, although they were concentrated in certain regiments (not unlike the preponderance of nobility in the British cavalry and guards).

Born in the Grand Duchy of Posen in 1865, Ludendorff attended cadet school and the academy at Lichterfelde. He was commissioned in the infantry at Wesel. Earning glowing plaudits all round, his natural abilities led him to the *Kriegsakademie*. There he gained the patronage of influential military leaders, the younger Helmuth von Moltke and Graf Alfred von Schlieffen, who in 1905 appointed him to the General Staff and secured him a key position in the department of mobilization. Ludendorff worked on the minutiae of the Schlieffen Plan, which was devised to allow Germany to fight a war on two fronts. In the shifting alliances that characterized the prelude to the First World War, this predicamant seemed ever more likely; Russia had made common cause with France and Britain.

The plan envisaged one enemy being effectively knocked out of the war in a

German infantry on the march through a war-ravaged town in East Prussia in the autumn of 1914. The Schlieffen Plan had envisaged that a swift knockout blow to the French in the West would release large numbers of German troops to overwhelm the Russians. In the event, the Germans were forced to fight on two fronts simultaneously.

Russians made progress in the east, panicky Prussians fled west, giving credence to the idea that if the enemy were not stopped, they would soon reach Berlin.

In August 1914, two Russian armies crossed the River Niemen with 800,000 men and 1,700 guns, intending to cut the German army off at Königsberg and head for the Vistula. As the former chief of the general staff Schlieffen had predicted, they split in two, remaining divided and out of touch with one another north and south of the 50-mile (80-km) chain of the Masurian Lakes. Schlieffen's strategy against the Russian threat was to deal with the lesser evil first, then withdraw the troops as quickly as possible to hit the other army.

Yet like many supposedly perfect staff plans, this one was scrambled in execution. The Russians arrived in far greater strength than the defending German Eighth Army: the Germans had 210,000 soldiers and 600 guns. The Russians had a chance of success. It was therefore decided to screen Russian general Paul von Rennenkampf's First Army, attacking from the northeast and shifting the Eighth Army's divisions to hit the left flank of Alexander Samsonov's 35-division-strong Second Army. The troops had to be transported around 100 miles (160 km) by train in difficult conditions due to the streams of German refugees fleeing west.

short time before the armies could be transferred to the other front *en masse*. The key to the strategy was rapid mobilization and deployment.

NOT GOING TO PLAN

In the opening act of the First World War, Ludendorff was responsible for the capture of the forts at Liège in Belgium, a task he executed with considerable aplomb. However, in a move not foreseen by the Schlieffen Plan, the Russians did not wait for the Germans to knock out the French and British before advancing on Germany's eastern borders in strength.

On the Western Front, the German advance was going smoothly, but as the

A DYNAMIC DUO

On 20 August, the Germans beat the Russians at Stallüponen before being beaten themselves at Gumbinnen, in the far east of East Prussia. However, the Russians failed to follow up their victory; Eighth Army commander Maximilian von Prittwitz had spotted the possibility of hiving off some of the forces north of the Masurian Lakes to relieve those to the south, while leaving a mere screen to face

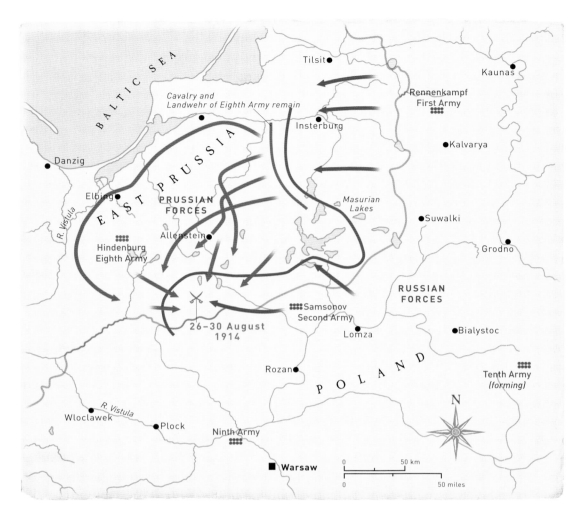

The map shows East Prussia and surrounding areas including the Baltic Sea, Danzig, Tilsit, Kaunas, Elbing, Insterburg, Rennenkampf First Army, Kalvarya, Masurian Lakes, Suwalki, Allenstein, Hindenburg Eighth Army, Grodno, Samsonov Second Army, 26–30 August 1914, Lomza, Bialystoc, Rozan, Tenth Army (forming), Wloclawek, Plock, Ninth Army, Warsaw, and Poland.

The clash between German and Russian forces in East Prussia in 1914, culminating in the devastating Battle of Tannenberg and the equally heavy Russian defeat at the Masurian Lakes. Ludendorff's staff officer Colonel Max Hoffmann came up with the idea of naming the Frögenau engagement 'Tannenberg' as a deliberate allusion to an historic setback for 'Teutonic' values at the hands of 'Slavs'.

the Russians. But his wider strategy was to abandon East Prussia entirely and withdraw behind the Vistula. This plan caused such great consternation at German Army HQ in Koblenz that Franco-Prussian War veteran Paul von Hindenburg was recalled from retirement to replace Prittwitz. Ludendorff was appointed as his chief of staff. They were given the assignment of seeing off the Russian army that had invaded East Prussia and was laying waste to everything that came within its reach.

Hindenburg and Ludendorff arrived at German eastern HQ, in the former fortress of the Teutonic Knights at Marienburg (Malbork), on 23 August. Moltke insisted on taking three corps and a cavalry division away from the Western Front to fortify the line, against Ludendorff's wishes.

On the 24th Hindenburg and Ludendorff went forward to consult Friedrich von Scholtz, who was commanding the XX Corps and who doubted his ability to fend off Samsonov. Employing methods reminiscent of the elder Moltke, the Germans used the railway network to deploy their armies at speed. They were, however, delayed by the late arrival of their artillery. Meanwhile the Russians moved further into the trap that Ludendorff was preparing for them. Ludendorff envisaged a battle of annihilation, so that he could transfer all his forces north to counter the threat posed by Rennenkampf's First Army.

On 22 August advance units of Samsonov's army came into contact with German forces. On 23, August the Germans retreated. Samsonov's superior,

Russian chief of staff Yakov Zhilinski, ordered him to attack, but the Germans held their ground, picking off the Russians as they advanced across the potato fields. One Russian regiment had nine company commanders killed out of 16.

Ludendorff issued orders to Hermann von François's I Corps to attack the Russian left on 25 August. He refused, saying his men were not ready and he needed more artillery. Not surprisingly, Ludendorff was incensed. He drove to see François on the 26th. In the meantime, encouraged by François's inaction, Samsonov was attacking the German centre, while Otto von Below and August von Mackensen were grappling with the Russian right. François was prevailed upon to obey orders. The German centre was thinned out while the strength was transferred to the wings. That day, Hindenburg learned from an intercept that Rennenkampf was not going to relieve Samsonov, but instead would advance to besiege Königsberg.

ENCIRCLED AND DESTROYED

On 27 August, the German I Corps destroyed the Russian Second Army's left while two more corps hammered General Artamonov's I Corps at Usdau on their right, putting the Russians to flight. By evening François was in Soldau, behind the Russian left. Undeterred, the Russian commander drove forward with his centre, pushing back Scholtz's XX Corps. However, this fatally exposed his flanks to François to the south and Mackensen and Scholtz to the north. By the 28th, the Germans had encircled the Russians.

Ludendorff now saw the possibility of a perfect encirclement. He ordered François to push on to Willenberg and Mackensen to attack the other wing. By now, the battlefield stretched across 60 miles (100 km) of marshes, woods and lakes. Despite there being no proper roads, just sandy paths, Mackensen and François were able to join up to the rear of the Russian centre. In part, they did this by disobeying Ludendorff's orders yet again. Samsonov was surrounded. At that point, Hindenburg's forces hit the Russians head on. They panicked and threw down their arms, but found themselves caught in a trap. In the battle, 50,000 Russians were killed and 90,000 captured. Only 10,000 men escaped. Samsonov was later found dead, supposedly by his own hand.

The master strategists Ludendorff (right) and Paul von Hindenburg discuss operations. Illustration by Hugo Vogel, from the 1928 German publication *Schlachten des Weltkrieges* ('Battles of the Great War').

TARNISHED REPUTATION

German losses amounted to just 5,000 killed and 7,000 wounded. A month later the Russian First Army was badly mauled at the Battle of the Masurian Lakes. Although there had been plenty of mishaps along the way, Ludendorff was able to present the two battles as a perfectly executed general staff strategy, a new 'Cannae' (which to some extent it was). But like Cannae, it failed to clinch the war.

The Eastern Front continued to be a mobile war, whereas on the Western Front advances rapidly stagnated into trench warfare. In Germany, the victories of Hindenburg and Ludendorff brought relief and a new-found belief in the invincibility of German arms.

Ludendorff is dishonoured by his later history. His role in wresting effective power from the kaiser and concentrating it in High Command and his own person; his engineering of the dismissal of Chancellor Bethmann-Hollweg, who opposed unrestricted submarine warfare; his behaviour during the abdication crisis, in which he sought to deny his own part in Germany's defeat; and his flirtation with Hitler and the Nazis, all tarnished his reputation as a commander in the field. He died in 1937. The Third Reich gave him a state funeral.

Defeated and downtrodden, captured Russian soldiers assemble at the railway station at Tilsit in East Prussia on 27 September 1914 for transportation west. The leadership of the Imperial Russian Army in the First World War was nothing short of woeful.

ANZAC COVE

Allied expeditionary force *v.* Turkish forces
25 April 1915–9 January 1916

IN THE FIRST MAJOR AMPHIBIOUS ASSAULT in history, in 1915 British and French warships attempted to take control of the Dardanelles Straits separating Europe and Asia. The Allies hoped to push their way through the Dardanelles, come to Russia's assistance and put Germany's ally Turkey out of the war. It would also provide a useful distraction from the Western Front. The full panoply of modern warfare was deployed in this elaborate operation, including aircraft (a prototype aircraft carrier saw action at Gallipoli), aerial photography, purpose-built landing craft, radio communications, artificial harbours and submarines. Turkish resistance proved unexpectedly strong, and the landings ended in bloody, ignominious failure. Yet important lessons were learned that paid dividends for the invasion of Normandy in June 1944 and even the landings at San Carlos Bay during the Falklands War of 1982.

The Dardanelles are less than 30 miles (48 km) long, and at their narrowest, under a mile (1.6 km) wide: here ships were in the greatest danger from shore batteries. The idea of opening a new theatre of war was originally mooted by the French. But making it a naval assault had been the brainchild of Winston Churchill, who was then First Lord of the Admiralty. The plan was enthusiastically endorsed by both Lord Kitchener – the Secretary of State for War – and the First Sea Lord, John Fisher. Fisher wanted the plan to go ahead in November 1914, using the oldest ships of the line. The Turks had yet to fortify the Dardanelles so the operation might well have succeeded.

A BOLD UNDERTAKING

When the Dardanelles operation was finally approved the following year, Fisher was keener on a Baltic landing, but still let Churchill have his old ships, as well as the new battleship *Queen Elizabeth*, fitted with 15-inch guns delivering impressive

firepower. Churchill was also assigned the hardened Imperial veterans of the 29th Division, the Royal Naval Division and ANZAC (Australian and New Zealand Army Corps) troops. The French sent their *Corps expéditionnaire d'Orient*. The operation began on 19 February, and drew in the Greeks and the Bulgarians, traditional enemies of the Turks.

The British bombardment did little damage and the disembarkation by the marines was ineffective. It was decided to 'force the narrows' on 18 March with 16 battleships, 12 British and four French. As John Keegan has written: 'even in the long naval history of the Dardanelles, such an armada had never been seen before.' They proceeded for a mile or so, knocking out some batteries before one French and two British ships were sunk by mines. The fleet withdrew. It was then decided that there would be a land assault to take the Gallipoli Pensinula on the European side of the straits and put the heavy artillery guns out of action.

'Midst Shot and Shell we made the Narrow Beach', lithograph depicting the ANZAC landing at Gallipoli (illustration by Cyrus Cuneo from *Told in Huts: The YMCA Gift Book*, published 1916).

This campaign, planned by Sir Ian Hamilton, came within an inch of success; but it was beset by logistical difficulties, and by a lack of men and ammunition. As the Turks were already at a high state of alert, Hamilton lacked the element of surprise and was forced to use subterfuge. From his base at Mudros on the island of Lemnos, Hamilton managed to deceive the commander of the Turkish 5th Army, the German field marshal Otto Liman von Sanders Pasha. He made a couple of feints to cover the landing of two divisions on the less well-defended western side of the peninsula by 25 April. The Turkish guns were all pointing onto the straits.

A fleet of 200 merchant ships ferried the troops to the landing beaches. The barrage began at 5 a.m. Two of the landings carried out by the 29th Division commanded by Major General Aylmer Hunter-Weston were unopposed, with the French at Kum Kale mopping up hundreds of prisoners, but elsewhere – at Sedd-el-Bahr or V Beach on the very tip of the spur – they were driven back.

The ANZAC force led by the British lieutenant general Sir William Birdwood were given the job of landing further north. Transported from Lemnos by three battleships, they were taken ashore by 12 tows of rowing boats. Birdwood decided against a preliminary barrage and landed by night, but selected the wrong beach: a small cove dominated on three sides by high ground. Even so, they found themselves largely unopposed and were able to move inland. It was vital, though, that they take the high ground before the main body of Turks arrived.

The reason for the paucity of enemy forces soon became clear: the Turks had dismissed the idea of the Allies choosing such an unsuitable spot to land. Crest succeeded crest, gully gave way to gully, spur to spur. In between, lay thick gorse-like scrub. The invaders needed to advance two and a half miles (4 km) to take the 3 mile (5 km) Sari Bair ridge that rose to 971 ft (296 m) and looked down on the Dardanelles. By the afternoon they had advanced only a mile and a half (2.4 km) when they came under fire. The ANZACs sustained 2,000 casualties that day.

KEMAL TO THE FORE

It was now that the creator of modern Turkey, Lieutenant-Colonel Mustapha Kemal 'Atatürk' ('Father of the Turks', a title bestowed in 1935) seized his moment. Kemal had prepared defensive plans for Gallipoli. Realizing that a full-scale invasion was underway, for three hours he sought instructions from his superiors, but when none was forthcoming, he took the initiative. Despite a lack of ammunition, he threw the whole weight of the Turkish 57th Infantry Regiment against the invaders, telling them: 'I do not expect you to attack, I order you to die.' He almost succeeded in driving the Allies into the sea. By 4 May, the ANZACs had lost 10,000 men to Kemal's 14,000, but the Turks were well dug in. Birdwood called for evacuation, but Hamilton resisted. The ANZAC's just held a narrow strip of land.

LIONS LED BY DONKEYS

While some of the British and French forces had had an easy time, at W and V Beaches the Lancashire Fusiliers, Dublins, Munsters and Hampshires died in droves as they tried to secure a beachhead near Cape Helles on the tip of the pensinsula. Their CO, Sir Aylmer Hunter-Weston was to 'receive opprobrium as one of the most brutal and incompetent commanders of the First World War' (Robin Prior). The sea was red from the blood of the dead and dying at W beach. Six Lancashire Fusiliers won VCs that morning.

'I do not expect you to attack. I order you to die.'

Throughout May and July, the Allied forces were plagued by heat, mosquitoes, dysentery and typhoid. They fought with great courage while their governments dithered about sending in reinforcements. On 19 May, the Turks launched an attack on Anzac Cove to destroy the bridgehead. The Australians and New Zealanders were prepared, as aerial reconnaissance had already picked up the Turkish troop movements. At one point in the line three companies were able to repel an entire Turkish division at a cost of 11 killed and 70 wounded. Between a third and a quarter of the attacking troops were lost. On 24 May, an armistice was declared so that the festering corpses could be buried.

Churchill was dismissed from his post in May. More men were sent in August, with 20,000 British and Gurkhas reinforcing the ANZACs.

The Australian 1st Division's assault on the Sari Bair Mountains of 6–7 August was led by British Major General Harold Walker. In an extraordinary feat of arms, they managed to take the supposedly impregnable Lone Pine position. There were 2,000 casualties on the first day and a further 1,000 on the second. More troops occupied Chunuk Bair with dreadful loss of life, but a delay meant that the left column got lost. The Gurkhas took Hill Q on the 8th before being driven back by a bombardment from their own side's guns. On the 10th, they were driven off Chunuk Bair by a charge led by Kemal. The operation had ended in failure.

Further landings at Suvla Bay to the north of Anzac Cove on 6–7 August were doomed from the outset as the site was well defended. A bloody battle on 21 August failed to gain any ground. Hamilton was relieved of his command in October, and his successor, Sir Charles Monro, decided to evacuate the army. His evacuation was perhaps the most brilliant moment of the whole campaign; from

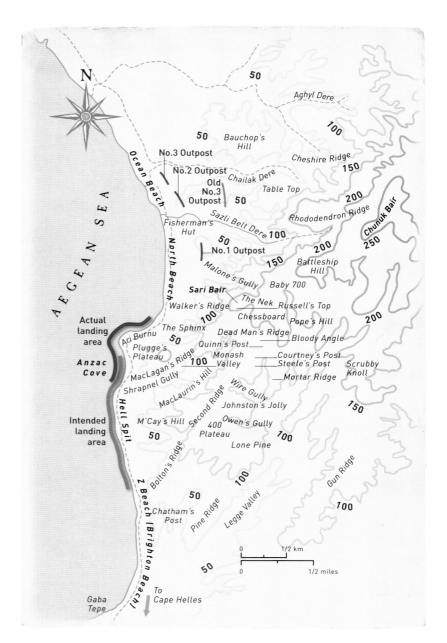

December 1915 to 9 January 1916 the men were taken off with just three casualties.

Many myths surround the Gallipoli campaign, the chief one being that the ANZACs were the only ones to fight and die in it. There were more Frenchmen at Gallipoli than Australians and they lost more men. In fact, of the 46,006 men who were killed, more than half were British. Around 200,000 or more Turks died. Yet the great heroism and sacrifice of the Australian and New Zealand forces has come to define national identities, and ANZAC Day is commemorated in both countries on 25 April every year.

Map of the landing site at Anzac Cove. The inhospitable terrain of high ridges and deep gullies choked with scrub made the landings an impossible venture. Some of the names given to topographical features (e.g. Hell Spit, Shrapnel Gully) testify to the soldiers' experience.

VERDUN

Crown Prince Wilhelm of Prussia *v.* French forces
21 February–16 December **1916**

VERDUN WAS ARGUABLY THE MOST SAVAGE BATTLE of all time, an epic struggle that almost sapped a nation's will to fight. Many have seen a clue to France's swift capitulation in 1940 in the terrible carnage of Verdun.

The fortress town of Verdun lies on the River Meuse south of France's ancient heartland of Champagne. A fortress since Roman times, rebuilt by Vauban and later by Napoleon III, its strategic importance only increased after the French loss of Alsace and parts of Lorraine in the Franco-Prussian War of 1870–71 placed it on the borders of France and Germany.

In 1885, the defences at Verdun were further strengthened by construction of a ring of forts made of iron and concrete. After the fall of the forts in Liège in Belgium in the opening weeks of the First World War, however, the value of such installations was cast into doubt and Verdun's guns were removed and reassigned for use in the field. Neglected and underdefended, the fortress was garrisoned by a relatively small force.

After Helmuth von Moltke the Younger's failure to effect the Schlieffen Plan in France, the chief of staff suffered a nervous breakdown and was replaced by the kaiser's favourite, Erich von Falkenhayn. Falkenhayn sought to re-energize the war in the West with a massive attack on Verdun. The German commander chose his objective with care, reasoning that only an attack on a major stronghold like Belfort or Verdun would force France to defend it to the last, even if it meant leaving her British allies in the lurch. France, he claimed, would throw in every man, and

'bleed to death' in the process. He was also anxious to pre-empt the planned Anglo-French attack on the Somme where already an Anglo-Belgian force of 45 divisions faced 30 German ones.

The state of Verdun's defences had caused concern for some time, not only to its governor, Colonel F.G. Herr, but also to Lieutenant-Colonel Emile Driant, a regular officer and politician commanding two battalions of chasseurs in the nearby Bois des Caures. General Joseph Joffre, the French commander who had drawn up his 'Plan XVIII' for a future war against Germany, refused to entertain the possibility that the Germans might advance through Belgium.

HELL ON EARTH

The kaiser's eldest son, Crown Prince Wilhelm of Prussia ('Little Willy'), was chosen to command the 5th German Army for the attack. He had his own army of 400,000 men, 1,400 guns and 168 aircraft. This force also had a new and terrifying weapon in the flamethrower. Some of the German artillery were the heavy-calibre weapons that had been used to destroy the Belgian forts. They also possessed a huge stockpile of ammunition, some two and a half million shells. Facing the Germans were Colonel Herr's two divisions of XXX Corps, plus two additional divisions of reserve troops.

A bayonet charge at the Battle of Verdun (colour print from *Le Petit Journal,* March 1916).

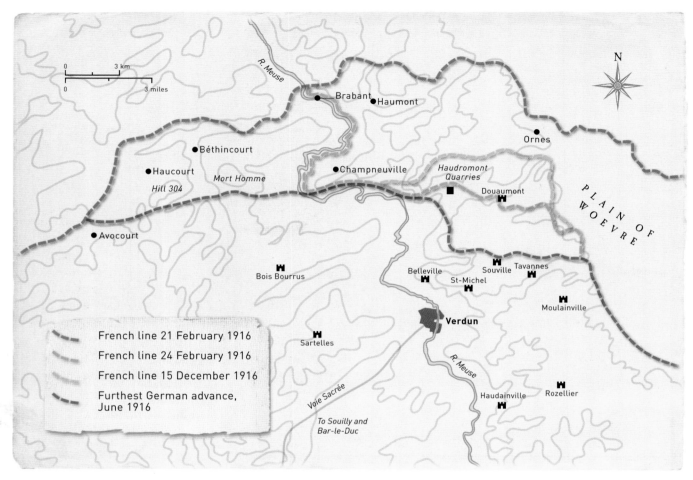

Map of the shifting battle lines at Verdun from February to December 1916. Though militarily of little significance, the town was defended to the death by the French for its symbolic value.

French weaponry was no match for the German guns. Many of the French cannon were antiquated, while the new ones from Saint Charmand and Le Creusot were only then leaving the foundries.

The battle was meant to start on 10 February, but bad weather delayed it until 21 February. That day opened with a shattering artillery barrage such as the world had never seen before, which took out guns and infantry positions. 'No line is to remain unbombarded, no possibilities of supply unmolested, nowhere should the enemy feel himself safe' said Falkenhayn.

Commander of the French Second Army, Philippe Pétain, wrote later: 'A storm of steel, iron, shrapnel and poison gas descended on our woods, ravines, trenches, shelters; smashing everything, transforming the sector into a field of carnage, turning the atmosphere to stench and carrying fires into the heart of the town... .'

A DESPERATE SITUATION

The idea was that the artillery would prove so destructive to men and morale that the infantry attack would be a walkover. The following day the German infantry went over the top, but were met by strong resistance from ragged *poilus* (French infantrymen) emerging from the ruins. In the Bois des Caures, Driant also put up a fierce fight, but was killed in action. On 23 February, a lieutenant in the French 72nd Division signalled: 'The commanding officer and all company commanders have been killed. My battalion is reduced to approximately 180

'They shall not pass!'

GENERAL ROBERT NIVELLE DEFIES THE GERMANS AT VERDUN

men. I have neither ammunition nor food. What am I to do?' The Germans finally came to a halt before Douaumont, the strongest of Verdun's forts. But this fell to a detachment of Brandenburg Grenadiers on the 25th led by a sergeant who bluffed the tiny garrison into surrendering. French High Command had failed to reinforce its garrison. From Douaumont, the Germans could rain down fire on Verdun itself.

The French defenders were gripped by panic. Food depots were pillaged and there was talk of blowing up the Meuse bridges. Joffre's belated response was to send in the Second Army to hold Verdun. His second-in-command, General Noel de Castelnau (called 'the Capuchin in boots' because he was a lay preacher), went to look at the lie of the land and decided it must be held at all costs. He assigned the already elderly General Philippe Pétain to command operations with instructions to hold both banks of the Meuse.

'THE SACRED ROAD'

More than a decade after the end of the First World War, Pétain justified his actions at Verdun: '... Verdun is not only the great fortress of the east that should sport the oak to its invaders, it is France's moral highway.' He established his headquarters at Souilly on the road to

Still pitted with shell holes almost a century after the end of the First World War, the landscape around Verdun still bears witness to the ferocity of the fighting that took place here in 1916.

Bar-le-Duc on 25 February, but almost immediately fell ill with pneumonia. Crucially, though, he had already organized the supply lines, and issued orders that there were to be no more counterattacks, but that the French were to defend the forts with their artillery. New units were drafted in and tired old ones withdrawn, in contrast to the Germans who kept the same divisions in their line for weeks on end. The tables now began to turn as the French rained down shells on the German positions. French popular opinion later credited Pétain as being the 'saviour of Verdun'.

The Bar-le-Duc road, leading north towards Champagne, now became the vital lifeline for the beleaguered fort. earning itself the name of *La voie sacrée* ('the sacred road'). In the week beginning 28 February, 190,000 men were sent along it to reinforce the position, while 3,500 lorries brought in the 2,000 tons of supplies the garrison needed daily. The number of lorries plying the road was to rise to 12,000.

BATTLE OF ATTRITION

The Germans launched another attack on 6 March, after a barrage every bit as lethal as the first, but failed to achieve their objectives. After the French strengthened their right, the Germans began to pummel the left. In April they hit both left and right simultaneously, advancing over a 9-mile (15-km) front over four days. They succeeded in taking Mort Homme and Hill 304 – the former at a cost of 100,000 casualties. The French had been hiding their artillery on the hill, but the Germans failed to capture it. The village of Vaux changed hands 13 times, but the Germans failed to seize the fort there. Meanwhile, the French achieved superiority in the air, thus enabling them to correctly appraise German troop movements.

On 8 May, an explosion in the captured fort at Douaumont emboldened the French to try retaking it. On 22 May, they managed to storm the outworks before they were repulsed. Between 1 and 7 June, the Germans launched an offensive against Fort Vaux. It was surrounded and blown up bit by bit. The French commander, Major Raynal, fought on bravely, but was finally obliged to capitulate for lack of water. When the French officer met the German commander, Prince Wilhelm gave him a sword to replace the one he had lost.

Mounting German losses now began to cause serious concern, and the crown prince was ready to call off the attack. Pétain was relieved by the artillery general Robert Nivelle, the French army's rising star. The Germans pressed home against Souville and Tavannes, briefly holding ground near Fort Souville with a clear view of Verdun. On 23 June, they began firing 'green cross' gas shells – containing

'A storm of steel, iron, shrapnel and poison gas descended on our woods, ravines, trenches, shelters; smashing everything, transforming the sector into a field of carnage, turning the atmosphere to stench and carrying fires into the heart of the town...'

General Philippe Pétain on the relentless German shelling of Verdun

a mixture of chlorine and phosgene – at the French artillery. The final German push took place on 11 July, but was repulsed once again at Fort Souville.

On 1 July, the Allies began their major offensive on the Somme, in an attempt to divert German troops away from the battle at Verdun. Falkenhayn was dismissed on 23 August and the French began recapturing lost ground. Nivelle despatched General Mangin to prise Douaumont away from them on 24 October by using his 'novel combination' of infantry and artillery. Pétain recognized

that by this time, the German batteries were already being starved of munitions.

By then Falkenhayn had fallen from grace. He was outmanoeuvred by the chancellor, Theobald von Bethmann-Hollweg, and replaced by Hindenburg, with his familiar lieutenant Ludendorff at his side as quartermaster-general.

The statistics of Verdun tell their own story of the appalling carnage that took place there: over the course of the battle no fewer than 20 million shells were fired, while each side lost in excess of 300,000 men.

FALL OF FRANCE

German forces *v.* French and British armies
May–June **1940**

THE GERMAN INVASION OF FRANCE in May 1940 took the world's breath away. Great War veterans listened with horror as familiar names appeared once more in the newspapers and on the wireless. But this time, there was to be no protracted trench warfare. Tanks and aircraft had come of age, and the Nazi *Blitzkrieg* crushed France within weeks.

Tanks had first been used by the British at the Battle of Cambrai in November–December 1917. In the final months of the First World War they had proved their worth in breaking the deadlock in the trenches. But it was not until the Second World War that they became the decisive battlefield weapon to replace cavalry.

Three Panzer corps were drawn up in three groups with armoured divisions forming the two in the vanguard and motorized divisions the third. Despite being assembled to a depth of 50 miles (80 km) east of the Rhine, Allied intelligence overlooked them.

A SWIFT STRIKE
The German campaign opened on 10 May, when Generalmajor (Brigadier) Erwin Rommel crossed the French border south of Liège. On the 13th, he had to force a passage across the River Meuse. Two days later the Netherlands had fallen and the French had collapsed on the Meuse, where the Germans had tried and failed to bleed France to death in 1916. Rommel proceeded to cross the Sambre on the 17th. In just two days, his division had taken 10,000 prisoners at a cost of just 35 dead and 59 wounded.

On the face of it the German strategy did not look greatly different from the Schlieffen Plan, only this time foreign minister Joachim von Ribbentrop's diplomacy had taken Soviet Russia out of the war. The eight-week campaign in Poland had annihilated the enemy at Germany's rear; they were now ready to push west.

The main German objective was to take the Channel ports. There was no desire to tie down huge numbers of men by occupying the whole of France. The leading general of the campaign was Erich von Manstein, chief of staff to Army Group A. Manstein had submitted a new battle plan after the original had fallen into the hands of the Belgians. He proposed taking seven of the ten Panzer divisions earmarked for the attack, move them to Army Group A and lead them on a surprise attack through the vast Ardennes forest. The Sedan–Dinant sector of the Meuse was regarded as the weakest section of the French defensive line. In the meantime, Army Group B was given the task of pinning down the Allied armies in Belgium.

By the end of the first day, Germany had 136 divisions in France. Only ten of these were armoured. Facing them were 126 French and 22 Belgian divisions, plus ten divisions of the British Expeditionary Force (BEF). The French had six armoured divisions and more tanks than the Germans (3,254 to 2,574), but they were technically inferior.

Hitler's *Blitzkrieg* in full swing, as a Panzer division sweeps across northern France in May 1940. The Allied withdrawal was hampered by roads crammed with French refugees escaping the German forces.

Stukas played a vital role in driving off the French counter-attacks.

The Germans now aimed their thrusts at the Second and Ninth French armies, which were made up of badly trained reserve units. A withdrawal of the Ninth ordered by General André Corap turned into a rout while the Second under General Charles Huntzinger fared little better. A largely British attempt to destroy the bridgehead from the air saw 85 (precisely half) of their aircraft shot down.

By 15 May, all three Panzer corps had crossed the Meuse and were proceeding unopposed to the rear of the Ninth French Army. Guderian and Rommel pushed on to the coast, which the Second Panzer Division struck on 20 May. Worries about over-extension proved unfounded and Belgium was now cut off – as well as the British Expeditionary Force. On 19 May, General Maurice Gamelin was replaced by Maxime Weygand who ordered a counter-attack to cut the Panzer units off from their supporting infantry, while the British prepared a strike at Arras on the 21st.

HITLER'S HALT-ORDER

At Arras, Rommel was attacked by two columns of tanks – 1st Army Tank Brigade and the 1st Armoured Division, plus two battalions of the Durham Light Infantry around Achicourt and Agny. Rommel thought he had the force of five divisions against him. The British overran the 42nd Anti-Tank Battalion, whose weapons proved incapable of penetrating the armour of their Matilda tanks. The fight lasted 12 hours before lethal fire from German 88-millimetre field guns and the appearance of Stukas forced the British force to retreat. Rommel pursued the British tanks to Acq, where the battle continued. The British lost seven tanks to Rommel's nine Mark IVs and Mark IIIs. The scrap at Arras may have made the German generals apprehensive; whatever

The bitter face of defeat: A Parisian weeps as he witnesses the entry of German troops into Paris on 14 June 1940. Rubbing salt into the wound, Hitler insisted on receivng the French surrender in the same railway carriage in the Forest of Compiègne in which the 1918 Armistice had been signed.

Nor could the Allies match the Germans in the air. Germany had 3,226 aircraft to France and Britain's 1,470. Most of the *Luftwaffe*'s aircraft were modern; most importantly, they had 342 Junkers Ju 87 'Stuka' dive-bombers, designed to give close support to ground forces on the battlefield.

By 12 May, the Germans had reached the River Meuse in two places. Tank commander General Heinz Guderian had taken Sedan in northern France, an historically significant site where Emperor Napoleon III had capitulated in 1870 at the end of the Franco-Prussian War. Meanwhile, Rommel had reached Dinant in Belgium. On 13 May, the Germans pressed on, establishing four bridgeheads despite stiff resistance from the French.

the case, the German advance suddenly ground to a halt, on Hitler's orders.

Although militarily there was still nothing to prevent Ewald von Kleist's Panzer army from taking Dunkirk, he received a direct order from the Führer on the 24th, expressly telling him not to advance. Officially this infamous 'Halt-Order' was given to allow the German infantry to catch up; it was hoped this would give them time to prepare the *coup de grâce* to the BEF at Dunkirk. But Guderian was livid, and tendered his resignation. It was not accepted, and he was told to go off and continue his 'reconnaissance in force'.

Hitler had overruled both the head of the army, Walther von Brauchitsch, and his chief of staff, Franz Halder. By the 25th, there was acute tension among the leading commanders of the *Wehrmacht*.

THE MIRACLE OF DUNKIRK

Gerd von Rundstedt, commanding Army Group A, consulted Kleist who desperately wanted to unleash the tanks, but Hitler insisted they could advance no further than was necessary to bring the port under artillery fire. Hermann Göring expressed the hope that the 'Tommies' could swim, as his *Luftwaffe* was planning to sink any vessel that came into the harbour – something that he failed to do. The British were faced by the need to evacuate 338,000 men (including 120,000 French) who were by now cut off by the German advance. The evacuation was managed by Field Marshal Lord Gort and Vice-Admiral Sir Bertram Ramsay. Gort decided against a counter-attack and in favour of an evacuation on 25 May. The operation was named DYNAMO. The evacuation began on 26 May.

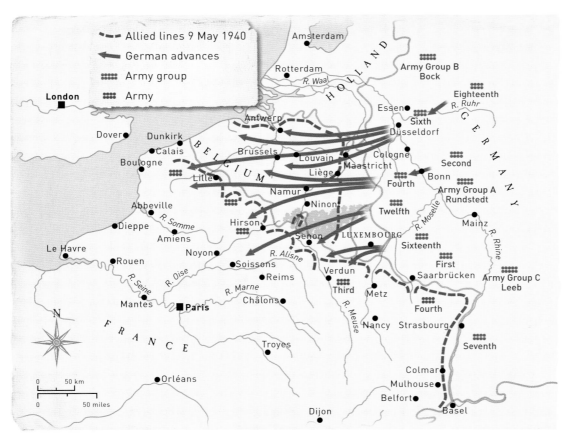

Map of the German invasion of France, showing the thrust towards Paris and the Channel ports. Farther south, the French had built the formidable Maginot Line as a bulwark against German invasion, but once again, Belgium proved the Achilles heel of France's defences.

'I hope the Tommies can swim....'

HERMANN GÖRING

The 693 vessels ranged from warships to privately owned boats. They were all subjected to fierce air attack. Two hundred boats were sunk, and RAF Fighter Command lost 106 aircraft. Although the BEF lost all its equipment, the successful evacuation of the only trained unit in the British army was of immense military importance, as well as providing a vital boost to morale.

FRENCH COLLAPSE

As the Germans pushed on to Paris, they could congratulate themselves on having captured a million men while suffering just 60,000 casualties of their own, mostly wounded. The Belgian and Dutch armies had been wiped out and the French had lost 30 divisions – around a third of their total strength and almost all their armour.

Weygand now had 66 divisions and no support from abroad. The Germans began phase two (codename: *Fall Rot*) on 5 June. Guderian commanded his own Panzer division in Army Group A. Army Group B contained Rommel's Seventh Panzer, which attacked across the River Somme. There was some fierce resistance from the British and French around Amiens and Abbeville in the final days of May. On 5 June, Rommel cut off the 51st Highland Division which was trying to make for Fécamp and St Valéry to board ships. The embarkation had already begun at Fécamp. At St Valéry was the HQ of General Fortune commanding the division. On the night of 10–11 June, Rommel seized the high ground to the west and poured artillery fire into the town: Fortune and 12,000 men surrendered on the 12th. The British sent reinforcements to Cherbourg, but were

obliged to withdraw them on 13 June. On the 14th, the German troops entered Paris. On 16 June, the aged Marshal Pétain took over command of French forces. Six days later, the former 'Saviour of Verdun' ordered his countrymen to lay down their arms.

STUNNING VICTORY

In just six weeks, Hitler and his generals – Manstein in particular – had managed to deliver a result that four years of the First World War had failed to achieve. France was out of the war; badly bruised British forces had limped back across the Channel; the military powers of Belgium and Holland had been swept aside and their countries occupied. Hitler was now ready to plan his main offensive: the invasion and annihilation of his ideological arch-enemy to the east, Stalin's Soviet Union.

MOSCOW

General Heinz Guderian *v.* Russian forces
December **1941**

HEINZ GUDERIAN WAS HITLER'S MARSHAL NEY. Like Napoleon's most famous lieutenant, he lost a vital battle, which Hitler never let him forget. That battle was Moscow. Guderian, a middle-class Prussian, originally trained as a cavalry officer and graduated to the general staff just before the First World War. After Germany's defeat he specialized in mechanized warfare and became the army's leading advocate of tanks.

Guderian's message struck a chord with the Nazis and he rose rapidly. At the outset of Operation Barbarossa – the German invasion of the Soviet Union, launched on 22 June 1941 – he was given command of his own Panzer group, originally called *Panzerarmee Guderian*. Within just six weeks of this operation, the largest land campaign ever fought, he had won a chain of victories, captured hundreds of thousands of men and come within 200 miles (320 km) of Moscow.

Not for the first time, Guderian found himself at odds with his supreme commander when Hitler decided that his tanks should be transferred to Army Group South, which was lagging behind. Kiev was taken, but Moscow was lost. He failed to convince the Führer that this strategy was wrong. Only in September was Guderian allowed to proceed to Moscow. Later Hitler dismissed him, although he was subsequently brought back to be Chief of the General Staff and humiliated all over again.

RAPID GAINS

The objective of the first phase of Barbarossa was to reach a line stretching from the Volga to Archangel within three months. No provision was made for winter fighting. German forces included over 3 million men in 152 divisions including 30 armoured and motorized divisions, 3,350 tanks, 7,106 guns and 1,950 aircraft. The Germans were supported by 14 Finnish divisions in the north and 14 Romanian divisions in the south. Like Napoleon's *Grande Armée* in its march on Moscow 130 years before, Hitler's forces were multinational. Later there were Hungarian, Italian, Spanish, Croatian and Slovakian armies, plus smaller units from every country under German occupation. They were arranged in three huge army groups: A, B and C.

The Germans employed the tactics that had been so successful in France when executed by generals of the calibre of Manstein, Guderian, Rommel and Kleist. They used concentrated columns of armour to smash their way through the enemy's defences and then encircle them from the rear. The infantry then went in to deal with the surrounded forces.

As the Germans advanced into Russia, huge numbers of prisoners were taken: 400,000 at Minsk, 300,000 at Smolensk, 500,000 at Kiev, and another 500,000 at Briansk and Viazma. They were so badly

In the first weeks of Operation Barbarossa, German troops made seemingly unstoppable progress deep into Russia and took large numbers of prisoners. Here, a motorized unit of the SS *Totenkopf* ('Death's Head') Division rests during a pause in the advance.

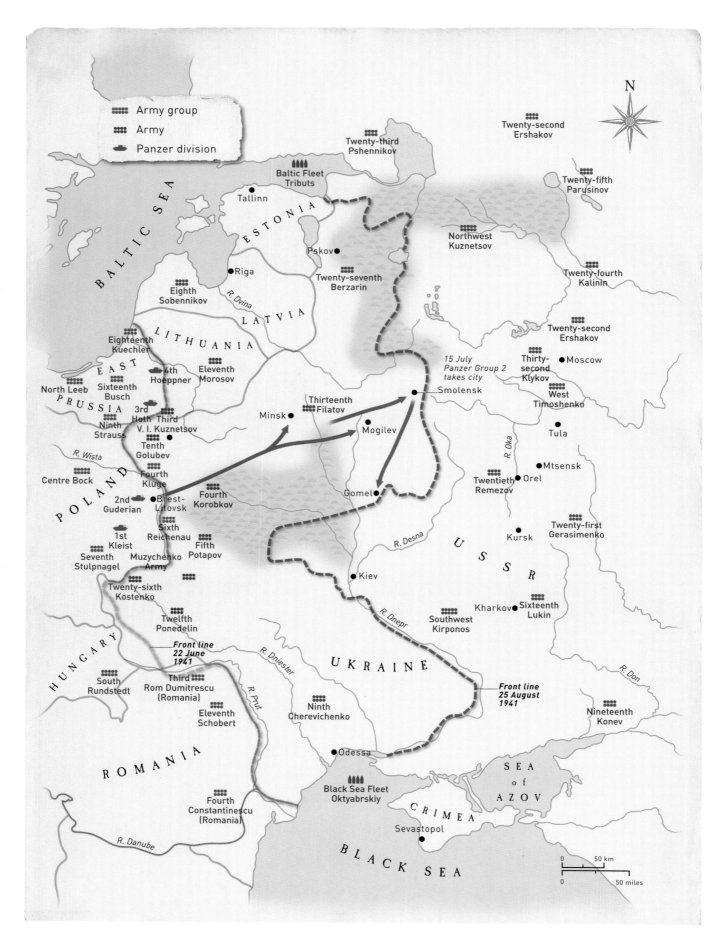

N

Army group

Army

Panzer division

BALTIC SEA

Twenty-second
Ershakov

Twenty-third
Pshennikov

Twenty-fifth
Parusinov

Baltic Fleet
Tributs

Tallinn

ESTONIA

Riga

Pskov

Twenty-seventh
Berzarin

Northwest
Kuznetsov

Twenty-fourth
Kalinin

Eighth
Sobennikov

LATVIA

R. Dvina

Twenty-second
Ershakov

Eighteenth
Kuechler

LITHUANIA

4th
Hoeppner

Eleventh
Morosov

15 July
Panzer Group 2
takes city

Thirty-
second
Klykov

Moscow

North Leeb

EAST
PRUSSIA

Sixteenth
Busch

3rd
Hoth

Third
V. I. Kuznetsov

Thirteenth
Filatov

Smolensk

West
Timoshenko

Ninth
Strauss

Minsk

Mogilev

R. Oka

Tula

Tenth
Golubev

R. Wista

Centre Bock

Fourth
Kluge

POLAND

2nd
Guderian

Brest-
Litovsk

Fourth
Korobkov

Gomel

R. Desna

U S S R

Twentieth
Remezov

Mtsensk

Orel

Kursk

Twenty-first
Gerasimenko

1st
Kleist

Sixth
Reichenau

Fifth
Potapov

Seventh
Stulpnagel

Muzychenko
Army

Kiev

R. Dnepr

Kharkov

Sixteenth
Lukin

Twenty-sixth
Kostenko

Southwest
Kirponos

Twelfth
Ponedelin

Front line
22 June
1941

R. Dniester

UKRAINE

Front line
25 August
1941

R. Don

HUNGARY

South
Rundstedt

Third
Rom Dumitrescu
(Romania)

R. Prut

Ninth
Cherevichenko

Nineteenth
Konev

Eleventh
Schobert

ROMANIA

Odessa

SEA
of
AZOV

Fourth
Constantinescu
(Romania)

Black Sea Fleet
Oktyabrskiy

CRIMEA

Sevastopol

R. Danube

BLACK
SEA

0   50 km
0   50 miles

treated that two-thirds of this almost 3
million were dead by February 1942.

THE FALL OF KIEV

On 6 July, the Red Army counter-attacked
on the Western and Central Fronts against
German Army Group Centre along the
Dnepr. These assaults included the limp
Timoshenko Offensive against Guderian's
Panzer Group on the River Sozh. Pin-
pricks though they were, the attacks on
German positions near Smolensk and
Kiev led Hitler to abandon his headlong
advance on Moscow and to attack targets
in the Kiev region instead, much to
Guderian's fury.

In late August, the *Stavka* (Russian
High Command) ordered the Western,
Reserve and Briansk Fronts to launch
huge offensives around Smolensk to
destroy Army Group Centre in a bid to
stop the Germans from taking Moscow
and Kiev. On 18 August, Stalin issued a
directive that Kiev must not be taken. The
city was exposed in a long and vulnerable
salient. Guderian was ordered to break off
his advance and head south with the 2nd
Panzer Army to attack the southwestern
front from the rear.

Stalin shored up the Briansk Front
under General Yeremenko with additional
troops and instructed his commander that
'the scoundrel Guderian ... and his whole
group must be smashed to smithereens'.
Precisely the opposite occurred, however,
and when Kiev fell on 17 September, it left
four whole Soviet armies encircled. More
than 600,000 men were lost in this action.
It was the high-water mark of the German
campaign, and Soviet Russia's worst disaster.

MOSCOW UNDER THREAT

Not only did these offensives fail, but
the Germans now began to advance on
Moscow in Operation Typhoon. Yet every
Soviet counter-attack, however costly,
delayed the German army from achieving

its main objective of taking the Russian
capital, and with each setback there was
an increased chance that the Germans
would end up fighting a winter campaign.

The Germans continued to push
forward rapidly, trapping no fewer than
seven Soviet armies and a million men in
the encirclements at Viazma and Briansk
in early October. These new catastrophes
for the Soviets quite eclipsed the losses of
June, August and September. By the 18th,
German tanks had reached the battlefield
of Borodino. When the Germans launched
their assault on Moscow later that month,
the defence of the city was initially in the
hands of Colonel-General Ivan Konev,
before passing to Marshal Georgi Zhukov
on 10 November. German High Command
had provided 70 divisions with a million
men for the task, together with 14,000
guns, 1,700 tanks and 1,000 planes. By
mid-November, the foremost German
units were within 40 miles (64 km) of the
capital, but resistance was still strong,
with the Russians making good use of
their main battle tank, the excellent T-34.

'General Winter',
one of Russia's most
formidable defensive
assets, began to play
his part when the
German advance on
Moscow stalled. Ill-
equipped for fighting in
subzero conditions,
the German armies
suffered the same
fate as Napoleon 130
years before.

**Left: The Eastern
Front** from 22 June
to 25 August 1941.
Guderian's 2nd Army
pushed forward further
than any other Axis unit,
reaching Smolensk
before being ordered
south to support Army
Group South.

The plan was to surround the city, and to this end German armies made for Kalinin, north of Moscow and Tula to the south.

DEFENDING MOTHER RUSSIA

But as the Russian winter set in, temperatures plummeted, motor oil congealed, and the ground froze so hard that troops found it impossible to dig in. Meanwhile, Stalin created ten reserve armies east of Moscow (during the battle nearly 100 divisions were used in the central theatre). Soviet intelligence also learned that the Japanese were not intending to attack in Manchuria or co-ordinate their campaigns with their new German allies. As a result, Stalin was able to redeploy badly needed forces from the Chinese border.

On 15 October, the Russians began a partial evacuation of the capital. It looked like 1812 all over again. Foreign diplomats and journalists and some ministries were despatched to Kuibyshev, 500 miles

(800 km) east of Moscow while the General Staff was stationed at Arzamas, halfway between the two. Secret police chief Lavrentiy Beria was ordered to mine the city lest the Germans take it. These measures caused many inhabitants to panic and flee. A broadcast by the city boss A. A. Shcherbakov on 17 October informed Muscovites that Stalin was remaining in the Kremlin and two days later an official state of siege was declared. Beria took over responsibility for security and five divisions of volunteers were formed to build defences and fight in the front line. Many were killed.

The original defensive line had been drawn 75 miles (120 km) west of the city. Zhukov brought it further east. By the end of the month, the Germans had breached the original line and were heading for the city from both the northwest and southwest. By early November they were just 50 miles (80 km) away.

Defiant in the face of this threat, Stalin went ahead and celebrated the

Destroyed Soviet T-34 tanks: This rugged tank proved an invaluable workhorse for Soviet armoured divisions in their defeat of Nazi forces. With the rapid German advances in the summer and autumn of 1941, production of the vital T-34 was hastily relocated east from the Ukraine to beyond the Ural Mountains.

> *'Guderian! Maintain your positions at any price! I shall send you reinforcements! I will mobilize everything I have! Just stick it out, whatever you do – stick it out!'*

INSTRUCTION BY HITLER TO HEINZ GUDERIAN IN DECEMBER 1941

anniversary of the Russian Revolution, though his rally on 6 November had to be held underground in Mayakovsky metro station. That day he gave a rousing speech underlining why Hitler would not win: he had failed to bring the Anglo-Americans in on his crusade; the Germans had staked too much on the Soviet Union imploding under its internal tensions; and they had underestimated the strength and morale of the Red Army. Yet he deliberately omitted to mention any historical comparison between Hitler and Napoleon, not wishing to remind his audience that the French emperor had actually succeeded in taking Moscow briefly in 1812.

The next day saw the traditional march-past in Red Square. Stalin called for patriotism as he pointed out the Soviet Union had been through worse and compared the current situation to 1918, when 14 nations invaded the infant republic. He then invoked the shades of Russian heroes from Alexander Nevsky to Kutuzov. His speech was printed and distributed among the armed forces.

BEGINNING OF THE END

On 30 November, the Germans reached Sheremetevo Airport. The Soviet line bent, but did not break. The Germans failed to take Tula, and then the attacks slowed down. Hitler's butler Heinz Linge later recalled his blind rage at the time and his furious attacks on the army leaders during the daily conferences in the Wolf's Lair (his Eastern Front military HQ in East Prussia). In early December, Linge heard the Führer's raised voice coming from the Conference Room. He was on the telephone to his Panzer commander: 'Guderian! Maintain your positions at any price! I shall send you reinforcements! I will mobilize everything I have! Just stick it out, whatever you do – stick it out!'

As Hitler's mood darkened, Stalin's morale went from strength to strength. Guderian's 2nd Panzer Army finally ground to a halt before Tula. Then the counter-attacks began: on 4 December and with increased force two days later. The 1st Shock Army and the 20th attacked to the north of Moscow while the 10th engaged the Germans near Tula. The Russians had the advantage, being used to the winter conditions, while the Germans were exhausted, ill-equipped and badly supplied. The Russians also had a seemingly unquenchable supply of men. Large groups of partisans were also active behind the German lines. The first shove pushed the Germans back 50 miles (80 km). By the end of the battle, the Red Army had driven the Germans back up to 248 miles (400 km), with the loss of half a million men, 1,500 tanks and 2,500 guns. However, all this was achieved at a massive cost: 926,000 Soviet soldiers killed.

On 16 December, the commander of Army Group Centre, Fedor von Bock, asked Hitler for permission to make a defensive withdrawal. Guderian became the scapegoat: his Christmas present from the Führer was his dismissal. The myth of the invincible *Wehrmacht* was eclipsed – it was the beginning of the end.

THE FALL OF SINGAPORE

Japanese Imperial guards *v.* British and Commonwealth forces
15 February 1942

DUNKIRK IS OFTEN SEEN AS A LOGISTICAL VICTORY, but it would be hard to put a positive 'spin' on the fall of Singapore. Churchill described it as 'the worst disaster and largest capitulation in British military history'. On its progress through Thailand and down the Malayan Peninsula, the Imperial Japanese Army took Singapore by the 'back door', while the British guns installed to protect the peninsula pointed the wrong way – out to sea.

The British had always been aware of the threat that Japan posed to the Far East, and it was that which decided them to build the naval base at Singapore in the first place, surrounded by heavy guns and airfields. The new harbour, though, had yet to play host to a permanent fleet.

INADEQUATE DEFENCES

It was also foreseen that the Japanese might land in Thailand, Japan's only ally in Asia, and then march into Malaya. In 1936, Major-General William Dobbie had highlighted the dangers of just such an invasion. Arthur Percival, who surrendered Singapore to the Japanese, was his staff officer at the time. The threat took on a new urgency once the Japanese joined the Axis Powers in September 1940. Now there was little to stop them from seizing those parts of Asia they coveted. Chief among these were Singapore and the Philippines, the centres of British and American power in the Pacific. Yet British military strategists fatefully decided that what little war material Singapore possessed could be better deployed elsewhere.

In October 1940, Air Chief Marshal Sir Robert Brooke-Popham was brought back from retirement to become C-in-C Far East. The appointment of an airforce officer might have signalled a new commitment to shoring up Singapore's defences, but when he asked for aircraft he was told there were none to spare. In May 1941, Lieutenant-General Arthur Percival took up an appointment as GOC Malaya, with two weak divisions – the 9th and the 11th at his disposal together with III Indian Corps.

Percival was a highly decorated officer who had fought the IRA in Ireland during the 'Troubles' of the 1920s, earning a reputation for ruthlessness. Having been posted to Singapore, he astutely mapped out a possible Japanese plan of attack that turned out to be very similar to the one actually used: 'to burgle Malaya by the back door.' He also approved the plan to strengthen the defences of Johore, just north of the island.

His opposite number in Singapore was Major-General Frank Simmons. He had the 8th Australian Division commanded by Major-General Henry Gordon Bennett. The Allied air force comprised 158 mostly obsolete aircraft. Tanks earmarked for Singapore had been diverted to Russia to help Stalin counter the German invasion.

On 8 December 1941, the Japanese 25th Army commanded by General Tomoyuki Yamashita landed at Khota Bharu in Malaya. The 25th was an élite unit that had been trained in amphibious landing and in the use of bicycles to cover long distances. Yet Yamashita's was only a diversionary attack; the main Japanese force was landed at Singora and Patani in southeast Thailand.

CO-ORDINATED CAMPAIGN

Japanese forces quickly achieved air superiority. The three landings took place just one hour before the attack on Pearl Harbor: the different date is accounted for by the international dateline. The timing of the attack was quite deliberate. Percival made the following announcement on 10 December: 'In this hour of trial the General Officer Commanding calls upon all ranks in Malaya Command for a determined and sustained effort to safeguard Malaya and the adjoining British territories. The eyes of the Empire are upon us. Our whole position in the Far East is at stake. The struggle may be long and grim but let us all resolve to stand fast come what may and to prove ourselves worthy of the great trust which has been placed in us.'

Accompanied by a tank unit at brigade strength, the Japanese fought their way south to Kuala Lumpur down the main roads, sweeping the British forces before them and winning battle after battle on the way: Jitra (11 December), Gurun (15 December), Kampar (2 January), Slim River (7 January, against the Indian Army) and Kuala Lumpur (11 January). Some Japanese forces advanced south in small boats. On the day of the disaster at Slim River, the British C-in-C of the entire

Japanese troops fight their way into Singapore behind a tank. The lack of landward defences and the absence of armour sealed the fate of the large British garrison on the island.

region, General Sir Archibald Wavell landed to inspect his forces. Appalled at what he saw, he ordered the army to fall back on Malaya's southernmost province of Johore. In Singapore, Wavell found not the shadow of a plan to resist a Japanese attack and voiced his misgivings in a telegram to Churchill.

A greater disaster had already overtaken Britain: in October it had been decided to send two brand new ships to Singapore, the battleship *Prince of Wales* and the aircraft carrier *Indomitable*. They were accompanied by an older battleship, HMS *Repulse*. The aircraft carrier was damaged during trials, but the other two ships left for the Indian Ocean as Force Z under the command of Admiral Sir Tom Phillips. On 10 December, they were attacked by Japanese bombers based in Indo-China. Both ships were sunk with the loss of 800 lives, including the admiral.

> *'.... the defence of Singapore Island be maintained by every means... No surrender can be contemplated.'*
>
> WINSTON CHURCHILL

Churchill was 'staggered' and ordered Percival to stand firm: 'Not only must the defence of Singapore Island be maintained by every means, but the whole island must be fought for until every single unit and every single strong point has been separately destroyed... No surrender can be contemplated.'

ASSAULT ON THE ISLAND

Percival was in a difficult position: the island was filled with refugees and water was running out, as 40 percent of it was delivered via pipes from the mainland. He was short of ammunition as well. What he did not know was that the Japanese had even less, and half the number of men.

The British continued to retreat down the peninsula. By midnight on 21 January, almost all of them had crossed the causeway into Singapore; a battalion of Argylls bringing up the rear. The causeway was blown up, but the water below was only 1.2 metres (4 ft) deep at low tide.

The Japanese fooled Percival with a feint. The Konoye Division landed on Pulau Ubin Island at midnight on the 7th with 400 men and two guns and shelled Changi fortress. The British rushed reinforcements east. On 8 February, Yamashita had concentrated his forces in the northwest and struck, in contrast to Percival who had spread his right round the coast. As 440 guns opened up, two divisions in 300 small boats landed on the northwest shore. During the night, they pushed back the defending Australian brigade and made for the reservoirs in the centre of the island.

But the following night, near the causeway that links Singapore to Johore, another wave of the Imperial Guards failed to achieve their objectives. Percival was still worried that the Japanese would make fresh landings when the bulk of their forces were already on the island. Wavell ran the gauntlet of the Japanese airforce to make a last visit. He furiously berated Percival for his ineptitude and ordered an immediate counter-attack.

VICTORY THROUGH BLUFF

On the night of 10–11 February, Yamashita's forces took the Bukit Timah Heights with a bayonet charge. Meanwhile, the Japanese were landing tanks and consolidating their hold on the reservoir area. Yamashita began to run short of ammunition on the 12th, and encouraged his men to fight with bayonets from then on. The British 18th Division, made up of raw troops, could make no headway against them. Yet Yamashita was aware that, with time, the situation might turn in

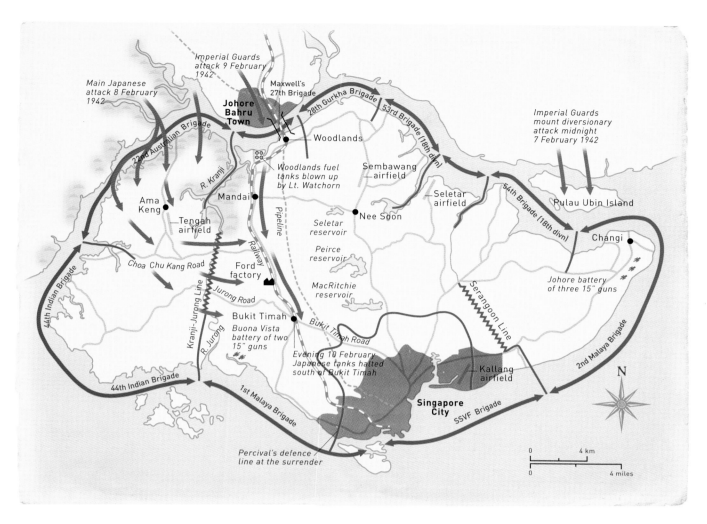

Defensive and attacking forces at the fall of Singapore. Throughout the battle for the island, Percival made the mistake of dispersing his forces, whereas Japanese commander Yamashita massed his troops on a narrow front.

Percival's favour. He therefore tried a bluff and demanded that Percival surrender.

Percival did not reply immediately, but at 9 a.m. on 15 February held his final conference at Fort Canning. He told his commanders that the situation was untenable and proposed surrender to the Japanese by 4 p.m. Wavell approved if there was no alternative.

That afternoon, Percival personally carried the white flag to Bukit Timah. Yamashita bullied him at the negotiating table. He was still fully aware that if the British stuck to their guns they might prevail: 'The time for the night attack is drawing near. Is the British army going to surrender or not? Answer YES or NO!' Percival tried weakly to stall for time, but finally conceded. The ceasefire came into force at 8.30 p.m.

Prior to the battle for Malaya and Singapore, Percival had 140,000 troops at his disposal. Around 9,000 of these were killed, but at the fall of Singapore the rest were taken prisoner. They suffered the most appallingly inhumane treatment at the hands of their captors. Only a few Allied troops, including Major-General Gordon Bennett, managed to escape. At 55,000 men, the Japanese army was less than half the strength of the Allied garrison. They lost some 3,500 killed. Yamashita had been given 100 days to take Singapore; he did it in just 70. Thereafter, he was known as 'the Tiger of Malaya'.

After the war, Percival was disparaged for his failure to defend Singapore and was denied a knighthood. He nonetheless fared better than Yamashita: an American military tribunal found the Tiger guilty of war crimes, especially the brutal treatment of Allied prisoners of war, and he was sentenced to death by hanging in 1946.

EL ALAMEIN

Lt-Gen. Bernard Montgomery *v.* Field Marshal Erwin Rommel
23 October–4 November **1942**

SOME MILITARY HISTORIANS HAVE CHALLENGED the traditional view that the British Eighth Army was transformed into a great fighting force by one man: the controversial Lieutenant-General Bernard Montgomery. What is beyond dispute is that 'Monty' had a talent for self-promotion that was rare among senior British officers at that time and was able to infect his subordinates with the same belief.

The Eighth Army had fared particularly badly before the summer of 1942, in one action losing 118 tanks to the enemy's three. Historians have suggested that the work of whipping the men into shape had already been done before Montgomery arrived on the scene. His predecessor Claude Auchinleck had established the strong defensive position adopted by British forces in Egypt. This comprised a 40-mile (64-km) line that could be held by two divisions and plenty of armour and could not be turned; the British right flank was protected by the Mediterranean while the left was anchored in the impassable quicksands of the Qattara Depression.

THE DESERT FOX AT BAY

The German Afrika Korps, commanded by Field Marshal Erwin Rommel (the 'Desert Fox'), had swept all before it in North Africa. It had pushed the British back over 1,000 miles (1,600 km) from Gazala to within just over 100 miles (160 km) from the Suez Canal and 60 miles (100 km) from Alexandria; official papers had been burned in Cairo and the fleet had sailed away from Alexandria. But overextended supply lines bedevilled Rommel; he was promised huge stocks of fuel, which he

never received. By July 1941, the British had checked his advance in what is sometimes called the 'First Battle of El Alamein' taking 7,000 prisoners. Thereafter, Auchinleck stabilized the front, established good defensive lines and advised that no offensive be undertaken before September.

Winston Churchill did not take kindly to any suggestion of inactivity, and sacked Auchinleck. William 'Strafer' Gott took over the Eighth Army, but was promptly killed while flying back from the front. Chief of the Imperial General Staff, General Alan Brooke, now suggested General Harold Alexander be given overall command for the theatre as C-in-C Middle East, with Montgomery in charge of the Eighth Army. In the interim, that force had taken delivery of 300 new American Sherman tanks, with 75-mm guns.

After the reforms made by Auchinleck, the Eighth Army had already begun to show its mettle at the Battle of Alam Halfa in August and September 1942. Auchinleck was aware from intercepted signals that Rommel was planning an attack and stopped him in his tracks at Miteirya Ridge using the artillery installed on Alam Haifa Ridge. Rommel had slight numerical superiority, but six of his

divisions were Italian. The Eighth Army now had the guns they needed and air superiority. Rommel's Afrika Korps was forced to withdraw and regroup. Attempts to pursue them failed and the Axis forces prudently laid extensive minefields as they retreated. Rommel returned to Germany with a swollen liver on 23 September, and Montgomery bided his time.

El Alamein was planned as part of the Anglo-American strategy for the further prosecution of the war. Germany was to be knocked out first, and then Japan. This was to be effected by a major offensive against the Afrika Korps followed by

landings that would neutralize Vichy French forces in Morocco and Algeria.

A FEINT AND A BARRAGE

Operation Lightfoot began on 23 October: Montgomery pitted his army of 220,000 men and 1,348 tanks against the combined German-Italian force of 112,000 men and 500 tanks led by Rommel's replacement General Stumme.

Of the Axis tanks, 340 were inferior Italian vehicles, while only 38 were the formidable German Mk IV, with its 75-mm gun. Montgomery not only possessed twice as many men, he had more of

Sappers Breaching the Minefields at El Alamein by the artist Terence Cuneo. Despite the availability of mine-clearing tanks, much of this dangerous work still had to be done by hand.

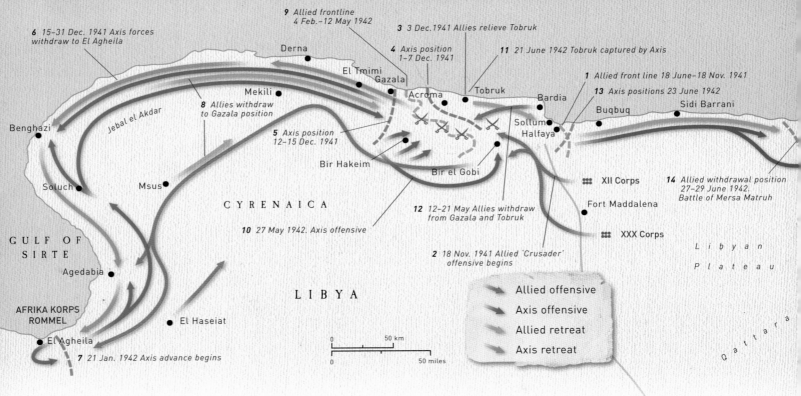

The Axis campaigns in North Africa from June 1941 to August 1942. The British scored major successes against Mussolini's Italian forces in North Africa before the arrival of Rommel's Afrika Korps, which was an altogether tougher nut to crack.

Map labels:

6 15–31 Dec. 1941 Axis forces withdraw to El Agheila

9 Allied frontline 4 Feb.–12 May 1942

3 3 Dec.1941 Allies relieve Tobruk

11 21 June 1942 Tobruk captured by Axis

4 Axis position 1–7 Dec. 1941

1 Allied front line 18 June–18 Nov. 1941

13 Axis positions 23 June 1942

Derna

El Tmimi

Gazala

Acroma

Tobruk

Bardia

Buqbuq

Sidi Barrani

Mekili

8 Allies withdraw to Gazala position

Sollum

Halfaya

5 Axis position 12–15 Dec. 1941

Jebal el Akdar

Benghazi

Bir Hakeim

Bir el Gobi

⊞ XII Corps

14 Allied withdrawal position 27–29 June 1942. Battle of Mersa Matruh

Soluch

Msus

C Y R E N A I C A

Fort Maddalena

12 12–21 May Allies withdraw from Gazala and Tobruk

10 27 May 1942. Axis offensive

⊞ XXX Corps

L i b y a n

P l a t e a u

GULF OF SIRTE

L I B Y A

2 18 Nov. 1941 Allied 'Crusader' offensive begins

Agedabia

AFRIKA KORPS ROMMEL

El Haseiat

El Agheila

7 21 Jan. 1942 Axis advance begins

Legend:
Allied offensive
Axis offensive
Allied retreat
Axis retreat

0   50 km

0   50 miles

Q a t t a r a

---

everything, including 531 Shermans and Grants (the latter also with 75-mm guns). Alongside Australians and New Zealanders, his forces also included Free French and Greek units. The only thing the Axis had in profusion was mines, laying half a million new ones to add to those already in place.

An elaborate charade was played out before the battle to convince the enemy that Montgomery would launch his attack in the south. One eyewitness reported: 'Hundreds of dummy vehicles were placed over tanks in the assembly areas; dummy lorries were placed in gun-positions so that the guns could be moved in at night and hidden under them; dummy tanks and dummy guns replaced the real articles in the staging areas as they went forward; mock dumps were started in the southern area and built up so slowly that they could not be ready until November; a fake wireless network was operated there with fake messages; a dummy pipeline, with dummy petrol stations and reservoirs was built in the wrong direction and deliberately not completed; the movement of every vehicle was controlled to guard against tell-tale tracks in the sand.'

El Alamein was a battle fought in three stages, preceded by a huge artillery barrage. Shortly after this, Stumme suffered a fatal heart attack. Temporary command passed to Major-General Wilhelm Ritter von Thoma. The first stage was the 'break-in' when Lieutenant-General Sir Oliver Leese's XXX Corps attacked the Axis centre along a 10-mile (16-km) front across minefields while Lieutenant-General Brian Horrocks with XIII Corps hit the enemy in the south. Neither was able to penetrate far enough to get behind the Axis armies. The second phase was Montgomery's 'dog-fight' between 26 and 31 October in the midst of the German-Italian positions. Their defences were ground down by superior firepower and greater strength in the air.

ROMMEL RETURNS

Rommel returned to command the Afrika Corps on 26 October. Like Napoleon at Waterloo, he was a sick man at a decisive battle. He admitted to one of his generals, Fritz Bayerlein, that the engagement was a foregone conclusion, but still made desperate attempts to restore the German line. Within a few hours, he ordered a counterattack against the British right, but it was broken up by artillery fire and aerial bombardment. The next day,

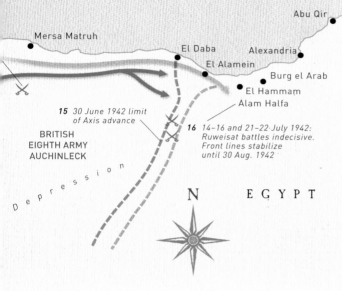

15 30 June 1942 limit of Axis advance

BRITISH
EIGHTH ARMY
AUCHINLECK

16 14–16 and 21–22 July 1942: Ruweisat battles indecisive. Front lines stabilize until 30 Aug. 1942

Rommel came up against the 2nd Rifle Brigade and the Australians.

THE BREAK-OUT

The next phase of the battle, the 'break-out,' took place from 1-4 November. Codenamed Operation Supercharge, it was spearheaded by the New Zealanders and the Ninth Armoured Brigade, who burst through the Axis lines north of Kidney Ridge. Prior to their assault, Matilda 'Scorpion' tanks drove through the fields of mines, detonating them with flail chains on revolving drums fitted to the front of the vehicles. Even so, the brigade lost 87 tanks. They cleared a path for X Corps to break through to the rear of the enemy positions. Although the Afrika Korps mounted counter-attacks, it failed to land a significant blow on Montgomery's forces. The mobile divisions retreated at speed, while the infantry surrendered. On 2 November, the ailing Rommel ordered a retreat. The next day a *Führerbefehl* (direct order from Hitler) ordered him to hold his ground. This threw Rommel into a quandary, but the British had already broken through to the south and captured von Thoma. By 4 November, the Afrika Korps was in full retreat.

Rommel was temporarily broken, but he rallied his forces and led an ordered withdrawal with great skill. He had only one division left, with eight tanks to the British 600. Heavy rain came to his aid, turning the desert into an impassable morass. On 23 January, the Eighth Army reached Tripoli, having driven the Axis Powers from Egypt and the Suez Canal. On the day Stalingrad fell, the British were already in Tunisia.

Once Rommel had recovered he went to see Adolf Hitler at his Wehrwolf HQ in the Ukraine on 10 March 1943. Although he had disobeyed orders, Hitler received him warmly and decorated him. Rommel had been forced to give ground because the reserves Hitler had promised had been ploughed into the Eastern Front. Rommel said frankly that he might have been able to take Alexandria had he had the men, and that the Italians were unreliable allies. For his part, Hitler explained that he had had to try and stem the tide at Stalingrad.

After the war, Montgomery magnanimously agreed with his old adversary: 'Had a proportion of the troops and equipment used against the Russians been sent to Africa, and particularly the armoured divisions, it is reasonable to presume that the Germans would have gained Egypt, the Suez Canal and possibly established a stronghold in the Middle East.'

The great significance of El Alamein lay in its timing, as it signalled the opening of the second phase of the war, when the Allies began to prevail over the Axis forces. As Churchill famously put it: 'Now this is not the end, nor is it even the beginning of the end, but it is, perhaps, the end of the beginning.' A few days after the British victory, the Allies conducted their 'Operation Torch' landings against French North Africa, while the Soviet counter-offensive at Stalingrad began on 19 November.

Monty in the desert: Montgomery was a dynamic leader, but could also be arrogant and high-handed. Churchill said of him: 'In defeat, unbeatable. In victory, unbearable.'

STALINGRAD

**Field Marshal Friedrich Paulus *v.* Russian forces
17 July 1942–2 February 1943**

OPERATION BARBAROSSA BEGAN TO FALTER in late 1941, with the failure to capture Moscow. As the campaign dragged on, the Germans grew desperately short of men and materiel. By contrast, Soviet Russia was increasingly well supplied and had plenty of reserves. To try and secure German fuel supplies and deny the Russians theirs, Hitler now ordered his forces to regroup and thrust south of the Caucasus to seize the Baku oilfields. To achieve this, they had first to occupy the territory west of the River Don.

Stalingrad was located in a bend on the Volga that was within 50 miles (80 km) of the most easterly point on the Don. The Germans wanted to establish a landbridge there between the two rivers to allow them to proceed to the oilfields farther south. This campaign, codenamed Operation Blau, was launched on 28 June 1942. By the end of July, Nazi forces had occupied much of the Don and reached the oilfields at Maikop. On 21 August, the German flag was flying from Mount Elbrus, the highest peak in the Caucasus.

General Friedrich Paulus's Sixth Army reached the outskirts of Stalingrad at the end of August. The Soviet High Command had already realized the danger and on 12 July opened the Stalingrad Front under General Timoshenko. The official date of the start of the battle is 17 July, when forward units of the 6th Army clashed with the Soviet 62nd and 64th on the River Chir. At the end of July Rostov fell. Stalin issued his famous Order 227 – *Ni shagu nazad!*: 'Not a step back!'

The Germans now laid siege to Stalingrad, beginning with an aerial bombardment on 23 August. The sprawling city stretched for some 30-40 miles (48-64 km) along the Volga and was divided into three parts: the old town in the south, the modern city in the centre, and the industrial area to the north. It was bisected by the River Tsaritsa and dominated by a 91-metre (300-ft) high hill called Mamayev Kurgan.

In their attempt to regain Stalingrad, Chuikov's 62nd Army successfully maintained four bridgeheads on the left bank of the Volga, which were whittled down to a thin strip of buildings by the water's edge. This 1958 painting by Soviet artist V.K. Dmitrievskii shows Red Army soldiers preparing to cross the river.

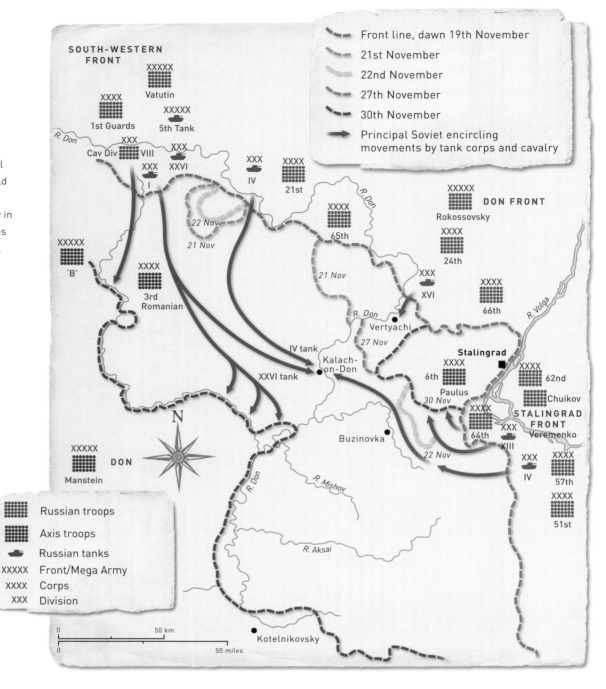

Map of the Soviet counter-offensive during the Battle of Stalingrad, showing the gradual encirclement of Field Marshal Friedrich Paulus's Sixth Army in a series of offensives by Red Army forces.

Front line, dawn 19th November
21st November
22nd November
27th November
30th November
Principal Soviet encircling movements by tank corps and cavalry

SOUTH-WESTERN FRONT

XXXXX Vatutin
XXXX 1st Guards
XXXXX 5th Tank
Cav Div XXX VIII
XXX I XXX XXVI
XXX IV
XXXX 21st
DON FRONT
XXXX 65th
XXXXX Rokossovsky
XXXX 24th
R. Don
22 Nov
21 Nov
21 Nov
XXX XVI
XXXX 66th
R. Volga
XXXXX 'B'
XXXX 3rd Romanian
R. Don
Vertyachi
27 Nov
Stalingrad
XXXX 6th Paulus
XXXX 62nd
Chuikov
IV tank
Kalach-on-Don
XXVI tank
30 Nov
XXXX 64th
XXX XIII
STALINGRAD FRONT
Veremenko
N
Buzinovka
22 Nov
XXX IV
XXXX 57th
XXXXX DON Manstein
R. Don
R. Mishov
XXXX 51st
Russian troops
Axis troops
Russian tanks
XXXXX Front/Mega Army
XXXX Corps
XXX Division
R. Aksai
0   50 km
0   50 miles
Kotelnikovsky

BATTLE IS JOINED

The *Luftwaffe* flew 2,000 bombing sorties in two days, killing 25,000 people. The next day Paulus reached the Volga, driving a wedge between the Soviet 62nd and 64th Armies. The Russians were outnumbered two to one, but another 50 divisions and 33 brigades were on their way, as well as 100,000 naval troops. General Vasilii Chuikov was appointed to lead the 62nd Army on 9 September.

Despite having fewer men, he successfully fought off Paulus's attacks. Chuikov needed to have control of the riverbank if he was to ensure his supply route.

By 26 September, the Germans were in control of the south and centre of the city, but had not yet secured Mamayev Kurgan. From the 27th onwards, they attempted to gain control of the hill and the industrial city in the north. A new assault on the factory district began on 14 October.

Paulus's last major attack was on 11 November; by the middle of that month the Germans were in control of more than 90 percent of the city. Chuikov had fought every inch and Paulus's troops were now exhausted. Russian casualties were massive: the 13th Guards' Division had gone in with 10,000 men. By the end of the battle there were 320 left.

BITTER STREET FIGHTING

The Russians had plenty of artillery on the right bank of the river, and the Germans certainly did not enjoy air supremacy. As the battle wore on, it became a *cause célèbre* in the Russian Great Patriotic War against the Nazi invader. Stalingrad was used to boost morale on the home front, thereby encouraging the courageous defenders. The Germans launched an all-out assault on the city on 17 November 1942. Fierce fighting erupted in the ruins. In one instance, a firefight took place in a factory where the Germans occupied the top floor, the Russians the middle, and more Germans the floor below.

Combat at such close quarters saw German officers revert to the tactics of the First World War, using the so-called 'stormwedges' devised in 1918: these groups of ten men, armed with machine guns, light mortars and flamethrowers, were sent in to clear the Russians out of cellars and sewers. On the Soviet side, T-34 tanks were dug in, half-buried in rubble. The Soviet forces tried to separate the German tanks from their infantry support by dropping mortar shells between the two.

Paulus realized that his flanks were vulnerable, and had anticipated a Soviet attack, but neither he nor High Command had expected the scale of this assault. Three Soviet armies – the South-Western Front, the Stalingrad Front and the Don Front – effected an encirclement. On 19 November, the South-Western Front commanded by the talented staff officer Colonel-General Nikolai Vatutin began 'Uranus', a counter-offensive directed against the Romanian Third Army north of Stalingrad. The next day, Colonel-General Andrey Yeremenko launched his Stalingrad Front against the Fourth Romanian and Fourth Panzer Army south of the city. With a total of 750,000 men, the two Russian armies had superiority from the start. Their spearheads linked up at Sovetsky, south of Kalach-on-the-Don on 23 November. Paulus's Sixth Army was surrounded, together with the Romanians, some Croatians and 50,000 Soviet auxiliaries – some of whom had been pressed into service by the Germans, while others had volunteered.

A DEADLY TRAP

Paulus and his 20 divisions could not break out on their own and Hitler refused to sanction his withdrawal. The Sixth Army was short of fuel, ammunition and transport. The only lifeline was provided by the *Luftwaffe*. The German High Command estimated that Paulus needed 700 tons a day. On 24 November, Göring assured Hitler that it was feasible to deliver 500 tons, while *Luftwaffe* command thought the figure would be closer to 350 tons. On 19 December, 295 tons were dropped, but the average was closer to just 100 and the weather meant that much of the time it was too overcast for pilots to locate the German positions. In addition, the aircraft had to fly through a heavy flak barrage; many were shot down.

Now only Hoth's 4th Panzer Army stood between the Soviets and the Sea of Azov, and it only possessed one intact division. The plan was to provide Hoth with reinforcements while Army Section Hollidt attacked from the north. However, this came to nought in the face of further Russian advances. Some Italian and Romanian units to the north and south

As the German Sixth Army attempted to take the northern industrial sector of Stalingrad, the area became the scene of intense fighting. Here, a group of Russian defenders fire at Nazi forces from the ruins of an abandoned factory.

now took the opportunity to quit the battle. A relief force was assembled, but the Soviets held it back. On 12 December, Army Group Don (which included Paulus's Sixth Army) launched Operation 'Wintergewitter', with Manstein in command. But at the same time, in Operation 'Little Saturn', the Soviet South-Western Front penetrated deep behind Army Group Don. Manstein did his best, with General Hoth advancing to within 30 miles (48 km) of the 6th Army, but Paulus's forces were too depleted to effect a breakout. By the end of December, the Germans knew surrender was inevitable.

On 10 January, the Polish Colonel-General Konstantin Rokossovsky, commander of the Don Front, executed Operation Ring, which resulted in Paulus's pocket being reduced by half. But Paulus still refused to lay down his arms.

THE FÜHRER'S FURY

On 13 January, the Chief of the General Staff, Kurt Zeitzler, sought to gain Hitler's permission to attempt a breakout and retreat from Stalingrad. Hitler was incandescent with rage: 'Paulus should not even dare to come to me with these things! He can't come out of there. I refuse his request.' Hitler's desire to hold on to Stalingrad at all costs may be explained by its name: as Stalin's own city, its fall would have been a terrible humiliation to the Soviet leader.

On 22 January, Paulus asked Hitler for permission to surrender. Hitler refused. The Führer was similarly incensed when General von Seydlitz-Kurzbach, the commander of LI Corps radioed to say he could no longer take responsibility for his corps: 'Reject responsibility – that is cowardice! I will not freely give up

Stalingrad, even if the whole Sixth Army perishes in the act!'

By the 26th, Paulus occupied two small pockets and elements of the 297th Infantry Division had already surrendered. On 31 January, Hitler made Paulus a field marshal, noting in his communiqué that no Prussian or German field marshal had ever been taken prisoner. The clear implication was that Paulus should commit suicide. Paulus surrendered the next day; on the expectation that he should take his own life, he contemptuously noted: 'I have no intention of shooting myself for this Bohemian corporal.' When news reached the Führer, his anger knew no bounds, as he swept the campaign map of Stalingrad from the table. The northern pocket carried on fighting until 2 February; by then up to 60,000 Germans had perished.

On 2 February, Hitler informed his closest aides: 'Last night I had a premonition that the Russians had taken Paulus prisoner. As a result I wanted to rescind his promotion to field marshal. The German people should not know that a German field marshal is in Russian captivity. The story of the Sixth Army's struggle and collapse must be told to the German people with the generals fighting shoulder to shoulder with their men in the trenches and dying with them at the end. I need a million new soldiers.'

ONWARD TO BERLIN

During the battle, POWs on both sides were reduced to cannibalism. Now, as many as 110,000 Germans were taken into captivity. By the time the final official group of released German POWs reached Germany in 1956, it was clear that fewer than 5,000 Stalingrad veterans had survived their internment. One of those who did was Friedrich Paulus, who died in Dresden in 1957.

In both its sheer savagery, and in the extraordinary tenacity shown by the defenders, the Battle of Stalingrad was reminiscent of Verdun. Yet the destruction of the Sixth Army also gave it something of the flavour of Cannae. But Hitler had no Fabius Maximus to grind down the Russians. Stalingrad marked the end of his expansionist dreams. From here on in, the forces of National Socialism were condemned to fight a rearguard action, as the Red Army began its relentless advance towards Berlin.

'Last night I had a premonition that the Russians had taken Paulus prisoner. As a result I wanted to rescind his promotion to field marshal. The German people should not know that a German field marshal is in Russian captivity. The story of the Sixth Army's struggle and collapse must be told to the German people with the generals fighting shoulder to shoulder with their men in the trenches and dying with them at the end. I need a million new soldiers.'

ADOLF HITLER REACTS FURIOUSLY TO NEWS OF THE DESTRUCTION OF THE SIXTH ARMY AT STALINGRAD

KORSUN-SHEVCHENKOVSKY POCKET

Colonel-General Ivan Konev *v.* German forces 24 January–16 February 1944

THE EASTERN FRONT WAS WEARING HITLER DOWN by the first months of 1944. Chief of Staff Kurt Zeitzler had to break it to him that the Germans would have to withdraw from Nikopol, in order to strengthen their line. At these words Hitler leapt up, threw himself across the table, screwed up the map in his left hand and screamed: 'If only the generals could finally understand why I cling to this area so much! We urgently need Nikopol manganese! They simply don't want to understand this. And as soon as they are a few tanks short, they go immediately to their radios and say, "without tanks we can't hold on. We ask for permission to retreat!" '

When Hitler's rage had subsided, Zeitzler informed him of the German army's other setbacks: the Eighth Army was having problems in the Korsun-Shevchenkovsky pocket. The operation to relieve the army was getting nowhere because the Russians were resisting ferociously.

The man who was perhaps most keen to see the German front shortened was Field Marshal Erich von Manstein. He went to see Hitler on 4 January and argued for a withdrawal of the troops in the Dnepr bend – the Korsun-Shevchenkovsky pocket. They were holding a stretch of river roughly 60 miles (100 km) long; a salient centring on Korsun, west of Cherkassy.

Naturally, Hitler wouldn't hear of it, and suspected Manstein of having designs on his supreme command. General Ivan Konev's Second Ukrainian Army Group had driven the Germans back to the River Dnepr near Dnepropetrovsk.

The Germans clung to their positions on the frozen river around Korsun, creating a bulge which Konev tried to surround. The suggestion that the salient might be 'pinched off' came from Marshal Georgi Zhukov. The idea was to create inner and outer rings around a cauldron: the inner ones to destroy the Germans within the pocket, while the outer one would defend the Soviets from any German army seeking to liberate their countrymen.

The strategy was similar to that employed at Stalingrad: Konev's Second Ukrainian Army Group drove northeast, while Vatutin's First Ukrainian Army Group struck southeast. Once the Germans had been encircled, they were ground down by aerial and artillery bombardment.

Konev employed a feint to try and dupe the German defenders, but they were not fooled. The battle was fought in the terrible conditions of a Russian winter and there were ten days of ferocious

Terrible winter conditions prevailed at the Battle of Korsun-Shevchenkovsky Pocket. This painting by Soviet artist Petr Krivonogov shows a German column marching past piles of their frozen dead.

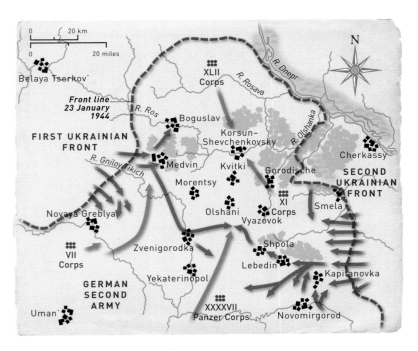

Soviet and German troop deployments in the Cherkassy pocket on a bend of the River Dnepr in the Ukraine. Amazingly, some two-thirds of the German force managed to escape this deadly encirclement.

fighting before the two Russian armies were united at the village of Zvenigorodka on 28 January. Konev wired to his leader: 'There is no need to worry, Comrade Stalin, the encircled enemy will not escape.'

German forces at Cherkassy comprised the XI Army, commanded by Lieutenant-General Wilhelm Stemmermann and XLII Army Corps with Lieutenant-General Theobald Lieb in charge. There was also SS Wiking Division, made up of Belgians from the SS Sturmbrigade Wallonien and Estonians of the SS Battalion Narwa together with several thousand Russian auxiliaries. All these were now trapped: around 54,000 men with 30 functioning tanks and 47 guns. There is a suggestion that their morale was further eroded by General von Seydlitz-Kurzbach and his Russian-based 'Committee for a Free Germany', which broadcast appeals to the German troops to surrender.

A RESCUE BID

Once again it was Manstein who was tasked with going to the rescue of the beleaguered Germans. However, the field marshal was short of equipment, especially tanks and aircraft. The Third

Panzer Division, for example, had just 27 tanks and 34 guns. The weather was appalling, and the German vehicles became bogged down in quagmires. Manstein wanted to direct his blow at a single point on the Russian line, but Hitler ordered him to spread his attack along the whole Soviet front.

The Russians tried to split the German forces inside the pocket. Stemmermann realized what they were doing and ordered the Wiking Division – the only one with armour – to hold the road to Korsun. Konev was able to ward Manstein off and on 8 February he sent a lieutenant-colonel and an interpreter under a white flag to parley with the Germans. He called on Stemmermann to lay down his arms. Stemmermann refused; Stalin once more feared the Germans would attempt a breakthrough.

One major difference between the Battle of Korsun-Shevchenkovsky and Stalingrad was in the effectiveness of *Luftwaffe* operations. Its Ju 52 transport planes were able to deliver 82,948 gallons of fuel, 868 tons of ammunition and four tons of medical supplies. They also airlifted 4,161 wounded men to safety.

On 11 February, III Panzer Corps ground to a halt on the River Gniloy Tikich. The following day, Konev was given sole charge of the operation. Manstein made a new thrust towards the south side of the pocket, getting to within 6 miles (10 km) of the German defenders before being driven back. Stemmermann now tried to mislead the Soviets. He withdrew a body of his troops to the north while mounting an assault on the villages in the southwest of the pocket. On 11 February, Major Robert Kästner's 105th Grenadiers captured Nova-Buda in a night assault. The next day the Germans took Komarovka, then Khilki. The village of Shanderovka changed hands several times. Once III Panzer became aware of these gains, they pushed towards their countrymen to relieve them.

On 15 February, Stemmermann received the following message: 'Capacity for action by III Panzerkorps limited by weather and supply situation. Gruppe Stemmermann must perform breakthrough as far as the line Zhurzintsy-Hil 239 by its own effort. There link up with III Panzerkorps.'

RIVER OF DEATH

Ordered to break out by any means at his disposal, Stemmermann remained in the north of the pocket with a rearguard of 6,500 men while Lieb attempted to force a way out in the south. Just over 4 miles (6.4 km) separated the two German armies at the nearest point. Shanderovka was now dubbed 'Hell's Gate' as it was peppered by Russian artillery fire and strafed by Red Air Force *Sturmovik* ground-attack aircraft. On 16 February, Manstein sent another message to Stemmermann: 'Password Freedom, objective Lysyanka 23.00 hours.' In the charge of their doctors, 1,450 non-walking wounded were left behind in Shanderovka while the others pushed forward in three columns.

Setting out with fixed bayonets, and followed by artillery and equipment, the soldiers thought they would walk into the arms of II Panzer Corps. Instead they faced well-armed Russian soldiers. Nonetheless, they still managed to push their way forward through not one but two Russian lines and several battalions and regiments reached the German lines at Oktyabr by 4.10 that morning.

Kästner managed to bring out his wounded and heavy weapons. The 105th entered Lysyanka at 6.30. The key to this success was the fact that Stemmermann remained in the north of the cauldron, which led the Soviets into wildly overestimating German strength there.

The left flank had less luck. They came up against Hill 239, which was occupied by T-34 tanks. The Germans abandoned their heavy equipment and fought on to the west. Finding their path blocked, they decided to make good their escape to the south, where they came up agains the River Gniloy Tikich. Here they were forced to abandon their small arms while the Russian T-34s took it out on their support troops and the wounded in Red Cross convoys.

Every possible means was found to cross the river, with its waters swollen by melting ice. Lorries, tanks and wagons were driven into the flood. Trees were felled and bridges hurriedly constructed. Lifelines were made from harnesses and belts, but still hundreds drowned. General Lieb swam across with his horse. A human chain made by SS commander Herbert Otto Gille, alternating swimmers and non-swimmers, broke and scores of men perished. Even so, some 35,000 troops led by their corps commanders managed to pick their way through the Soviet lines.

What is remarkable about the battle is not so much the resounding Russian victory, but the fact that two-thirds of the Germans managed to escape.

Konev attacked the rearguard, slaughtering the Germans, including Stemmermann, whose body was found on the battlefield. Soviet records claim that 77,000 Germans were killed in the battle but the real figure is more like 19,000, including soldiers under Manstein's command. After the victory Konev was made a marshal of the Soviet Union. Now the road was open for the Red Army towards the southern Ukraine.

> '*There is no need to worry Comrade Stalin, the encircled enemy will not escape.*'
>
> GENERAL IVAN KONEV

D-DAY

THE SOVIET UNION HAD BORNE THE BRUNT OF THE WAR, and repeatedly urged America and Britain to open a 'second front' against Nazi Germany. On 6 June 1944, after assembling troops and equipment along the south coast of England for months, the Western Allies invaded the coast of Normandy in force. Operations Neptune (naval) and Overlord (ground forces) were originally planned for 'not later than the 5th', but were delayed by bad weather. The Allies chose Normandy because the Germans had built the strongest fortifications at the obvious point they expected a landing, the narrower Pas de Calais. Prior to the invasion, to make the Germans believe that the Allies would indeed disembark there, a massive deception plan – codename Operation Fortitude – was enacted. This involved mustering a complete, fictititous army group in southeast England under General George Patton, complete with inflatable dummy tanks and landing craft.

Invasion troops of the US 1st Infantry Division disembark from a landing craft at Omaha Beach on 6 June 1944. German defences were unexpectedly strong at Omaha, and the Americans took heavy casualties. By the end of a gruelling day, just two small footholds had been established here.

In the disastrous Dieppe Raid of 1942, the British had learned to their cost that a port could not be captured in head-on assault by landing troops. The main fruit of this bitter experience was the 'Mulberry' floating dock, an artificial harbour that obviated the need to seize a port. On 6 June, these remarkable constructions were towed across the Channel in sections.

German occupation forces in France had been softened up in readiness for the attack with relentless bombing – especially in the Pas de Calais. Some 60 percent of the railway network had been knocked out too, to prevent the Germans from bringing up troops quickly.

Western forces were commanded by General Dwight D. Eisenhower, with Sir Bernard Montgomery in charge of the ground forces in 21st Army Group. He had to reckon with a well-defended coastline: the Atlantic Wall was meant to inhibit just this sort of operation, although the German commander in the west,

Field Marshal Gerd von Rundstedt, was unimpressed by the coastal defences, and referred to them as 'a propaganda wall'.

THE INVASION BEGINS

On 6 June, an armada of 5,000 vessels (including 1,213 warships) left the British coast. A total of 3,200 aircraft were on standby and around 3 million men were involved in the operation – although only a small minority of these were involved in the attack. The British landed 83,000 men, the Americans around 10,000 fewer. At the same time, 23,000 parachutists and glider-borne troops boarded their aircraft. Just after midnight on the 6th, Operation Tonga began as D Company, the 2nd Oxfordshire and Buckinghamshire Light Infantry commanded by Major John Howard, seized the bridges over the Caen Canal and the River Orne.

Howard's force of 181 men, including a handful of Royal Engineers and men of the Glider Pilot Regiment, made their

landings from 'Horsa' gliders and secured the eastern flank to prevent German armour from reaching the British 3rd Infantry Division, due to land on Sword Beach later that day.

The Ox and Bucks landed very close to their objectives at 16 minutes past midnight – the first Allied troops to set foot in France. They completely surprised the German defenders, and took the bridges within ten minutes.

These 'water obstacles' might have been lethal for the seaborne forces, and Montgomery had decided they had to be removed before the landings. The airborne divisons landed soon after – although some went astray, landing in the sea or in rivers swollen by the recent rain. Many of the US airborne troops were drowned.

Yet the airborne assault did achieve its aim of sowing confusion among the Germans. Field Marshal Rommel was actually on leave on D-Day; he had gone back to Germany to celebrate the birthday of his wife.

MIXED FORTUNES

As Operation Overlord began, Hitler was preoccupied with the Eastern Front and the fate of Army Group C in particular, which was teetering on the brink of collapse: 'The road to Germany leads

The Normandy landings on D-Day, 6 June 1944, showing the Allied beachheads and airborne objectives.

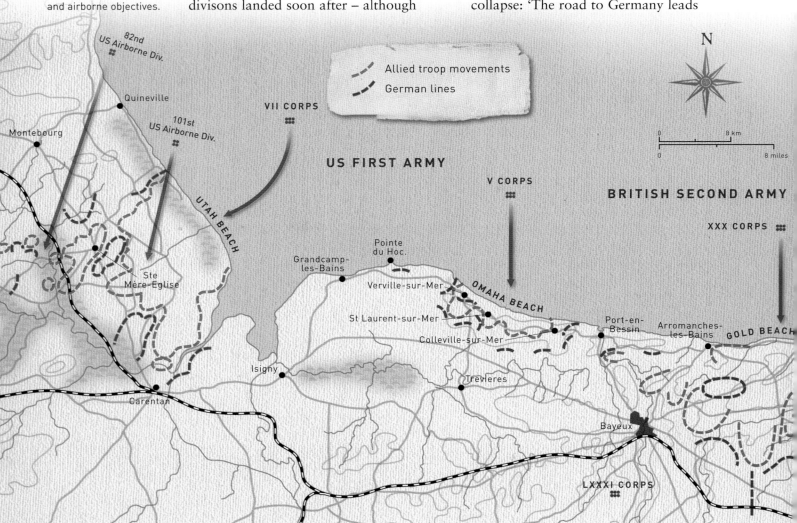

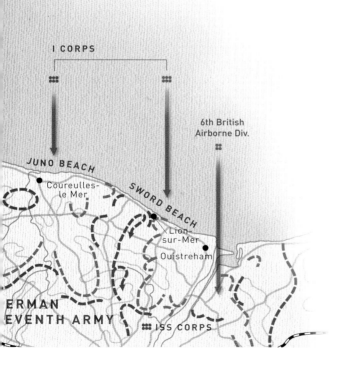

directly through this army group! We must not retreat a single step here!' He was confident that Rundstedt – who had about 59 divisions in France and the Low Countries, including six armoured divisions – would be able to keep the Allies at bay. There were two German army groups: A, commanded by Rommel, and G, led by Colonel-General Blaskowitz as well as Panzer Group West, under the command of General Geyr von Schweppenburg and Colonel-General Kurt Student's paratroop army. Rundstedt's plan was to mop up the Allies once they had moved out of range of protection by their naval guns. Rommel's experience in North Africa made him less sanguine, as he knew that Allied air superiority would hamper the movement of his armour.

The British landings, at Gold and Sword beaches, went ahead as planned. Innovations in weaponry for the invasion

By mid-June 1944, the Allied invasion was in full swing. Their tenuous hold on Omaha Beach had been transformed into a major beachhead, as thousands of men, jeeps, trucks, tanks and half-tracks were landed under the protection of barrage balloons.

included the Sherman 'DD' (duplex-drive) amphibious tank, with canvas flotation screens and propellers to drive it to shore. Once on land the screen was lowered and the tank could fire immediately while negotiating the German beach defences or 'hedgehogs'. The Canadians, landing at Juno Beach, encountered heavy resistance from the defenders. A third of their landing craft were sunk or damaged.

BATTLES IN THE *BOCAGE*

Even after a beachhead had been established at Juno, the Canadians and British made slow progress, being badly mauled on the 7th by 12th SS Panzer Division commanded by Standartenführer Kurt Meyer. Elsewhere the advance was impeded by the damp *'bocage'* countryside of western Normandy, with its small fields and tall hedgerows, which offered poor visibility. The British-led forces faced Colonel-General Dollmann commanding the Seventh Army with its 12 infantry divisions occupying the sector that encompassed the River Orne, the Cotentin Peninsula and Brittany. The British 3rd Division tried but failed to seize Caen, 9 miles (14 km) away. Over the following weeks, the city was largely flattened by bombing.

At Utah Beach, the Americans fared relatively well, but they encountered fierce resistance at Omaha where the length and pitch of the beach made an assault particularly perilous. It had been hoped that the mostly Polish and Russian defenders there would not fight hard. As it

was, the crack German 352nd Division had recently arrived. Many US landing craft and amphibious tanks were sunk and 600 troops were killed – a quarter of all those who perished on D-Day. Later the American 'Mulberry' fell victim to a storm.

On 6 June, over 150,000 soldiers were landed and the element of surprise was maintained. The Germans failed to counterattack and even the 21st Panzer Division near Sword was sent in far too late to be effective.

Thereafter, the Allies established a firm bridgehead, with the Americans taking the right of the line and the British the left. The Americans advanced up the Cotentin Peninsula to take the important port of Cherbourg, which fell at the end of June. Montgomery was left battling for Caen, which resisted doggedly. A new offensive, 'Epsom', was launched from 24–30 June. The 7th Armoured Division was halted before Villers-Bocage on 12–14 June in an action that has been branded the 'nadir of British incompetence' by historian Gordon Corrigan. The British force was intercepted by 101st SS Heavy Panzer Battalion with its five Tiger tanks commanded by Obersturmführer Michael Wittmann. They wiped out the British vanguard of 20 Cromwell tanks, with Wittmann supposedly destroying ten of them single-handed. Villers-Bocage was not recaptured until 4 August.

The campaign in the *bocage* had some similarities to the trench fighting in the First World War, with the vital difference that in Normandy the Allies always enjoyed air superiority. By 17 June, they had successfully disembarked over half a million men and 81,000 vehicles. On 18 June, amid concerns that the assault was beginning to stall, Montgomery issued a directive calling for the capture of Caen and Cherbourg. The Allies had already suffered 61,700 casualties, but crucially the Germans lost 80,000 in the same period.

PAINFULLY SLOW PROGRESS

German morale was low; Colonel-General Dollmann took his own life on 28 June. When Gerd von Rundstedt voiced his view that the only solution was to make peace, he was sacked and replaced by Gunther von Kluge. Kluge would later be linked with the conspirators who tried to assassinate Hitler on 20 July. There is a suggestion that he tried to negotiate a ceasefire with the Allies, but was thwarted by his inability to locate their HQ. He commited suicide rather than answer for his conduct and was replaced by Field-Marshal Walther Model.

By early July, the Allies were supposed to have taken Alençon, Rennes and St Malo, but in no case were they more than 15 miles (24 km) inland. On 17 July, Rommel was strafed by Allied fighters in his staff car; after the July Plot misfired, in which he was also implicated, he was forced to take poison. Many in the German camp had had enough of the war and were in favour of striking a deal with the Western Allies. As the war turned against them, the Germans' greatest fear was being overrun by Soviet forces in the east.

A new thrust to capture Caen was ultimately successful, but at huge cost. In Operation Charnwood, Air Chief Marshal Trafford Leigh-Mallory proposed carpet bombing the city in the way that the Italian fortress of Monte Cassino had been levelled in February. There was fierce fighting within the city itself, but most of Caen was in Allied hands by the 10th.

Montgomery's job was to hold the Germans in the east to allow the Americans to break through in the west. On 18 July, he launched Operation Goodwood, east of Caen, to clear the Germans off Bourgébus Ridge with three armoured divisions. The British advanced just 7 miles (11 km) at the rate of 1,000 tons of bombs a mile. Montgomery's failure to make headway almost brought about his dismissal as commander of the ground forces. This costly action claimed 6,000 British casualties and 400 tanks and produced no positive result.

On 19 July, the town of St Lô, which according to plan should have fallen a month before, finally capitulated. This resulted in the desired breakthrough towards Avranches. But finding himself deadlocked by German resistance west of the city a week later, US general Omar Bradley launched Operation Cobra on 25 July. By now the war had become more mobile, and Patton swung into action, taking command of the US Third Army. US forces wheeled south and headed for Paris, while the British and the Canadians continued to slug it out in northern France.

Remains of a German bunker at Pointe du Hoc, west of Omaha Beach. On D-Day, US Rangers scaled the cliffs here on rope ladders and destroyed the heavy gun emplacements. Many remnants of the German 'Atlantic Wall' can still be seen along the Normandy coast.

THE PHILIPPINES

Field Marshal Douglas MacArthur *v.* Japanese forces
20–27 October 1944

THE JAPANESE HAD BEEN WAITING TO POUNCE. After the fall of France in 1940, they invaded Indochina, waging a short but bloody war before the Vichy government capitulated. The United States responded with an oil embargo and other economic sanctions. But these backfired when, in order to ensure their fuel supplies, the Japanese set their sights on Malaya and the Dutch Indies. By December 1941, Japan was poised to subsume much of the region into its 'Greater East Asia Co-Prosperity Sphere'. The British had long anticipated this move, but still left their territories in southeast Asia woefully underdefended.

On 7 December, the day of their infamous attack on the American fleet at Pearl Harbor on Hawaii, the Japanese also struck the Philippines and Malaya. The Americans had wrested the Philippines from Spain in 1898. Despite enjoying nominal independence since 1935, there was still a strong American presence on the islands. The Japanese attack destroyed a third of the fighters and half the bombers at the US Air Fleet base at Clark Field near Manila. They followed up with landings on the island of Luzon. Manila was evacuated. Field Marshal Douglas MacArthur (the only American to hold that rank) had to be evacuated on 11 March, escaping by the skin of his teeth. As he left, he uttered his famous pledge: 'I shall return!'

MacArthur left behind Lieutenant-General Jonathan Wainwright, who held on until 7 May. When Japan finally took the Philippines, POWs were treated abominably in the Bataan Death March, in which thousands of Americans and Filipinos were slaughtered by their Japanese captors.

MACARTHUR RETURNS

Appointed SWPA – Supreme Commander Allied Forces in the Southwest Pacific – MacArthur based himself in Australia. He elaborated the strategy of 'island-hopping': taking small, poorly garrisoned islands and then allowing the bigger, better-defended ones to 'wither on the vine'. His promised return occurred on 20 October 1944, when he landed on the island of Leyte.

The invasion of the Philippines, while strategically unnecessary, was symbolically of immense importance, and so in October 1944 the biggest army ever assembled in the Pacific campaign sailed to Leyte. The fleet commanded by Admiral William F. Halsey included ships from the Royal Australian Navy. The armada counted 701 vessels, including 127 warships.The Royal Australian Airforce also took part in the operation.

The Japanese under General Tomoyuki Yamashita (the 'Tiger of Malaya') devised a brilliant plan to defend the archipelago, but lacked the troops to put it into effect. They also miscalculated the strength of

Island-hopping:
American troops of the 7th Cavalry Regiment advance towards San José on Leyte Island in the Philippines on 20 October 1944.

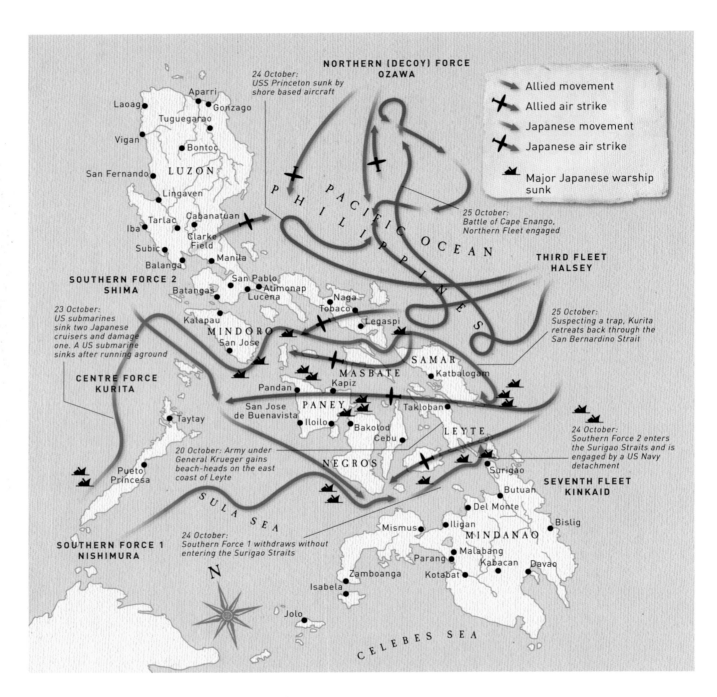

Within the map:

NORTHERN (DECOY) FORCE
OZAWA

24 October:
USS Princeton sunk by
shore based aircraft

25 October:
Battle of Cape Enango,
Northern Fleet engaged

THIRD FLEET
HALSEY

25 October:
Suspecting a trap, Kurita
retreats back through the
San Bernardino Strait

Allied movement
Allied air strike
Japanese movement
Japanese air strike
Major Japanese warship
sunk

Aparri
Laoag
Gonzago
Tuguegarao
Vigan
Bontoc
San Fernando
LUZON
Lingayen
Tarlac
Cabanatuan
Iba
Clarke
Subic
Field
Balanga
Manila

SOUTHERN FORCE 2
SHIMA

23 October:
US submarines
sink two Japanese
cruisers and damage
one. A US submarine
sinks after running aground

San Pablo
Batangas
Atimonap
Lucena
Naga
Tobaco
Katapau
Legaspi
MINDORO
San Jose
SAMAR
Katbalogam
MASBATE

CENTRE FORCE
KURITA

Pandan
Kapiz
PANEY
San Jose
de Buenavista
Iloilo
Taytay
Bakolod
Cebu
Takloban
LEYTE

24 October:
Southern Force 2 enters
the Surigao Straits and is
engaged by a US Navy
detachment

20 October: Army under
General Krueger gains
beach-heads on the east
coast of Leyte
NEGROS

Pueto
Princesa
Surigao
Butuan

SEVENTH FLEET
KINKAID

SOUTHERN FORCE 1
NISHIMURA

SULA SEA

24 October:
Southern Force 1 withdraws without
entering the Surigao Straits

N

Del Monte
Mismus
Iligan
Bislig
MINDANAO
Parang
Malabang
Zamboanga
Kotabat
Kabacan
Davao
Isabela
Jolo

CELEBES SEA

The Battle of the Philippines, 20–27 October 1944.

the attacking force. The first Americans to arrive in the Philippines landed at Suluan at the mouth of the Gulf of Leyte on 17 October. When American POWs heard that their countrymen were back they allowed themselves a weak joke: 'better Leyte than never!'

A landing took place on neighbouring Homonhon the next day. The gates to Leyte were now secured and GIs arrived on the east coast and on Samar to the northwest on 20 October. MacArthur had been watching the landings from the bridge of the cruiser *Nashville*. After lunch he changed into a clean khaki uniform, sunglasses and a marshal's cap. Several members of the press corps were present on the barge that took him to the beach. A photograph shows MacArthur wading ashore. As he reached dry land he proclaimed 'People of the Philippines, I have returned! By the grace of Almighty God, our forces stand again on Philippine soil.' In language worthy of Joan of Arc, MacArthur gathered the journalists around him and invoked the 'Holy Grail of righteous victory!'

Japanese forces tenaciously clung on to Ormoc City on Leyte, but air superiority prevented them from dislodging the invaders. The Americans laid down temporary airstrips, but failed to stop the Japanese from landing 13,000 reinforcements from Luzon. The next time the Japanese tried bringing in 10,000 troops, however, their convoys were shot up and only a small number succeeded in making land.

The Japanese fought an intense battle from *takotsubo* dugouts, shaped like Christmas stockings, and other well-concealed positions, forcing the Americans to wrest every inch of territory from them. The Japanese would suddenly appear as if from nowhere, detonating explosives under tanks, and shooting the American attackers from behind. At Carigara Bay in November, the Americans moved against some Japanese positions that inhibited their artillery attack on Ormoc ('Breakneck Ridge' 5 – 16 November 1944). The Japanese fought tooth and nail from their earthworks, but by the 23rd, the Americans under General Sibert broke through.

All the while, American forces were subjected to *kamikaze* suicide attacks. Even after the Japanese had been swept from the plains, they continued to fight on in the mountains. Ormoc City fell to the Americans on 10 December and the port at Palompon on Christmas Day. But the fanaticism of the defenders meant that the battle for Leyte dragged on for months, even after the Japanese had lost the ability to provision their army.

'**Divine Wind**': The light aircraft carrier USS *Belleau Wood*, with Grumman Avenger torpedo bombers on board, blazes after being hit by a Japanese *kamikaze* plane during operations off Leyte on 30 October 1944. Aircraft carrier USS *Franklin* is seen ablaze in the background.

THE BATTLE OF LEYTE GULF
In the interim, the Japanese refusal to concede the Philippines had seen the largest naval battle of the entire war. On

'Better Leyte than never!'

American POWs, on learning that US forces had landed on Leyte

25 October, Admiral Soemu Toyoda despatched a large fleet to Leyte Gulf to confront the Americans and thwart the invasion. It was an almost suicidal mission. Although the Japanese had only 116 aircraft on their combined carriers, with another 180 in Manila to counter the American landing forces, the Japanese ships still possessed the biggest guns the world had ever seen. The battle went on into the night, as the sky was lit up by blinding streams of tracer bullets. US air and naval superiority eventually prevailed. Over the following four days, the Japanese lost 28 ships to the Americans' six. In the later stages of the engagement, the Japanese sent in *kamikaze* planes

laden with 250 kg (550 lb) bombs to attack the carriers. These succeeded in sinking the USS *St Lo*, but by then the pride of the Japanese Imperial Navy had been effectively destroyed.

The *kamikaze* missions were a new tactic. The idea was conceived by Vice Admiral Takijiro Onishi, who arrived in Luzon to find he had fewer than 100 planes left, and wondered how to deploy them to best effect. The name *kamikaze* ('divine wind') was originally applied to typhoons that dispersed two Mongol fleets in the 13th century, and saved Japan from foreign invasion.

After the destruction of its fleet, Tokyo ordered an all-out land battle on Leyte. Yamashita tried to get Field Marshal Terauchi to persuade the General Staff to

The liberator of the Philippines, Douglas MacArthur makes his famous landing at Homonhon on Leyte. This is one of the most enduring images of the entire Pacific War.

change its mind. Reinforcements would have the greatest difficulty getting past the American fleet. Moreover, Yamashita suspected that Leyte was a feint, and that the real objective of the Americans was to take the main island of Luzon. He was right: the Americans disembarked at Mindoro, just south of Luzon, at 7.32 a.m. on 15 December, pushing 7 miles (11 km) inland by that afternoon.

There were only 1,000 Japanese on Mindoro, and Yamashita gave it up for lost. On 28 December, the Americans had retaken the two airbases on the island. He had also quietly given up on Leyte despite the fact the Japanese prime minister Kunaiki Koiso had committed his government to victory there. He was more intent on holding Cebu and Negros, which he deemed 'highly suitable for self-sustaining action'.

MOVING ON MANILA

The landings on Luzon – home to the Philippines' capital, Manila – commenced on 9 January. It was America's biggest campaign of the war. Close on 175,000 men were landed at Lingayen Gulf under the command of General Walter Krueger – one of the very many German-Americans who distinguished themselves in the Pacific Theatre. The preliminary bombing only managed to hit some transport ships taking American POWs to Japan; hundreds were killed. Encountering only token resistance, US forces were deployed south towards the capital, covering 8 miles (13 km) by dusk. Yamashita had seen them coming and built strong defensive positions in the hills around the bay, but decided that the 'decisive battle' would be fought in the hills in the north of the island.

The Americans pounded the Japanese defensive positions from their ships, but several of them were sunk by *kamikaze* aircraft. But by the last week of January, the Americans were back at Clark Field, the scene of their humiliation three years previously.

On 3 February, elements of the 1st Cavalry Division entered the capital. Corregidor held out until the 27th, while it took until 3 March to clear the Japanese from Manila. On 13 April, to put an end to the fierce resistance from Fort Drum in Manila Bay, an American team pumped 3,000 gallons of diesel oil into the fort and ignited it. There were no survivors.

It was time to mop up: Palawan Island was attacked on 28 February when the 8th Army landed at Puerto Princesa. On 17 April, they landed on the last island in the archipelago, Mindanao, and from there retook Cebu, with its naval base, Panay and Negros. Once again the Japanese withdrew in small units to the jungle and fought on until 2 September 1945. On Lubang Island, the last to surrender – Second-Lieutenant Hiroo Onoda – was only rediscovered in 1974, claiming he was waiting for someone to give him orders to lay down his arms!

More than 336,000 Japanese lost their lives in the course of the Philippines Campaign. The American dead totalled 14,000. On Leyte only one in 13 of the 75,000 Japanese defenders survived. They had faced an army of a quarter of a million well-armed Americans.

'People of the Philippines, I have returned! By the grace of Almighty God, our forces stand again on Philippine soil.'

FIELD MARSHAL DOUGLAS MACARTHUR AFTER LANDING ON THE PHILIPPINES

DIEN BIEN PHU

General Vo Nguyen Giap *v.* French colonial forces
23 March–7 May 1954

JAPANESE-OCCUPIED INDOCHINA SURRENDERED to the Allies in 1945. In 1940, the United States had refused to assist French Vichy forces there and was strongly opposed to France reclaiming its former colony after the war. The ensuing power vacuum was exploited by Communist leader Ho Chi Minh, who sought full independence for his country. Ho asked General Vo Nguyen Giap, a former schoolmaster and journalist, to form the nucleus of a Vietnamese national army. The force he created, the Viet Minh ('League for the Revolution and Independence of Viet-Nam') prepared to square up for conflict with French colonial troops, who arrived at Haiphong in 1946 to take possession of Indochina.

French forces in Indochina relied heavily on their airforce, which was equipped with a motley collection of British Spitfires, German Ju52s and American C-47 Dakotas. Trained and equipped by Communist China, Giap's guerrillas began a campaign of harassment against the French, seizing entire tracts of land that became no-go areas for the colonial forces. In the words of historian Bernard Fall, with the loss of a string of forts along the Chinese border: 'the French had suffered their greatest colonial defeat since Montcalm had died at Quebec.'

STEMMING THE TIDE

In a short space of time, the Viet Minh developed into a proper army with a regimental and divisional structure. In 1950, as it closed in on Hanoi, the French began to make provisions for the evacuation of women and children from the city. In a last-ditch attempt to stem the tide, France now sent in one of its two greatest generals of the Second World War, Marshal Jean de Lattre de Tassigny. He defeated Giap at the Battle of Vinh

Yen in the Red River Delta in the first weeks of 1951, but lost his only son at the battle for Nam Dinh in May. Even so, de Lattre went on to record a series of victories that forced Giap and his Chinese advisors to revise their strategy. In late 1951, illness forced de Lattre to return to Paris, where he died of cancer within a few months.

The Battle of Hoa-Binh, which lasted from November 1951 to February 1952, witnessed what Bernard Fall has called 'some of the bloodiest river battles since the American Civil War'. In this long engagement, despite losing more men than the French, Giap emerged victorious. Refusing to be drawn out into the open to fight on French terms, he bided his time before going on the offensive and forcing the French to withdraw.

To counteract the increasingly modern equipment used by the French and their command of the air, the Viet Minh became masters of camouflage. They wore palm-leaf helmets with wire mesh disks attached to them, adorned with the foliage of the local terrain.

In shallow trenches at the centre of the camp at Dien Bien Phu, exhausted French paratroops await another Viet Minh assault on their position. This photograph was taken on 24 March 1954.

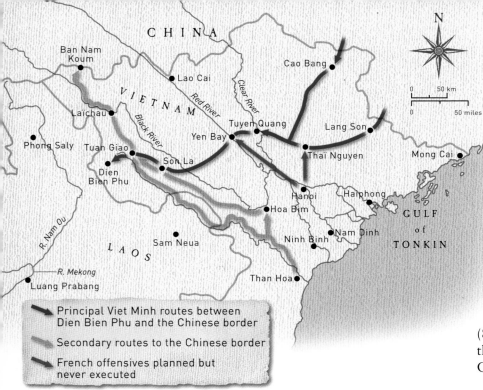

The Viet Minh's links across Vietnam to Dien Bien Phu, 1954.

Legend on map:
- Principal Viet Minh routes between Dien Bien Phu and the Chinese border
- Secondary routes to the Chinese border
- French offensives planned but never executed

OPERATION LORRAINE

In October–November 1952, in Operation Lorraine, French troops were despatched to Nghia Lo. This operation was intended to seriously disrupt the enemy's lines of supply and communication along the Red River. Victory would, it was hoped, force Giap to withdraw a large part of his forces from the northwest.

A four-stage strategy envisaged opening up a bridgehead across the Red River to Phu-Tho, which would link up with a task force heading north from Viet-Tri. These two forces would progress to Phu-Doan, where they would be joined by Airborne Group 1 and a *Dinassault* (Naval Assault Division). The French could then provision the various supply depots and materiel in the region. The result would be the withdrawal of Giap's forces to prevent their total destruction.

This was the largest army the French had ever assembled in Vietnam: four mobile groups, one airborne group and three parachute battalions plus five commando units, two armoured sub-groups as well as tank-destroyer and reconnaissance squadrons, two *Dinassaults*, two artillery battalions and sundry engineers – a total of more than

30,000 men. The troops were assigned the job of establishing a number of strong points, at the centre of which would be a 0.6-mile (1-km) -long airstrip.

Because of the size of the taskforce, an infrastructure of roads and bridges had to be created, a taxing undertaking for French engineers. The bridgehead was secured by 4 November 1952. The French advanced steadily, taking some 500 miles (800 km) by 7 November. By 14 November, they had achieved their objectives and General Salan ordered a withdrawal.

Yet as they advanced, the French realized that the Viet Minh were stronger than they thought. They were receiving aid not only from the Chinese, but also from the Soviet Union. The withdrawing French found the road blocked on 17 November. The force was ambushed at the Chan-Muong gorge, a surprise attack that turned into a massacre. The French had miscalculated the strength of their opponents and relied on their artillery to dislodge them from the hills that commanded the position.

JUNGLE FORTRESS

On 24 July 1953, the fateful decision was taken that, in order to protect northern Laos, the French should occupy the Dien Bien Phu valley, situated in the highlands west of Hanoi and close to the Laos border. Dien Bien Phu was selected rather than other sites because of the size of the valley floor (10 x 5.6 miles/16 x 9 km) and the relative distance from the commanding hills (6.5–7.5 miles/10–12 km), which put them out of range of Viet Minh artillery. It also had a small airstrip.

The new French commander-in-chief in Indochina, Henri Navarre, set about fortifying Dien Bien Phu. From 20 November onwards, Operation Castor saw 9,000 French Union troops dropped or flown into the area. The arrangement chosen for the French strongholds (each of which was named after a former mistress of the commanding officer, Colonel Christian de Castries) was ill-conceived. The southernmost one, 'Isabelle,' where three of the 12 infantry battalions were stationed together with a third of the guns and tanks, lay 4.4 miles (7 km) to the south of the main position. This effectively prevented the defenders from concentrating their forces. Also, aside from the French positions at Gabrielle (491 metres/1,610 ft) and Beatrice (509 metres/1,670 ft) none of the other

French defensive positions at Dien Bien Phu (right and below). In the siege, the French lost around 8,000 killed, wounded or missing in action, while estimated Viet Minh casualties were in excess of 25,000.

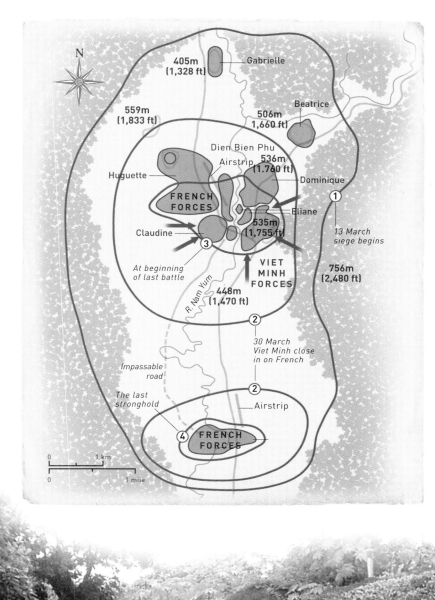

To the rescue, temporarily:

Paratroops of the French Foreign Legion land near the fortress of Dien Bien Phu on 16 March 1954. Their deployment brought only brief respite for the defenders.

strongholds was higher than 380 metres (1,250 ft). There were also two ridges, with a respective average height of 1,100 and 550 metres (3,600 and 1,800 ft), within 2,500 metres (1.6 miles) of Dien Bien Phu. This meant that, once Gabrielle and Beatrice were lost (which they were on Day One), the Viet Minh commanded several high points from which they could look down on the French positions.

In the four months before the Viet Minh attacked Dien Bien Phu, the fortress was inspected many times by French and American experts. No one suggested it was anything other than sound.

As Operation Castor proceeded, Giap was also busy. A force of 50,000 Viet Minh, advancing on bicycles, surrounded the position and began digging tunnels under the hills. A network of perfectly camouflaged paths allowed the Viet Minh to deliver ammunition to their gun emplacements. The enemy positions were, according to Navarre, 'a human ant-hill'. Moreover, the Viet Minh had taken sound advice from the Chinese on how to site their batteries, sinking single artillery pieces into shell-proof dugouts. This made them impervious to French artillery fire or aerial bombardment. It was also too wet for the use of napalm (deployed in war for the very first time by the French in 1949). Before long, the French found themselves outnumbered and outgunned.

THE SIEGE COMMENCES

The siege of the French position began on 13 March 1954. The opening Viet Minh barrage knocked out both the airstrip and the French artillery. Now French aircraft had to drop provisions from too great a height to ensure accuracy.

Despondency reigned among the defenders, who left the fighting to relief forces of parachutists commanded by the likes of Pierre Langlais and the legendary Marcel Bigeard, which were dropped in to save them. The Viet Minh assaults employed tactics reminiscent of Vauban's time, sapping the defensive positions and digging to within a few feet of the French before blowing up the wire with bangalore torpedos (explosive charges at the end of long, extendable tubes). The French defended the fort with impressive bravery. The heaps of Viet Minh dead littered beside Beatrice prompted Giap to seek a truce on the 14th. Of the 3rd Battalion, 13th Half-Brigade defending, there were only a few survivors, and no officers.

The situation at Gabrielle was similar. The sandbags were blown to bits by the artillery fire. The defenders – the 5th Battalion, 7th Battalion and the Algerian Rifles – all fought with great courage. On 14 March, Colonel Langlais counter-attacked towards Gabrielle with his paratroopers and two tank platoons. They succeeded in breaking in, but could not create adequate defences. The situation was comparable to Verdun, where the topsoil had been ground into fine sand by repeated shellfire. All Langlais could do was to gather up the survivors and fall back. This setback effectively signalled the beginning of the end for the French defenders.

The relentless bombardment drove the French troops crazy. The final landing on the airstrip occurred on 28 March when an ambulance aircraft landed to take out 25 casualties. But departure was delayed by a mechanical problem, and before the plane could leave the Viet Minh artillery blew it to pieces.

The defenders were running out of ammunition and grenades. On 15 April, C-119 transport planes provisioning the garrison accidentally dropped 19 tons of ammunition onto enemy lines. The last strong points fell on 7 May, when 12,000 French soldiers capitulated. The next day, the 13th Half-Brigade of the Foreign Legion staged a last-ditch bayonet charge. Dien Bien Phu was a defeat on a scale of the Fall of France. Only 70 men succeeded in breaking out of the fortress.

The reasons for this military catastrophe were threefold; over-reliance on air resupply; entrenchment within a fortress that was insufficiently compact, so that Isabelle could not be used to defend Gabrielle, Beatrice or Anne-Marie; and a fatal underestimation of the enemy's capabilities.

On 20 July 1954, at the conference table in Geneva, the French had to accede to Vietnamese demands. All of Vietnam north of the 17th Parallel was to be ceded to the Communist government of Ho Chi Minh. It was a foretaste of the bitter defeats the French were to suffer over the next decade in North Africa. The French retired hurt from Indochina, leaving the United States to hold the line against Communist expansion in southeast Asia.

'The French ... suffered their greatest colonial defeat since Montcalm had died at Quebec.'

HISTORIAN BERNARD B. FALL ON FRENCH HUMILIATION IN INDOCHINA (VIETNAM)

THE SINAI CAMPAIGN

General Moshe Dayan *v.* Egyptian forces
October–November **1956**

IN 1956, GREAT BRITAIN AND FRANCE invaded Egypt to compel its leader, Colonel Nasser, to rescind his nationalization of the Suez Canal. Yet the United States and the Soviet Union, which had emerged from the Second World War as the world's new superpowers, forced their former allies to stage a humiliating withdrawal. 1956 also marked another chapter in the history of deteriorating Arab–Israeli relations.

The state of Israel was founded in 1948. As soon as its first prime minister, David Ben-Gurion, announced its creation it was attacked by surrounding Arab nations. Israel emerged victorious from the war that ensued.

A rising military star in this struggle was Moshe Dayan. A native of Palestine (unlike most Israelis, then and now), Dayan was a member of the *Haganah*, the clandestine Zionist army trained by the maverick British counter-insurgency expert, General Orde Wingate. Dayan was active in *Haganah*'s suppression of an Arab revolt in Palestine in 1936. He lost his left eye fighting for the British in the Second World War. Promoted to Army Chief of Staff in 1953, Dayan was to play a leading role in the events of 1956. The Suez Crisis saw Israel make common cause with Britain and France, in order to secure its borders against a hostile, nationalist-led Egypt still smarting from defeat in 1948. Later in life, Dayan was recalled to the colours and led the Israeli Defence Forces to victory in the Six-Day War of 1967.

Jubilant Israeli troops celebrate the capture of the coastal city of Gaza in 1956, which had been occupied by Egypt since the war of 1948.

A LOOMING CRISIS

In the lead-up to the Suez Crisis 1956, Israeli intelligence had been watching with concern the growing friendship between Egypt's leader Gamal Abdel Nasser and the Soviet Union. The Soviets offered to loan Egypt $1,120,000,000 for the building of the Second Aswan Dam, and now Nasser had a powerful ally to help him rid Egypt of the French and British – the guarantors of the Suez Canal, which, until 1954, had been defended by detachments of British soldiers.

In 1955, Nasser bought a huge stock of arms from Russia's Warsaw Pact ally Czechoslovakia, including 50 jet bombers, 100 MiG fighters, 300 tanks, over 100 self-propelled guns, 200 armoured personnel carriers, two destroyers, four minesweepers and 20 torpedo boats. This greatly alarmed Israel, which hoped that the Britain and France would respond. At the time both Egypt and Israel had around 45,000 men under arms. On 26 July 1956, Nasser felt strong enough to nationalize the Suez Canal.

Moshe Dayan (back row, with eye patch) and commanders of the Israeli 202nd Parachute Brigade during the Suez Crisis of 1956. Ariel Sharon is on Dayan's right, while in the front row (squatting, far right) is Raful Eitan.

Dayan sketched his plans for a pre-emptive strike across the Sinai Desert on the back of a cigarette box, but it took more time to convince Ben-Gurion of the need for action. Yet when faced with the prospect that the Egyptians might hit targets in Israel, he agreed to Dayan's strategy. For its part, Israel had been able to purchase large quantities of materiel from the French: 60 Mystère IV fighters, 36 Vautour fighter-bombers, 2,000 tanks and stocks of rockets totalling nearly $100 million. The French discreetly asked the Israelis how long it would take them to reach the canal. They were assured that it could be done in 5–7 days. This was the basis of the co-ordinated attack made by France and Israel.

Dayan was anxious not to provoke the Egyptians so far that they would bomb cities in Israel. The idea was to stay well clear of Cairo, but prepare the ground for a lightning thrust to seize control of the Sinai Peninsula.

SEIZING THE MITLA PASS
On 29 October 1956, Dayan launched Operation Kadesh. Israel had a small army of 11,000 regulars and 40,000 conscripts. There was just one general,

Dayan, but because of the two-and-a-half year conscription, a call-up could muster a force of 200,000 trained soldiers. Dayan first employed a feint by despatching Colonel Ariel Sharon's 202nd Parachute Brigade to the Jordanian border, then cut Egyptian communications with Sinai by having P-51 Mustang fighters fly as low as 3.7 metres (12 ft) off the ground to sever the wires to Egyptian Army HQ at Ismailia.

Still the Egyptians suspected nothing, as the Sinai Desert – over 9,000 square miles (23,000 sq km) of sand and rock – seemed an unlikely place to do battle. Sharon's force was a battalion short, but on 29 October, 16 Dakota transports flew in below Egyptian radar before climbing to 460 metres (1,500 ft) and dropping the remaining 395 paratroops of 202rd Brigade under the command of Lieutenant-Colonel Raful Eitan 15 miles (24 km) east of the Mitla Pass and 40 miles (64 km) east of Suez. Located around 90 miles (145 km) from the Israeli border, the Mitla Pass was a key objective, since it is virtually the only way of crossing the mountain ranges that separate the desert from the canal. The Israelis marched to the pass and dug in as the sun set, a task made easier by a ruined Turkish fort there. There was another drop at 9 p.m. that evening: jeeps, weapons, ammunition, water, food and medicine. Supplies were also dropped by the French Air Force.

The 30,000-strong Egyptian Sinai force was taken completely by surprise at first. Unaware of the Israeli landing, an Egyptian unit of troop carriers received a nasty surprise when it approached and was shot up in an ambush. 'We captured several of their vehicles and were lucky to find a generous supply of drinking water as well', wrote Eitan.

The rest of the brigade, under Sharon, now made a smart about-turn away from the Jordanian border and headed across

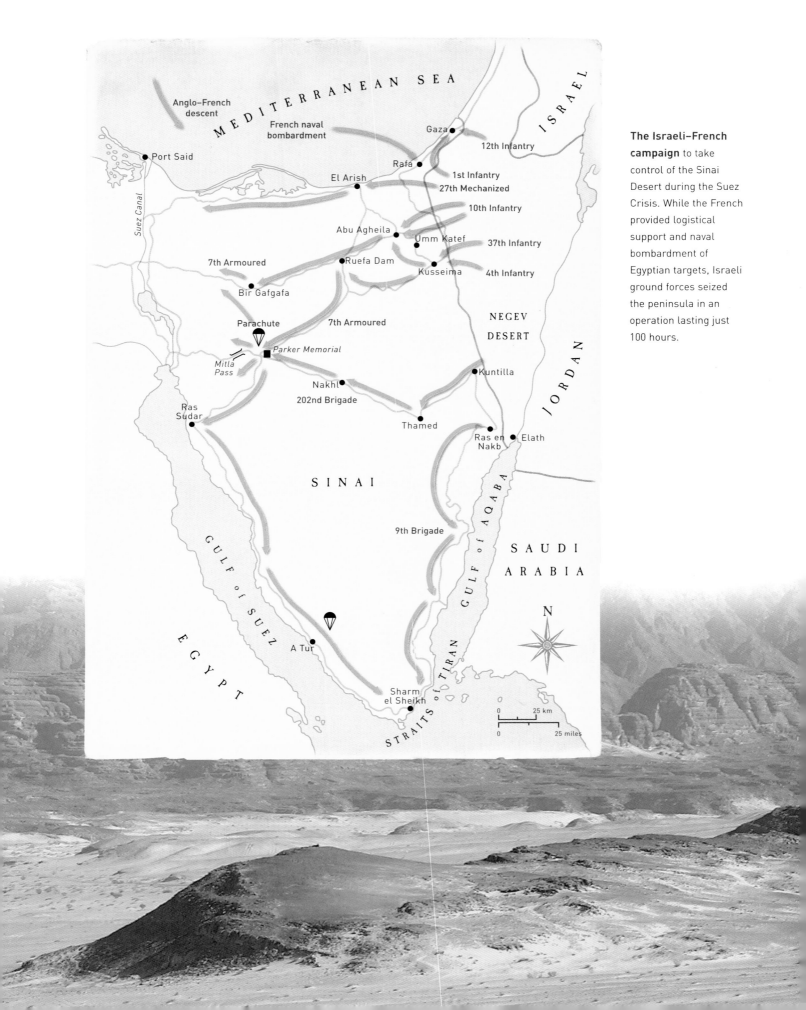

MEDITERRANEAN SEA

Anglo-French descent

French naval bombardment

Port Said

Suez Canal

Gaza

Rafa

12th Infantry

El Arish

1st Infantry

27th Mechanized

10th Infantry

Abu Agheila

Umm Katef

37th Infantry

7th Armoured

Ruefa Dam

Kusseima

4th Infantry

Bir Gafgafa

ISRAEL

NEGEV DESERT

Parachute

7th Armoured

Mitla Pass

Parker Memorial

Nakhl

202nd Brigade

Kuntilla

JORDAN

Ras Sudar

Thamed

Ras en Nakb

Elath

SINAI

GULF of SUEZ

9th Brigade

GULF of AQABA

SAUDI ARABIA

EGYPT

A Tur

N

Sharm el Sheikh

STRAITS of TIRAN

0   25 km

0   25 miles

The Israeli–French campaign to take control of the Sinai Desert during the Suez Crisis. While the French provided logistical support and naval bombardment of Egyptian targets, Israeli ground forces seized the peninsula in an operation lasting just 100 hours.

the desert to join up with Eitan at the Mitla Pass. Sharon's first target was the border town of Kuntilla.

Israeli radio justified its actions by claiming that the army was neutralizing *fedayeen* (Arab insurgent) bases in Sinai, but as Ariel Sharon later revealed all too frankly in his memoirs, this was a smokescreen: there were none. At Themed, Sharon's unit encountered resistance from two companies of Egyptian infantry, but soon swept them aside and advanced.

A HARD-FOUGHT VICTORY

By this time, the Egyptians had realized what was afoot, and rushed troops up to the Mitla Pass. Eitan's force was subjected to a pounding, but held out for 30 hours before Sharon relieved them, having covered 90 miles (145 km) in four days. As he approached Mitla, Sharon saw a sign in Modern Hebrew that read: 'Border Ahead. Stop!'

Yet the Israelis' hold on Mitla was still extremely tenuous. Their positions were being shelled by the Egyptian 2nd Infantry Brigade and strafed by MiG-17s. (The Egyptian Air Force also carried out largely ineffective attacks on airbases in Israel.) Eitan and Sharon had just 1,200 men, three light tanks and a few field guns. Sharon was in favour of scaling the heights around the pass to find a better defensive position. The Egyptians now poured in reinforcements in anticipation of a decisive victory. High Command refused Sharon's request to storm the pass, but he went ahead on his own initiative and eventually succeeded in getting through, at a cost of 38 Israeli troops killed and 120 wounded. Dayan was furious, seeing this sacrifice as pointless, since it had never been part of the Israeli plan to advance beyond this point.

Dayan now despatched further units to Sinai. The Central Task Force led by

Debris of war: abandoned Egyptian tanks and lorries litter the Sinai Desert after fierce fighting during the war of 1956. The United Nations forced Israel to relinquish control of this buffer zone after the conflict.

> *'How could we possibly support Britain and France, if in doing so we lose the whole Arab world?'*
>
> US President Dwight D. Eisenhower, 31 October 1956

Yehudah Wallach went north towards Abu Agheila and engaged the enemy at Umm Katef.

Aside from air drops, the French also provided naval support. On 31 October, the Egyptian destroyer *Ibrahim al-Awal* began shelling the harbour and oil refinery at the northern Israeli port of Haifa. The French destroyer *Kersaint* intervened, and with Israeli help, the Egyptian warship was driven off and forced to surrender.

EGYPT ROUTED

That same day saw the start of the Anglo-French assault on Egypt and the Suez Canal. Flying from bases in Malta and Cyprus, and from aircraft carriers in the Mediterranean, British and French aircraft bombed Port Said and other key targets. More than 100 Egyptian planes were destroyed. In haste, Egyptian forces in the Sinai sabotaged most of their heavy equipment and began to withdraw.

With the help of the French, Dayan set about attacking the Egyptian fortifications in central and northeastern Sinai, where the bulk of their forces were concentrated. The Israeli plan was a two-pronged attack across the minefields protecting the Gaza Strip to envelop the Egyptians at Rafa. Israeli engineers began work on the mines on the night of 30–31 October. By 9.00 a.m. on 31 October, the road junction at Rafa was in Israeli hands. From there, they proceeded to El Arish. On 2 November, Gaza itself fell, with around 7,000–8,000 Egyptians taken prisoner. The Israelis lost just 10 men in the battle for the city. In the face of the Israeli onslaught, many Egyptian troops simply deserted, shedding their uniforms, burying their weapons in

the sand and beginning the long march home in just their underwear. They survived by living off dates, which fortunately were ripe at this time of year.

El Arish also fell; the Israeli advance was now unstoppable. There remained just one final objective: Sharm el Sheikh, at the southern tip of the peninsula. Dayan called this: 'the most ambitious mission of the Sinai Campaign.' On 2 November, Colonel Avraham Yoffee set out from Kuntilla with the 9th Brigade and two paratroop companies provided by Dayan at the last minute.

On 3 November, the assault on Sharm el Sheikh began with an Israeli Air Force bombardment, which destroyed two of the three big guns guarding the Straits of Tiran at Ras Nasrami. However, interrogation of the pilot of a downed Israeli plane alerted the commander of the town to the imminent ground assault, and he had time to prepare his defences. Yoffee and his men began their attack on 5 November. The first wave was repulsed, but later that morning the Egyptians surrendered. Israeli forces now proceeded to their objective and stopped 10 miles (16 km) short of the canal.

Aside from Sharon's misjudged action at the Mitla Pass, the Israeli plan had worked flawlessly. For the destruction of three Egyptian divisions, Moshe Dayan's forces had lost only 170 men.

The Suez Crisis was a political disaster for Britain and France. The United States exerted intense diplomatic and economic pressure (on Britain) to withdraw. Faced with international condemnation, the two former great colonial powers were forced to comply.

INDEX

Words and page numbers in **bold type** indicate main references to the various topics; page numbers in *italic* refer to illustrations

BIBLIOGRAPHY

Allmand, Christopher. *Henry V*. Yale University Press, New Haven and London, 1997.

Anderson, M.S. *The War of the Austrian Succession 1740-1748*. Longman, London, 1995.

Asprey, Robert B. *The German High Command at War: Hindenburg and Ludendorff and the First World War*. Little Brown, London, 1993.

Barlow, Frank. *Edward the Confessor*. Yale University Press, New Haven and London, 1997.

Barnet, Correlli, ed. *Hitler's Generals*. Weidenfeld & Nicolson, London, 1989.

Boardman, John, Jasper Griffin and Oswyn Murray. *The Oxford History of the Classical World*. Oxford University Press, Oxford, 1986.

Browning, Reed. *The War of the Austrian Succession*. Alan Sutton, Stroud, 1995.

Caesar, Julius (translated with an introduction by Jane Gardner). *The Civil War*. Penguin Books, London, 1967.

Cary, E., ed. *Dio's Roman History, Books XII-XXV*. Harvard University Press, Cambridge, Massachusetts and London, 1989.

Craig, Gordon A. *The Politics of the Prussian Army 1640-1945*. Oxford University Press, Oxford, 1964.

Duffy, Christopher. *Frederick the Great, A Military Life*. Routledge, London, 1985.

Eberle, Henrik and Matthias Uhl, eds. (translated by Giles MacDonogh). *The Hitler Book: The Secret Dossier Prepared for Stalin*. John Murray, London, 2005.

Fall, Bernard B. *Street Without Joy: The French Debacle in Indochina*. Pen & Sword, Barnsley, 2009.

Gibbon, Edward (edited with an introduction by Felipe Fernàndez-Armesto). *The History of the Decline and Fall of the Roman Empire, Volume VIII: The Fall of Constantinople and the Papacy in Rome*. The Folio Society, London, 1990.

Gibbon, Edward (edited with an introduction by Betty Radice). *The History of the Decline and Fall of the Roman Empire, Volume IV: The End of the Western Empire*. The Folio Society, London, 1986.

Goldsworthy, Adrian. *Caesar: the Life of a Colossus*. Weidenfeld & Nicolson, London, 2006.

Gregg, Edward. *Queen Anne*. Yale University Press, New Haven and London, 2001.

Herodotus (translated by Aubrey de Sélincourt). *The Histories*. Penguin Books, London, 1996.

Holmes, Richard and Martin Marix Evans. *Oxford Guide to Battles*. Oxford University Press, Oxford and New York, 2006.

Horne, Alistair. *The Age of Napoleon*. Weidenfeld & Nicolson, London, 2004.

Housley, Norman. *Fighting for the Cross: Crusading to the Holy Land*. Yale University Press, New Haven and London, 2008.

Howard, Michael. *War in European History*. Oxford University Press, Oxford, 2009.

Keegan, John. *The American Civil War: A Military History*. Hutchinson, London, 2009.

Keegan, John. *The First World War*. Hutchinson, London, 1998.

Keegan, John. *The Face of Battle*. Jonathan Cape, London, 1976.

Keegan, John and Andrew Wheatcroft. *Who's Who in Military History from 1453 to the Present Day*. Routledge, London, 1987.

Kinross, Lord. *The Ottoman Empire*. The Folio Society, London, 2003.

Lendon, J.E. *Soldiers and Ghosts: A History of Battle in Classical Antiquity*. Yale University Press, New Haven and London, 2005.

Livy (translated by Aubrey de Sélincourt with an introduction by Betty Radice). *The War with Hannibal*. Penguin Books, London, 1965.

MacDonogh, Giles. *The Last Kaiser: William the Impetuous*. Weidenfeld & Nicolson, London, 2000.

MacDonogh, Giles. *Frederick the Great: A Life in Deed and Letters*. Weidenfeld & Nicolson, London, 1999.

MacDonogh, Giles. *Prussia: The Perversion of an Idea*. Sinclair-Stevenson, London, 1994.

Mansel, Philip. *Constantinople: City of the World's Desire, 1453-1924*. John Murray, London, 1995.

Montgomery of Alamein, Field-Marshal Viscount. *A History of Warfare*. Collins, London, 1968.

Morley, John. *Life of William Ewart Gladstone*. Macmillan, London, 1903.

Morley, John. *Oliver Cromwell*. Macmillan, London, 1900.

Nepos, Cornelius (translated by John C. Rolfe). *Cornelius Nepos–On The Great Generals and Historians*. Loeb Classical Library, Harvard University Press, Cambridge, Massachusetts, 1984.

Orme, Robert. *A History of the Military Transactions of the British Nation in Indostan*. F. Wingrave, London, 1799.

Pausanius (translation by Peter Levi). *Guide to Greece, Volume I: Central Greece*. Penguin Books, London, 1979.

Plutarch (translated by Robin Waterfield). *Roman Lives*. Oxford University Press, Oxford, 1999.

Plutarch (translated by Robin Waterfield). *Greek Lives*. Oxford University Press, Oxford, 1998.

Prior, Robin. *Gallipoli: The End of the Myth*. Yale University Press, New Haven and London, 2009.

Riall, Lucy. *Garibaldi: Invention of a Hero*. Yale University Press, New Haven and London, 2007.

Riley-Smith, Jonathan, ed. *The Oxford History of the Crusades*. Oxford University Press, Oxford, 1999.

Roberts, Andrew, ed. *The Art of War: Great Commanders of the Ancient and Medieval World*. Quercus Books, London, 2008.

Roberts, Andrew. *Salisbury, Victorian Titan*. Weidenfeld & Nicolson, London, 1999.

Roberts, Geoffrey. *Stalin's Wars: From World War to Cold War, 1939-1953*. Yale University Press, New Haven and London, 2006.

Showalter, Dennis E. *The Wars of Frederick the Great*. Longman, London, 1996.

Stenton, Frank. *Anglo-Saxon England* (3rd ed). Oxford University Press, Oxford, 1971.

Stone, Norman. *The Eastern Front 1914-1917*. Penguin Books, London, 1998.

Tacitus (translated by Michael Grant). *The Annals of Ancient Rome* (revised edition). Penguin Books, London, 1989.

Thucydides (edited with a translation by Sir Richard Livingstone). *The History of the Peloponnesian War*. Oxford University Press, Oxford, 1960.

Tincey, John. *Blenheim 1704: The Duke of Marlborough's Masterpiece*. Osprey, Oxford, 2004.

Toland, John. *Rising Sun*. Pen & Sword, Barnsley, 2005.

Tranquillus, Gaius Suetonius (translated by Robert Graves). *The Twelve Caesars*. The Folio Society, London, 1964.

Trevelyan, G.M. *Blenheim*. Fontana, London, 1965.

Trevelyan, G.M. *Ramillies and the Union with Scotland*. Fontana, London, 1965.

Turner, Barry. *Suez 1956: The Inside Story of the First Oil War*. Hodder, London, 2006.

Wedgwood, C.V. *The King's War 1641-1647*. Fontana, London, 1977.

Weintraub, Stanley. *Victoria*. John Murray, London, 1987.

Worden, Blair. *The English Civil Wars 1640-1660*. Weidenfeld & Nicolson, London, 2009.

Worthington, Ian. *Philip II of Macedonia*. Yale University Press, Newhaven, 2008.

PICTURE CREDITS

2 Wikimedia Commons/United States Coast Guard; 4(b) Wikimedia Commons/Vaggelis Vlahos; 4(t) Wikimedia Commons; 5(t) Wikimedia Commons/Imperial War Museum; 5(b); Wikimedia Commons/United States Army Center of Military History; 9 Shutterstock/Nagib; 11 Wikimedia Commons/Golf Bravo; 13 Galleria Civica d'Arte Moderna di Torino, Turin, Italy/Alinari/Bridgeman Art Library; 14 Wikimedia Commons/Fkerasar; 15 Wikimedia Commons/Vaggelis Vlahos; 17 Shutterstock/Steba; 19 akg-images; 23 Wikimedia Commons/Campana Collection, 1861/Louvre Museum, Paris; 26 Wikimedia Commons/Jastrow/British Museum, London; 27 Wikimedia Commons/Ken Russell Salvador; 29 akg-images; 33 © Petit Palais/Roger-Viollet/TopFoto/TopFoto.co.uk; 35 akg-images/De Agostini Pict. Li; 37 Shutterstock/Jule Berlin; 40 Hervé Champollion/ akg-images; 43 Wikimedia Commons; 45 Wikimedia Commons/Nikater; 47 Shutterstock/Steba; 48 Wikimedia Commons/Historia No121; 51 Wikimedia Commons; 53 Â©ullsteinbild/TopFoto/TopFoto.co.uk; 57 akg-images; 59 Wikimedia Commons; 61 Shutterstock/Andy Poole; 62 Wikimedia Commons; 65 akg-images/Erich Lessing; 69 akg-images; 73 © Stapleton Collection/ Corbis; 74 National Portrait Gallery, London, UK/Bridgeman Art Library; 77 Wikimedia Commons; 78 Wikimedia Commons/Giraud Patrick; 81 Wikimedia Commons/Art Renewal Center Museum; 82 Wikimedia Commons/Sina Bey/Topkapi Museum; 87 © Fotomas/TopFoto/TopFoto.co.uk; 88 Wikimedia Commons/Bartholomeus Willemsz. Dolendo/Rijksmuseum Amsterdam; 91 Wikimedia Commons; 92 akg-images; 95 akg-images; 97 The Granger Collection/TopFoto/TopFoto.co.uk; 98-99 © Cheltenham Art Gallery & Museums, Gloucestershire, UK/The Bridgeman Art Library; 100 Wikimedia Commons; 103 Wikimedia Commons/Steve Partridge; 105 IMAGNO/ Austrian Archives/TopFoto/TopFoto.co.uk; 106 Wikimedia Commons/The Library of Congress; 109 World History Archive/ TopFoto/TopFoto.co.uk; 110-111 © 2004 Topham Picturepoint/Topfoto.co.uk; 115 Lauros/Giraudon/ The Bridgeman Art Library; 119 Private Collection/Peter Newark Military Pictures/The Bridgeman Art Library; 121 Wikimedia Commons/National Portrait Gallery, London: NPG 526; 123 akg-images; 127 © TopFoto/ TopFoto.co.uk; 131 Wikimedia Commons/von Junst; 133 Wikimedia Commons/ Pudelek (Marcin Szala); 134-135 Wikimedia Commons/ JoJan; 137 Wikimedia Commons/Nicolas Illy; 139 State Central Artillery Museum, St. Petersburg, Russia/The Bridgeman Art Library; 142-143 akg-images; 146 Wikimedia Commons; 149 The Granger Collection/TopFoto/TopFoto.co.uk; 152-153 The Granger Collection/ TopFoto/TopFoto.co.uk; 154 Wikimedia Commons; 156-157 Wikimedia Commons/U.S. Army; 159 Newberry Library, Chicago, Illinois/Bridgeman Art Library; 161 Wikimedia Commons/Andrew J. Russell/Mfield; 163 Private collection/The Stapleton Collection/The Bridgeman Art Library; 165 Shutterstock/Christa DeRidder; 167 The Granger Collection/TopFoto/TopFoto.co.uk; 171 akg-images; 173 Wikimedia Commons/D.J. Mueller; 174-175 Private Collection/© Malcolm Innes Gallery, London, UK/The Bridgeman Art Library; 178-179 © Print Collector/HIP/TopFoto/TopFoto.co.uk; 181 © TopFoto/ TopFoto.co.uk; 182 Wikimedia Commons/Deutsches Bundesarchiv (German Federal Archive); 184 Wikimedia Commons/Verlag Gerhard von Stalling, Oldenburg/Berlin 1928/Lars Helbo; 185 Wikimedia Commons/Berliner Illustrirte Zeitung/R.Minzloff; 187 The Granger Collection/TopFoto/TopFoto.co.uk; 191 akg-images; 193 Wikimedia Commons; 195 Wikimedia Commons/German Government, Department of photos and film/ Dr. Alexander Maye; 197 Â©ullsteinbild/TopFoto/TopFoto.co.uk; 198 Wikimedia Commons/US National Archives and Records Administration; 200-201 The Granger Collection/TopFoto/TopFoto.co.uk; 203 Wikimedia Commons /Deutsches Bundesarchiv (German Federal Archive); 205 Wikimedia Commons/Deutsches Bundesarchiv (German Federal Archive; 206 Â©ullsteinbild/TopFoto/TopFoto.co.uk; 209 © 2003 Topham Picturepoint/TopFoto.co.uk; 213 © TopFoto/TopFoto.co.uk; 215 Wikimedia Commons/U.S. federal government; 216-217 The Granger Collection/TopFoto/TopFoto.co.uk; 220 Wikimedia Commons/ Deutsches Bundesarchiv (German Federal Archive); 222-223 State Central Military Museum, Moscow, Russia/The Bridgeman Art Library; 227 Wikimedia Commons/United States Coast Guard; 229 Wikimedia Commons/United States Coast Guard; 230 Wikimedia Commons/Conseil Régional de Basse-Normandie/Archives Nationales du Canada; 231 Shutterstock/Bryan Busovicki; 233 Wikimedia Commons/United States Army Center of Military History; 235 Wikimedia Commons/U.S. Navy; 236 Wikimedia Commons/U.S. Army; 239 © 2004 Topham Picturepoint/TopFoto.co.uk; 241 Wikimedia Commons/Pilip; 242 Â©ullsteinbild/TopFoto/TopFoto.co.uk; 245 © 1999 Topham Picturepoint/TopFoto.co.uk; 246 Wikimedia Commons/National photo collection, Israel; 247 Wikimedia Commons/DokiC; 248 Wikimedia Commons/United States Army Heritage and Education Center.

Quercus Publishing has made every effort to trace copyright holders of the pictures used in this book. Anyone having claims to ownership not identified above is invited to contact Quercus Publishing.

ACKNOWLEDGEMENTS

For Gay McGuinness
Who helped me with my Irish.

This book was spawned from the two volumes of *The Art of War* edited by Andrew Roberts and published by Quercus Books in 2008 and 2009, to which I contributed the article on Frederick the Great. My starting point in each of these battles, has been the essay contributed by the following authorities in their various fields: John A. Barnes, Ian Beckett, Stephen Brumwell, Michael Burleigh, John Childs, Anne Curry, Ben Dupré, Philip Dwyer, Carlo D'Este, Antonia Fraser, John Gillingham, Adrian Goldsworthy, Robert Hardy, Robert Harvey, Peter Hart, John Haywood, Tom Holland, Alistair Horne, Robin Lane Fox, John Lee, Adrian Murdoch, John Julius Norwich, Richard Overy, Alan Palmer, Geoffrey Perret, Jonathan Phillips, Lucy Riall, Andrew Roberts, Trevor Royle, Simon Sebag Montefiore, Richard J. Sommers, Charles Spencer, Jonathan Sumption, Joyce Tyldesley, Andrew Uffindell, Martin van Creveld, Alan Warren, Robin Waterfield and Charles Williams.

I'd also like to thank my friends Richard Bassett and Roddy Matthews for their helpful suggestions and my family for their forbearance once again. Chiefly, however, I am grateful to my son Joseph for lending me books and magazines (many of which I gave him in the first place) and for unravelling the stories of many of these battles with me.

Giles MacDonogh

First published in Great Britain in 2010 by

Quercus Publishing Plc
21 Bloomsbury Square
London
WC1A 2NS

A CIP catalogue record for this book is available from the British Library

UK and associated territories: ISBN-978-1-84916-490-0

Printed and bound in China

10 9 8 7 6 5 4 3 2 1

Designed and edited by BCS Publishing Limited, Oxford.